YOUTH & DRUGS AND MENTAL HEALTH:

A RESOURCE FOR PROFESSIONALS

Elsbeth Tupker, MSW

Clinical Services Consultant

Education and Publishing Department

Centre for Addiction and Mental Health

camh
Centre for Addiction and Mental Health
Centre de toxicomanie et de santé mentale

YOUTH & DRUGS AND MENTAL HEALTH: A RESOURCE FOR PROFESSIONALS

For professional advice to help your client with an alcohol or drug problem, please call:
Addiction Clinical Consultation Service, 9 a.m. to 5 p.m. Monday to Friday
1 888 720-ACCS
416 595-6968 in the Toronto area

For information on other Centre for Addiction and Mental Health resource materials or to place an order, please contact:
Marketing and Sales Services
Centre for Addiction and Mental Health
33 Russell Street
Toronto, Ontario
Canada M5S 2S1
Tel: 1 800 661-1111 or 416 595-6059 in Toronto
E-mail: marketing@camh.net
Web site: www.camh.net

Disponible en français sous le titre
Les jeunes, les drogues et la santé mentale : Ressource pour les professionnels

ACKNOWLEDGMENTS

Many people were involved in the development of *Youth & Drugs and Mental Health: A Resource for Professionals*. Their contributions are gratefully acknowledged.

Editor and project leader:

Elsbeth Tupker

Needs assessment for this resource:

Angela Barbara

Research and first draft of Chapters 1 to 4 written by:

Liz Hart   Greg Graves

Virginia Carver   Wanda Jamieson

Section 2.3: Drugs and how they work and Chapter 5: Pharmacotherapy written by:

Wende Wood

Appendices D & E and sections in Chapter 4:

Darryl Upfold

Youth & Drugs and Mental Health project advisory committee:

Daniel Coté, Children's Mental Health System, Northeast Mental Health Centre, Sudbury

Patti Dryden-Holmstrom, Youth Addictions Program, Kenora

Anne Edmondson, East Metro Youth Services, Toronto

Linda Gray, Bruce-Grey Children's Services

Joanne Johnston, Children's Mental Health Ontario

Russ Larocque, Algoma Family Services

Steve Martin, Open Doors for Lanark Children and Youth, Carleton Place

Jim Sauve, Chatham-Kent Integrated Children's Mental Health Services

Smita Thatte, Royal Ottawa Hospital

Paul Wilson, Nexus Youth Services, Peel Children's Centre

Youth & Drugs and Mental Health CAMH project team:

Jennifer Barr   Elizabeth Hendren-Roberge

Gloria Chaim   Louise LaRocque-Stuart

Mark Erdelyan   Marty McLeod

Jane Fjeld   Brian Mitchell

Julia Greenbaum

Key informants and reviewers:

Jean Addington
Ed Adlaf
Sharon Armstrong
Bruce Ballon
Lindley Bassarath
Lorena Dolinar
Jane Fjeld
Leah Fraser
Araujo Gonzalo
Umesh Jain
Colleen Kelly
Megan McCormick

Catherine McPherson-Doe
Peter Menzies
Robert Millin
Cherry Murray
Gary Roberts
Charles Senior
Joanne Shenfeld
Susan Smither
Jennifer Speers
Chrissoula Stavrakaki
Leslie Viner
Christine Wekerle

References:

Alexandra Chtyrlina

Copy editor:

Honey Fisher, Fishtales Productions

Design:

Up Inc

Production co-ordination:

Creative and Production Services, CAMH

CONTENTS

PART 1.
YOUTH & DRUGS AND MENTAL HEALTH:
A RESOURCE FOR PROFESSIONALS

CHAPTER 1: AN OVERVIEW OF YOUTH SUBSTANCE USE AND MENTAL HEALTH

CHAPTER 2: PREPARING TO RESPOND: KEY ATTITUDES, KNOWLEDGE AND APPROACHES

CHAPTER 3: IDENTIFYING, ASSESSING AND PLANNING TREATMENT FOR SUBSTANCE USE AND MENTAL HEALTH PROBLEMS

CHAPTER 4: TREATMENT AND SUPPORT

CHAPTER 5: PHARMACOTHERAPY

APPENDICES

PART 2.
FIRST CONTACT: A BRIEF TREATMENT FOR YOUNG SUBSTANCE USERS WITH MENTAL HEALTH PROBLEMS

YOUTH & DRUGS AND MENTAL HEALTH:

A RESOURCE FOR PROFESSIONALS

ABOUT THIS RESOURCE

This is a resource for people who work with youth, but is intended primarily for service providers who work in settings dealing with youth substance use and mental health treatment.

The resource provides up-to-date information about addressing substance use among young people—including doing so in the context of other mental health problems that they may be experiencing.

Our knowledge of treatment for young people with substance use and other mental health problems is at an early stage of development. Despite the need for comprehensive approaches, there currently is relatively little consensus about what works and does not work. Consequently, this resource draws upon available published information and integrates it with the advice of experts who work in addiction and mental health programs for youth.

This new resource replaces *Youth & Drugs: An Education Package for Professionals* (Addiction Research Foundation and Health and Welfare Canada, 1991) and has new information on:
· youth substance use and mental health
· screening and assessment
· integrated treatment and support
· cultural competency
· Motivational interviewing
· Stages of change

- family involvement
- pharmacotherapy.

Part two of this resource is the treatment manual *First Contact: A brief treatment for young substance users with mental health problems.*

Depending on the setting in which you work, some of the information in this resource will be familiar to you, while other sections will be new. We encourage you to use the information that is most relevant to you to integrate your understanding of, and approach to treating young people with substance use and other mental health problems.

CHAPTER 1

OVERVIEW OF YOUTH SUBSTANCE USE AND MENTAL HEALTH PROBLEMS

1.1 ADOLESCENT DEVELOPMENT, SUBSTANCE USE AND MENTAL HEALTH

"Physical, emotional, and social well-being among youth is important for numerous reasons, not the least of which are the long-lasting effects into adulthood. Childhood and adolescence are pivotal developmental stages during which many life-long health behaviours, beliefs and attitudes become established. Therefore, healthy children will likely become healthy adults" (Adlaf, Paglia & Beitchman, 2002, 1).

As they grow and learn, all young people in our society are exposed to and affected by the behaviours and experiences of the adults in their lives. This includes exposure to widespread use of alcohol and other drugs, as well as to the degree of mental health—or in some cases mental health problems—experienced by those adults. In turn, most young people will experiment, at some point, with alcohol and/or other drugs. While the majority will go on to lead healthy, productive lives, many will have experiences that affect their sense of well-being and, in more serious circumstances, that negatively affect their mental health and reduce their ability to function.

Throughout this primer, we use the terms "young people" and "youth" to acknowledge the fact that the broad time period from birth to early adulthood can be affected by the pervasiveness of substance use and mental health problems in our society. Our primary focus, however, is on adolescents.

1.1.1 ADOLESCENT DEVELOPMENT

Adolescence is a time of opportunity and growth—a time when young people explore their identities and roles. Through this process of experimentation, learning and development, young people "lay down the foundations for physical, psychological and social maturity" (Centre for Addiction and Mental Health (CAMH), 2002a).

Adolescence is also a time when young people take risks that can have long-term effects on their health and well-being. As part of their exploration and experimentation, adolescents often engage in high-risk behaviours such as drinking and driving, unsafe sexual practices and harmful sleeping and eating patterns that can have serious consequences for themselves and others. Some adolescents engage in violence, including, in rare circumstances, homicide or suicide.

Adolescence is, above all, a period replete with significant life changes and emotional upheaval. Entering puberty and making it through high school can be stressful times for young people. For some, this period of transition can lead to emotional and/or behavioural problems and difficulties with school or other areas of life (Adlaf et al., 2002). Among marginalized groups of young people, vulnerability is compounded by factors such as dislocation, racism, sexism, homophobia, poverty, social isolation and street-involvement.

1.1.2 RISK AND PROTECTIVE FACTORS

Although many adolescents experiment with substances and stop using them relatively quickly, some do remain occasional or recreational users. A few become heavy users. Some young people are at greater risk of developing substance use problems than others.

There is no definitive "cause" of drug use problems among young people, but experts have suggested many reasons why young people who decide to experiment with drugs, go beyond experimentation or transition to regular use.

Within the context of adolescent development, some experimentation with alcohol and other drugs is considered normal. Young people might experiment with substances because:
· Drugs are available and provide a quick, often inexpensive way to have "fun."
· They are curious and want to find out what the fuss is about.
· Using substances expresses opposition to adult authority and can be part of the process of separation from parents.
· Using substances symbolizes developmental transition (e.g., moving from a less mature to a more mature stage). In some families, the "first drink" is a rite of passage.

Once adolescents have some experience with a drug and know what the effects are, they might continue to use drugs because:
· Drug use becomes a coping mechanism for dealing with anything from poor grades and social rejection to family conflict, family dysfunction and child abuse. Drug users might be trying to quell feelings of anger, frustration, stress, fear of failure or failure itself.

- Drug use can be an attempt to self-medicate symptoms of mental health problems such as depression or anxiety.
- Drug use can demonstrate a personal identity. It can be a way of showing that they are "cool" or have characteristics valued in adolescent culture.
- They might view drug use as a way to gain admission to a peer group.
- They might believe drug use will make others perceive them as adults.
- They feel omnipotent and immortal and therefore not at risk.

Some experts believe that mental health problems are risk factors for substance use (substance use as a self-medicating or coping strategy), but others prefer the suggestion that mental health and substance use problems among young people may emerge from a common pre-existing factor such as stress (Adlaf et al., 2002).

We now know a great deal about the factors that put young people at increased risk for substance use and mental health problems as well as the factors that help protect them. Much of what we have learned suggests there is overlap in both risk and protective factors and their potential outcomes (Offord, Boyle & Racine, 1989).

The more risk factors a young person is exposed to, the more they are at risk. The impact of risk and protective factors depends, in part, on a young person's stage of development and factors that affect early development can be the most crucial (National Institute on Drug Abuse [NIDA], 1997). Appendix A provides an overview of the often overlapping risk and protective factors that have been linked to substance use and/or mental health problems among young people.

1.2 ADOLESCENT SUBSTANCE USE

Many young people experiment with alcohol and other drugs, much like they test out other "adult" behaviours. Often, this is a way for them to express independence and autonomy. But not all substance "use" leads to "abuse." In fact, most young people who use substances "do not progress to problem use or dependency" (CAMH, 2002a).

At the same time, given the fact that young people have not reached full maturity, physically, psychologically or socially, substance use may interrupt those crucial developmental processes. If a young person's use of alcohol or drugs hampers his or her ability to master key developmental tasks, he or she may experience difficulties in reaching full potential.

All young people will not develop dependence on the drugs they use. Those who do become dependent can develop either psychological or physical dependence. Psychological dependence means they are emotionally or psychologically driven to continue taking drugs to maintain their sense of well-being. Physical dependence refers to the adjustment of bodily

Risk factors make it more likely that individuals will experience poor overall adjustment or negative outcomes such as mental health or substance use problems. Risk factors may include biological, psychological or social factors in the individual, family and environment.

Protective factors reduce the potentially negative effects of risk factors. Protective factors may include biological, psychological or social factors in the individual, family and environment (Braverman, 2001).

The DSM-IV distinguishes between *substance abuse* and *dependence*.

Substance abuse refers to:
· use that results in failure to fulfil role obligations at work, school or home and/or legal problems
· use in situations that are physically hazardous
· continuation of use despite persistent social problems.

Substance dependence refers to:
· use that leads to tolerance and/or withdrawal (see section 2.3.2)
· use of large amounts over a long period of time
· unsuccessful efforts to control the use
· a great deal of time spent on drug-use related activities
· reduction of important social, recreational and occupational activities
· continued use despite serious physical or psychological problems (Health Canada, 2002).

tissues in response to the continued presence of a drug, such that withdrawal symptoms develop when use of the drug is discontinued.

Our concern is not so much with what might be called "abuse," but primarily with the "continuum of use." In young people, the significance of a minimal-use pattern cannot be foretold. It may pass uneventfully or turn into a destructive lifestyle. From this standpoint, we must be concerned about all adolescent drug use.

1.2.1 ONTARIO DATA ON STUDENTS' SUBSTANCE USE

The Ontario Student Drug Use Survey (OSDUS) data confirm that substance use among young people is very common. Across the province, two-thirds of all students in grades 7 to 13 reported having used alcohol during the year prior to the survey (Adlaf & Paglia, 2001). One-third of students in grades 7 to 13 reported having used an illicit drug at least once during the year prior to the survey (Adlaf & Paglia, 2001). There are key differences in drug use patterns and trends across the province. For more specific information about the experiences of young people in different regions, consult the OSDUS reports.

- -

SOME PUBLIC HEALTH FLAGS FROM THE OSDUS

· **One quarter of students smoke cigarettes.**
· **Heavy drinking (i.e., binge drinking, getting drunk) remains at an elevated level among all students, compared to a decade ago.**
· **Over the past decade, there has been a steady increase in illicit drug use among students, even when cannabis is excluded.**
· **One in seven students drink and drive and one in five report driving after cannabis use.**
· **About one-third of all students report being a passenger with a driver who had been drinking.**
· **Fewer students today disapprove of drug use compared to students a decade ago.**
· **The reported availability of drugs (except for LSD) is increasing.**
· **Use of ecstasy has increased substantially (from less than one per cent in 1991 to about six per cent in 2001).**
· **A substantially larger percentage of students today use hallucinogens such as mescaline and psilocybin compared to 1979.**
· **Daily cannabis use has increased significantly over the past decade.**
· **Over the past decade, cocaine use has been steadily increasing among all students and among several demographic subgroups. One example is the dramatic rise in cocaine use since 1993 among 11th-grade students.**
· **Over the past decade, there has been a steady increase in stimulant use (e.g., diet pills) among female students.**

(Adlaf & Paglia 2001)

Substance use patterns and prevalence vary among specific groups of young people:

· Although young women and young men have a relatively similar prevalence of substance use, there are some differences. For example, in 2001, young women reported higher rates of non-medical (not medically prescribed) stimulant use compared to young men. Young men reported higher rates of heavy drinking, use of cannabis, glue, methamphetamine, LSD and hallucinogens (Adlaf & Paglia, 2001).

· Aboriginal youth are at a two-to-six times higher risk for every alcohol-related problem compared to other young people.

· Aboriginal youth use solvents more frequently than other young people. One in five Aboriginal youth report having used solvents. One-third of those who have used solvents are under the age of 15 and more than half began using solvents before the age of 11.

· First Nations and Metis youth are more likely to use illicit drugs than other young people.

· Aboriginal youth are likely to begin using substances such as tobacco, solvents, alcohol and cannabis at a much earlier age than other young people (Canadian Centre on Substance Abuse [CCSA] and CAMH, 1999).

· The majority of young people entering the youth justice system have significant substance use problems (Trupin & Boesky, 2001).

· Homeless and street-involved youth report much higher levels of substance use than other young people. One-quarter to one-half report frequent heavy drinking. 66 to 88 per cent report using cannabis and 18 to 64 per cent report using cocaine. Many street-involved youth report having used injection drugs (11 per cent in a national study; 48 per cent of males and 32 per cent of females in a Vancouver sample; and 36 per cent in a Montreal sample). More than half (58 per cent) of a sample of street youth in Montreal had shared needles (Health Canada, 2001).

1.3 ADOLESCENT MENTAL HEALTH

Young people's ability to cope with and enjoy life and its challenges is strongly linked to their mental health and their overall sense of well-being. If they have mental health difficulties in their formative years, the effects on their ability to function may last for the rest of their lives.

Resilience (also referred to as resiliency) is a concept that incorporates two components:

· exposure to significant stressors or risks

· demonstration of competence and successful adaptation.

(Braverman, 2001)

Mental health is a continuum that ranges from optimum mental health at one end to severe and persistent mental health disorders at the other end, with emotional problems lying somewhere in the middle (Adlaf et al., 2002).

Mental health problems are diminished cognitive, social or emotional abilities but not to the extent that the criteria for mental disorders are met.

Mental disorders (often used interchangeably with mental illness) are diagnosable illnesses characterized by alterations in thinking, mood or behaviour (or some combination thereof) associated with distress that significantly interferes with an individual's cognitive, emotional or social abilities.

1.3.1 RESILIENCE

Some consider resiliency to be a "balance" between an individual's level of stress and adversity versus her or his coping abilities and support systems (Mangham, McGrath, Reid & Stewart, 1995). The role of service providers is to assist youth to develop resiliency by reducing risks and enhancing protective factors.

The good news is that resiliency is not a special set of characteristics or traits. It is a fairly ordinary phenomenon that stems from our innate human ability to adapt (Masten, 2001).

Young people's natural ability to adapt is threatened by conditions that interfere with brain development, caregiver-child relationships, regulation of emotion and behaviour, and motivation to learn and engage in the environment. Fostering resilience involves ensuring that young people have positive connections with competent, caring adults, helping them develop cognitive and self-regulation skills, promoting their positive self-image and motivating them to be effective in their environment.

In order to promote resilience among young people, we have to find ways to:

· Promote their competence.
· Ameliorate their symptoms and problems.
· Build upon their strengths.
· Minimize their risks and stresses.
· Facilitate protective mechanisms and processes.
· Treat illness.
· Reduce harmful processes (Masten, 2001).

Unfortunately, according to studies in Canada and the United States (Adlaf et al., 2002) many young people experience serious mental health problems:

· About one in five children and adolescents in the United States display symptoms of a mental health disorder in any given year, and about five in one hundred experience a serious emotional disturbance with functional impairment.
· Among young children and adolescents studied in Canada, the prevalence of a mental health problem ranges from 18 to 22 per cent, and is about 25% among young adults.
· Suicide is the third leading cause of death for adolescents in Canada and the United States (after deaths from motor vehicle and other accidents).

There is evidence that the prevalence of mental health problems among young people may be increasing (Adlaf et al., 2002).

1.3.2 ONTARIO DATA ON STUDENTS' MENTAL HEALTH AND WELL-BEING

The OSDUS found that a considerable minority of students reported some form of impaired well-being or functioning. The OSDUS assesses moderate functional impairment rather than psychiatric disorders that are based on clinical criteria (Adlaf et al., 2002, 5).

- -

SOME PUBLIC HEALTH FLAGS FROM THE OSDUS:
- **About one in four students report elevated psychological distress.**
- **About one in three females report elevated psychological distress.**
- **About one in four students report being bullied at school.**
- **About one in three students report bullying someone at school.**
- **About one in five males report fighting at school.**
- **About one in seven to ten students report either poor health, physical inactivity, visiting a mental health professional, low self-esteem, suicide ideation, engaging in three or more delinquent activities, carrying a weapon, some type of gambling problem, or concern about personal safety at school.**
- **About one in twenty students are at high risk for depression.**
- **About one in twenty males report a pathological gambling problem.**

(Adlaf et al. 2002)
- -

Patterns and prevalence of mental health problems vary among specific groups of young people:
- OSDUS data for 2001 indicate that young women are more likely to experience internalizing problems such as depression, psychological distress and suicide ideation (Adlaf et al., 2002).
- Male students are more likely to engage in risk behaviours (or externalizing behaviours) such as delinquent acts and pathological gambling (Adlaf et al., 2002).
- Gay, lesbian, bisexual or transgendered youth are at high risk for mood-related disorders, self-mutilation and suicide.
- At least one in five young people entering the youth justice system experience a serious mental or emotional disorder (Trupin & Boesky, 2001).

- -

1.4 ADOLESCENT CONCURRENT DISORDERS

Young people who develop substance use problems are often dealing with many other issues, including mental health problems. This is evident among those who present for drug treatment. The combination of substance use problems and mental health concerns is referred to as "concurrent disorders" (CAMH, 2002a).

According to the OSDUS report (Adlaf et al., 2002), survey research in Canada and the United States has found links between substance use and mental health problems among young people:

- A Canadian survey of adolescents aged 12 to 16 found a strong association between an existing mental disorder (e.g., conduct disorder) and substance use, especially among females.
- A United States household survey found that adolescents aged 12 to 17 with severe emotional or behavioural problems were much more likely to be dependent on alcohol or illicit drugs compared to young people without those problems.
- The *United States National Comorbidity Survey* found that half of all those aged 15 to 54 who have had a mental disorder during their lifetime have also had a history of substance use problems. Moreover, the 15- to 24-year-old group was most likely to have had a concurrent disorder.

1.4.1 ONTARIO DATA ON COEXISTING SUBSTANCE USE AND MENTAL HEALTH PROBLEMS AMONG STUDENTS

The OSDUS provides some information about the extent of overlap between substance use and mental health problems among Ontario students.

OSDUS FINDINGS

About one in 25 (36,600 of Ontario students) report both elevated psychological distress (symptoms of anxiety and depression) and hazardous drinking. Young women and young men are equally likely to report a concurrent problem (Adlaf et al., 2002).

Among students reporting alcohol problems, almost half also report psychological distress (Adlaf & Paglia, 2001).

1.5 THE RELATIONSHIP BETWEEN SUBSTANCE USE AND MENTAL HEALTH PROBLEMS

A young person's substance use and mental health problems are interrelated and they may affect each other in a number of different ways. For example, mental health problems may precede substance use and a young person may be using substances to cope with or "self-medicate" mental health symptoms. Alternatively, he or she may have developed mental health symptoms as a result of substance use (Ballon, in press; CAMH, 2002a).

The following information can be helpful in thinking about how the two disorders might be related.

RELATIONSHIP BETWEEN SUBSTANCE USE AND MENTAL
HEALTH DISORDERS

"There are several ways in which substance use and mental health problems affect each other:

CREATE—Substance use can create psychiatric symptoms. Example: Alcohol is a depressant—if any youth uses alcohol long enough, the youth could develop depressive symptoms and eventually meet criteria for major depression.

TRIGGER—Substance use can trigger the emergence of some mental health disorders if a youth is predisposed to mental illness. Example: A youth whose mother has bipolar disorder may have never experienced symptoms of mania until the youth uses PCP.

EXACERBATE—Symptoms of mental illness may get worse when a youth uses alcohol and drugs. Example: A youth with suicidal ideation may make an actual suicide attempt after drinking alcohol because the youth becomes more depressed and less inhibited.

MIMIC—Substance use can look like symptoms of a psychiatric disorder. Example: A youth with no history of psychiatric symptoms can develop paranoid delusions after heavy methamphetamine use.

MASK—Symptoms of mental illness may be hidden by drug and alcohol use. Example: A youth with attention-deficit/hyperactivity disorder may be less distractible when using cocaine. Psychiatric symptoms may not emerge until the youth stops using substances for a significant period of time.

INDEPENDENCE—A mental health disorder and substance abuse disorder may not be related to each other, but a common factor may underlie them both. Example: A youth's genetic makeup may make the youth vulnerable and more likely to develop mental illness and/or substance abuse."

(Trupin & Boesky, 2001)

1.6 THE MOST COMMON CONCURRENT MENTAL HEALTH PROBLEMS

There are a number of mental health problems that often overlap with substance use problems. Some, such as attention-deficit/hyperactivity disorder (ADHD), depression, anxiety, conduct and learning disorders can emerge in childhood and later increase the risk that a young person develops substance use problems. Others, such as bipolar disorder and schizophrenia tend to onset during adolescence and young adulthood, at the same time that substance use problems tend to emerge.

Attention-Deficit/Hyperactivity Disorder (ADHD)

- Symptoms are impulsivity, inattentiveness, hyperactivity and distractibility.
- ADHD starts at an early age and must be evident before age seven to be diagnosed correctly.
- Children with ADHD often do not completely "grow out of it" and go on to develop an ADHD residual syndrome.
- ADHD, conduct disorder and substance use problems often co-occur.
- ADHD frequently goes undiagnosed, sometimes resulting in self -medication through the use of stimulants or depressants depending on the symptoms the youth wants to modify.
- It is frequently misdiagnosed as other disorders or behaviours that mimic the symptoms of ADHD or that coexist with ADHD such as substance use, learning disability or Fetal Alcohol Spectrum Disorder (FASD).
- Substances such as cannabis are used by youth with ADHD to reduce impulsivity, although cannabis can also increase inattentiveness.
- Ritalin, the stimulant commonly prescribed to youth with ADHD, is the most effective treatment for ADHD symptoms, even in youth with substance use problems (Ballon, in press).

Bipolar disorder

- Bipolar disorder manifests in discrete episodes of manic moods, characterized by irritability or euphoria, alternating with depression.
- The age of onset of bipolar disorder is controversial, though most clinicians feel bipolar disorder doesn't fully manifest until age 12.
- Among youth with bipolar disorder, substance use may begin at an early age.
- Substance use can cause bipolar symptoms to appear mixed or it can create a rapid-cycling effect.
- Substance use is found more often among people in manic episodes than in any other psychiatric disorder. Stimulants can be used to maintain the manic state and avoid or delay the depressive state. The chronic use of stimulants, however, eventually brings on depression (Ballon, in press).
- Bipolar disorder can be difficult to diagnose when there is abuse of cocaine or other major stimulants. Usually, a period of abstinence is needed for a correct diagnosis.

Conduct disorders

- Conduct disorders refer to long-standing problem behaviours such as defiance, impulsivity or anti-social behaviour that may include vandalism, fire-setting, bullying, fighting, drug use or criminal activity and a lack of concern for others (Chaim & Shenfeld, in press).
- Conduct disorders are highly linked with problem substance use and usually precede it. They are also commonly associated with ADHD.

- Youth with conduct disorders are typically risk-takers and heavy users of multiple substances because of the excitement and rush they get from drugs (camh, 2002a).

Depression
- Depression manifests as irritable moods, physical complaints (e.g., headaches, stomach cramps), insomnia, decreased academic functioning and/or decreased social activities.
- Depression often precedes problem substance use. It is a common practice for youth to use substances to alleviate negative feelings associated with depression.
- Stimulants can be used to increase energy in clients with depression, but they can also increase anxiety.
- Many of the drugs that depressed youth use (e.g., alcohol, marijuana) can cause greater depression with chronic use (CAMH, 2002a).
- It should be noted that withdrawal from certain substances could induce depression.

Eating disorders
- The likelihood of developing a concurrent substance use problem increases by 12 to 18 per cent among people with anorexia and by 30 to 70 per cent among people with bulimia.
- The onset of eating disorders usually occurs during adolescence.
- Young people with eating disorders tend to use substances such as nicotine, alcohol or stimulants (e.g., diet pills, caffeine pills, speed, cocaine) to suppress their appetites (CAMH, 2002a).

Fetal Alcohol Spectrum Disorder (FASD)
- FASD is a spectrum of neurological, behavioural and cognitive deficits that interfere with growth, learning, and socialization and are caused by maternal alcohol use during pregnancy.
- The symptoms of FASD can mimic many of the symptoms of ADHD, learning disorders and conduct disorders and often coexist with ADHD.

Learning disorders
- Learning disorders are caused by "conditions of the brain" that affect the ability to take in, process or express information.
- There is a very high rate of substance use among youth with learning disorders, since they are likely to experience many of the symptoms that are high risk for drug use such as low self-esteem, academic difficulties, loneliness and depression (Chaim & Shenfeld, in press).

Post-traumatic stress
- Post-traumatic stress can manifest through symptoms such as anxiety, depression, self-harming, preoccupation with death, suicidal thoughts or gestures, and flashbacks.

- The incidence of post-traumatic stress is much higher when the young person has been emotionally, sexually or physically abused.
- People experiencing post-traumatic stress often use substances to help numb painful emotions and deal with anger (camh, 2002a).

Schizophrenia

- Symptoms of schizophrenia, such as psychosis, hallucinations and paranoia, usually first appear in the late teens or early twenties.
- People with schizophrenia use alcohol primarily for its euphoric and relaxing effects. Alcohol can enhance central nervous system (CNS) side effects of antipsychotic drugs, worsen extrapyramidal side effects (EPS) and also accelerate appearance of Tardive Dyskinesia. It can also increase the risk of anxiety, sleep disorders and sexual problems.
- Some research has shown that people with schizophrenia who use cannabis heavily have earlier onset of illness by five to 10 years compared to others who have not used cannabis.
- The rate of tobacco use in this population is much higher than in the general public, partially because nicotine blunts the side effects of antipsychotic medications. The incidence of Tardive Dyskinesia is much higher in smokers than non-smokers with schizophrenia.
- Psychotic symptoms that mimic schizophrenia (hallucinations, delusions, anxiety, depersonalization and paranoia) can be induced by hallucinogens such as cannabis. Hallucinogens usually cause visual effects, and chronic hallucinogen use can result in Hallucinogen Persisting Perception Disorder (HPPD), more commonly known as "flashbacks." Flashbacks are visual pseudo-hallucinations appearing as trailing effects, halos and shifting movements from out of the corner of one's eye. Usually people with HPPD know they are experiencing unreal phenomena, unlike those who are suffering from a psychotic illness (Ballon, in press).
- Cocaine can reduce negative symptoms and relieve feelings of depression.

Social anxiety

- Symptoms of social anxiety usually manifest as school-avoidance behaviours, poor self-image and social isolation, fear of humiliation and negative judgment.
- Initially, avoidance behaviour can protect a young person from using a substance. However, when she or he tries alcohol or other drugs, the anxiety-reducing effect of the substance can promote ongoing use (CAMH, 2002a).
- Use of substances can alleviate the symptoms of social anxiety, and youth who self-medicate in this way appear to be functioning reasonably well. However, as tolerance develops, the effects of the drugs diminish and symptoms of the anxiety can be exacerbated.
- Social anxiety can be mistaken for shyness or social skill deficits that are common developmental deficits during adolescence.

- Excessive caffeine or stimulant use by a person with anxiety disorder can mimic symptoms of anxiety and increase insomnia. It can also lead to increased heart rate, nervousness, flushed face, gastrointestinal disturbances, muscle twitching, palpitations and sweating.

Dual Diagnosis
- Young people with developmental disabilities and mental health disorders have what is referred to as a "dual diagnosis."
- There are some specific characteristics associated with substance use among individuals with developmental disabilities.
- Substance-related disorders, like mental health problems, are linked to the degree of cognitive impairment/potential. The higher the IQ, the higher the prevalence of these disorders (Campbell & Malone, 1991; Edgerton, 1986).
- The commonly held belief that people with dual diagnosis and substance-related disorders would be more vulnerable to the intoxicating effect of the substance of use has been, in part, borne out.
- People with developmental disabilities tend to drink alcohol or use illicit drugs in lower amounts compared to the general population. As a result, they are more difficult to identify. Often, caregivers consider this to be part of the individual's "life pattern."
- The inherent limitations that people with developmental disabilities face in their lives and the resulting anxiety and depressive disorders (Stavrakaki, 1999; Stavrakaki & Mintsioulis, 1995; 1997) tend to render these individuals more vulnerable to substance use for self-medication or stress relief (Longo, 1997; Ruf, 1999).
- Mental disorders that are common in this population, such as bipolar disorder, and schizophrenia, tend to increase the prevalence of substance-related disorders in this group (Longo, 1997; Stavrakaki, 2002; Westermeyer et al., 1988).

CHAPTER 2

PREPARING TO RESPOND: KEY ATTITUDES, KNOWLEDGE AND APPROACHES

You probably already know, from your own experience, that you have to be prepared to deal with almost anything when you work with young people! This chapter provides an overview of some key areas that, if you are not already familiar with them, may be helpful to you. The sections address key attitudes, knowledge and approaches that may influence how you work with young people to address their substance use and mental health problems, as well as other issues.

Depending on your setting, you may find the following topics helpful:
· Integrated approaches
· Common myths and stigmas about substance use and mental health
· Basic concepts of substance use
· Harm reduction
· Stages of Change model
· Motivation and behavioural change
· Cultural competency
· Outreach
· Promoting disclosure
· Managing behaviour
· Legal issues

2.1 INTEGRATED APPROACHES TO ADDRESSING YOUTH SUBSTANCE USE AND MENTAL HEALTH PROBLEMS—AN EMERGING AREA OF PRACTICE

Given that substance use and mental health problems occur together so often, integrated treatment approaches make sense because they reflect the reality of many young people's lives.

An integrated approach means addressing *both substance use and other mental health problems* when they occur among young people. It requires:

· screening and assessment of both substance use and mental health

· a comprehensive treatment and support plan which addresses all of the young person's relevant issues and

· collaboration with other service providers to implement the plan in a co-ordinated manner.

In an integrated treatment program, you and the other members of your team work together to provide both substance use and mental health treatment for young people. Another option is to collaborate with colleagues in other parts of your agency or in other community agencies to provide a range of both simultaneous and sequential services that meet youth's needs for treatment and support. (For more information about program- and systems-level integration, see Health Canada, 2002, 14-18, 82-85.)

It is important to integrate your response to substance use and mental health problems because they interact with each other in many different ways and tend to result in poorer outcomes for young people when not dealt with concurrently. To be effective, you need to understand the ways in which a young person's substance use may be affecting his or her mental health, and vice versa.

Regardless of whether a young person enters through the substance use treatment door or mental health treatment door, as a service provider, you have a responsibility to identify both substance use and mental health problems and ensure they are addressed in a co-ordinated way.

2.1.1 WHAT CAN YOU DO TO PROMOTE INTEGRATION?

There are a number of ways you can become more responsive to young people's substance use and mental health problems. For example, you can:

· Increase your understanding of the basic concepts of substance use.

· Increase your knowledge of youth substance use and other mental health problems, the prevalence of these problems, and their interactions.

· Increase your understanding of the differences and similarities between the approaches to substance use and mental health services for young people. This may help you understand how young people's needs may be interpreted and prioritized differently.

· Increase your knowledge of the range of mental health and substance use programs and services available for young people in your community.

- Develop some crossover skills in identifying, assessing and treating substance use and mental health problems.
- Enhance the co-ordination of your services with other youth mental health and substance use services in your community so young people do not "flip-flop" between services, or worse, fall between the cracks.
- Be prepared to co-ordinate case management and ensure that there is an integrated response to young people with substance use and mental health problems.

2.1.2 CO-ORDINATING SUBSTANCE USE AND MENTAL HEALTH TREATMENT SERVICES FOR YOUTH

Historically, the substance use and mental health spheres have been very separate worlds, but this is beginning to change. There is increasing recognition that young people being served by substance use treatment or mental health services tend to have multiple needs that demand comprehensive, integrated responses.

Some of the initiatives to increase linkages between substance use and mental health services include, for example, joint staff training, staff exchanges and secondments and consultation (Schwartz, 1997). Other ways to enhance co-ordination include co-location, information and referral, centralized intake and referral, inter-agency networks such as multidisciplinary teams, case management, staff sharing, financing models, training and education, shared data systems and linkages with the broader health, social, and correctional service system (Health Canada, 2002).

Appendix B: Substance use and mental health services for youth in Ontario: A comparative overview illustrates some of the differences and, perhaps more importantly, the similarities among substance use treatment and mental health services for young people.

- -

2.2 COMMON MYTHS AND STIGMAS ABOUT SUBSTANCE USE AND MENTAL HEALTH

Regardless of your expertise or experience, there may be times when you feel:
- uncomfortable or frightened about dealing with young people who use drugs
- somewhat less empathetic toward young people who use alcohol or drugs compared to young people who are, for example, depressed or anxious
- uneasy around young people who exhibit unusual or extreme behaviours such as cutting themselves or speaking in sentences that do not make sense
- reluctant to ask young people about their substance use
- hesitant to ask about potential mental health problems.

"This is a new focus in Ontario. Traditionally, substance abuse has been sectored in one corner while children's mental health has been sectored in another. The two are beginning to meet, to work together, to take on the challenge of [meeting the needs of adolescents struggling with substance abuse and mental health problems]. The opening chapter is being written." (Schwartz, 1997, 1)

"Adolescents who come to children's mental health centers are much the same as adolescents who are going to addictions programs for help. It's the same child! The same risk factors. Similar problems. Similar families. Similar mental health issues, fears and anxieties." (Schwartz, 1997, 1)

Your feelings probably reflect some of the myths and stigmas that still cling to the issues of substance use and mental health in our society.

Some common myths about substance use and mental health

Myth	Truth
Treatment of substance use is a highly specialized field and a youth who is using drugs should be immediately referred to an addiction specialist	Although education and training in substance use, identification, assessment and treatment is required, you can deliver effective interventions without being a specialist.
Nothing can be done until a drug user hits "rock bottom."	"Rock bottom" suggests something dramatic has to happen before change can occur, which is definitely not true! Negative consequences from substance use, however, often do lead a young person or their parent(s) to seek help.
Treatment for substance use only works for those who are highly motivated.	Motivation is not an intrinsic characteristic, but rather a fluid process or a continuum that can be enhanced. Your style of communication—empathetic, warm, objective and committed—can lower resistance and enhance a young person's level of motivation to change their behaviour.
Soft drugs like alcohol, marijuana and tobacco are not addictive. Young people who use only these drugs do not need help.	All drugs have the potential to be addictive and cause significant problems.
Young people who use substances must become abstinent before they receive treatment for mental health disorders.	Making abstinence a prerequisite for treatment is often "pie in the sky." This approach has contributed to the ineffective shuffling of young people from one system to another.

Myth	Truth
Young people with mental health disorders are all potentially violent and dangerous.	Young people with mental health disorders are not more dangerous than other young people. Depending on their disorder, however, they may be more likely to be violent toward themselves than toward others. Almost half of people with schizophrenia attempt suicide and one tenth succeed.
Young people with mental health problems are somehow responsible for their condition. It reflects some kind of weakness or character flaw. The condition can be "brought on" by their parents or themselves to get attention.	Someone diagnosed with a mental health disorder has an illness. It is not something that is their "fault." It occurs among all races, cultures and social classes.
Young people with mental health issues cannot live independently and have nothing positive to contribute to the community.	Many people who have had mental health problems have made significant contributions to our society in politics, culture, academic life, athletics, journalism, business, art and science. Many have been leaders and visionaries.
Young people with mental health problems must receive treatment before their substance use can be addressed.	If someone is experiencing severe or life-threatening symptoms related to their mental health issues, these must be addressed as quickly as possible. Otherwise, it is often best to treat both mental health and substance use issues at the same time.

(Addiction Research Foundation and Health and Welfare Canada, 1991; Centre for Addiction and Mental Health and Canadian Mental Health Association, 2001; Schwartz, 1997)

2.2.1 IMPORTANCE OF A POSITIVE ATTITUDE

Your attitudes and expectations about the young people with whom you work can have an important impact on what happens to them. Debunking myths and stigmas is part of building positive attitudes towards youth's potential for change. Focussing on their natural strengths and resources, and not just on their problems, is also crucial to building rapport and enhancing their motivation to explore and resolve problems.

If you recognize that working with young people who may be using substances and dealing with mental health issues is rewarding and you feel entitled and equipped to deal with substance use and mental health issues, then you can make an important difference.

The bottom line is recognizing that each young person is a unique individual who is coping with difficult and sometimes devastating circumstances. It would be misguided to make assumptions or generalizations based on the enormity of their problems.

2.3 DRUGS AND HOW THEY WORK

In this section, we will define basic concepts and describe basic processes of drug use. The section is designed to answer the fundamental questions: "What are drugs?" and "What do they do?"

First, what is a drug? The Greek word *pharmakon* means both medicine and poison— a confusion of fact and attitude which is still with us today. Some "drugs" (e.g., medicines) are designed for their positive effects on the mind and/or body but, used incorrectly, they can be toxic. Other substances normally used as foods or beverages (e.g., mushrooms, alcohol) or for purposes other than human consumption (e.g., gasoline; solvents) can also have powerful effects on the mind and/or body. What all these substances have in common is their capacity to change the mood, state of mind, or state of being of the user.

People take drugs for one primary reason— because they change the chemistry of the CNS, especially the brain. The effects may be physiological, biochemical or psychological, but in all cases, drug use produces "altered states"—altered feelings, altered perceptions, even altered capacities.

At what point does this alteration become drug abuse? The phrase "drug abuse" is really a value judgement rather than a scientific term. The distinction between socially acceptable use, dangerous use, and what counts as "abuse" varies with time and place and cultural context.

"The counselor's own expectations about a person's likelihood of change can have a powerful effect on outcome, acting as a self-fulfilling prophecy" (Miller & Rollnick , 2002, 41).

A drug is any substance used to change the mood, state of mind or state of being of the user.

The American Medical Association defines drug abuse as:

"... the ingestion of a psychoactive substance that is capable of producing physical or psychological dependence, in an amount and frequency likely to result in overt intoxication or to lead to physical or psychological problems or anti-social behaviour. Said in another way, when the continued use of a mood-altering substance means more to the individual than the problems associated with such use, that person can be described as abusing drugs." (Wilford, 1981, p. 7)

In order to understand drug effects, you will need to be familiar with two major processes influencing their intensity:

· the concentration of the drug at the site of action in the body, and the factors which determine it

· the responses of the body to a given concentration of the drug, which change and develop over time. This is referred to as tolerance.

2.3.1 CONCENTRATION OF THE DRUG AT THE SITE OF ACTION

The intensity of a drug effect depends largely on its concentration at the site of action. Concentration, in turn, depends on the dose administered; the way in which the substance is absorbed, distributed, metabolized and eliminated by the body; drug interactions; and other factors. All are discussed below. The primary site of psychoactivity is the CNS, but actions at other sites (e.g., the heart) may produce psychological effects (e.g., excitement).

Dose

Dose refers to the amount consumed. In the case of legal substances, the dose of a drug either is known or can be estimated. For prescription or non-prescription medication, it is normally written on the label. A dose of alcohol can be estimated by using the concept of the "standard" drink, illustrated below.

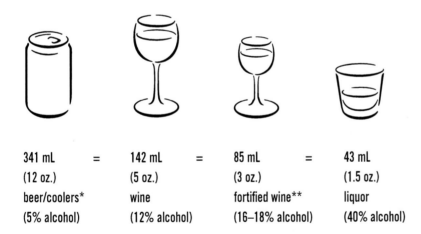

341 mL	=	142 mL	=	85 mL	=	43 mL
(12 oz.)		(5 oz.)		(3 oz.)		(1.5 oz.)
beer/coolers*		wine		fortified wine**		liquor
(5% alcohol)		(12% alcohol)		(16–18% alcohol)		(40% alcohol)

*Note that regular beers and many coolers have an average alcohol content of five per cent, but some have as much as six or seven per cent, making them stronger than a "standard" drink. "Light" beers have an average alcohol content of four per cent.

**such as sherry, port or vermouth

Figure 2.1: "Standard" drinks consisting of a bottle of beer, a glass of table wine, a small glass of dessert (fortified) wine, or a "shot" of spirits. Each contains the same amount of alcohol.

In the case of illicit drugs, the dose is often unknown because of the great variability of these preparations. In the case of drugs derived from plant sources (e.g., marijuana), differences in strains of plants and cultivation techniques can greatly affect potency. In the case of synthetic drugs, potency varies according to:

· the chemical techniques of the manufacturer

· the care with which these are carried out

· age and storage conditions

· purity.

Absorption

In order for a psychoactive drug to have an effect on the brain, it must be able to:

· cross the cell membranes of the small intestine, lungs, mucous, etc., in order to be absorbed into the bloodstream

· cross the blood-brain barrier (the specialized cell membranes of the small capillaries in the brain which are set closely together) in order to pass from the bloodstream to the brain which is the site of action.

Most psychoactive drugs are able to cross cell membranes with relative ease, but the speed with which they enter the bloodstream and the brain depends on the route or mode of administration.

The routes most commonly used for ingestion of drugs are:

Ingestion: Oral administration (swallowing a drug) is the most common and convenient method of drug administration. However, the rate of absorption of substances by this route tends to be rather slow since, for the most part, they must pass from the stomach into the small intestine before they can enter the bloodstream.

Absorption via ingestion may be affected by:

· the presence of food in the stomach

· stomach contents that dilute the drug

· stomach contents that are highly acidic or highly basic. (Some drugs [e.g., insulin, some antibiotics, some hormones] are destroyed entirely by stomach acid or digestive enzymes and must be given by injection if they are to be effective.)

Inhalation: Volatile substances (gases) and aerosols (suspensions of particles or liquid droplets in a gas) are usually inhaled. Absorption in the lungs occurs rapidly: the effects of a puff of smokable cocaine or tobacco can be felt within seconds. Drugs that can be taken in this manner include solvents, propellant gases, cannabis and tobacco, some drugs given in the treatment of asthma and many general anaesthetics.

The dose of an inhaled drug can be controlled by an experienced user. Absorption, and therefore the intensity of effects, depends on how deeply the user inhales, how long she holds her breath, etc. For this reason, the amount of drug in a smoke or vapour that is actually absorbed is difficult to measure.

Absorption across mucous membranes: Mucous membranes (the linings of the mouth, nose, eye sockets, throat, vagina, rectum, etc.) are more permeable than surface skin. Therefore, absorption through mucous membranes is both fast and effective for fat-soluble drugs. The effects of drugs that are "snorted" into the nose, such as cocaine and nicotine in the form of snuff, can be felt within a minute or two. Cocaine and nicotine can also be absorbed through the lining of the cheek. Rectal administration can be used for many drugs, as well.

Injection: Injection bypasses normal biological barriers, drastically decreasing the time needed to produce an effect. Injection produces a rapid rise in concentration of the drug in the blood if done quickly. Blood with a high drug level (or "bolus") can reach the brain within a few seconds of administration. The resulting rapid rise in drug concentration in the brain accounts for the "rush" or brief period of intense drug effect that is experienced by the user.

Drugs can be injected into many of the body's tissues or cavities. The most common routes of injection are listed below:

· *Subcutaneous (S.C.) injection ("skin popping"):* This term refers to injection under the skin. It is used as a route of administration for some therapeutic drugs (e.g., insulin), and by street users who are either inexperienced with needles or can no longer inject into badly scarred veins. Absorption is slower than when the same drugs are given intravenously, but faster than when they are taken orally.

· *Intramuscular (I.M.) injection:* This involves the administration of a drug directly into muscle tissue. It permits a larger volume of solution to be injected than with S.C. administration, but there is usually more pain involved. I.M. injection is frequently used with therapeutic drugs but is not popular with street users.

· *Intravenous (I.V.) injection ("mainlining"):* Intravenous injection delivers drugs directly into the bloodstream resulting in the most rapid route of absorption. It requires considerable skill, and therefore tends to be employed by the more experienced users. I.V. injection is extremely hazardous because of:

  – the risk of overdose

  – the risk of infections (including HIV/AIDS) from impure solutions or contaminated needles

  – the risk that small particles (e.g., from crushed tablets that have not been filtered) or air bubbles (emboli) in the injected solution may block the normal flow of blood through the organs, which may be fatal.

Distribution

Drugs travel through both the bloodstream and, to a lesser extent, the lymphatic system, to get to their sites of action. But not all drugs are distributed as easily as others. Some drugs bind easily to blood particles such as plasma proteins. Others dissolve in body fat. A few may

Many of the hazards of taking drugs are inherent in the process of administration. In other words, smoking, in itself, is harmful regardless of the substance that is being smoked. Injecting is also a dangerous behaviour, no matter what the drug is that is being injected.

be deposited in bone tissue. Drugs must be a relatively small molecule size, highly fat-soluble and not attached to blood particles in order to cross the blood brain barrier and enter the brain. Most drugs can cross through the placenta of pregnant women and affect the fetus. They can also pass into the milk of lactating women.

Metabolism

Drugs are eliminated from the body in both changed and unchanged states. In order to facilitate excretion, the body transforms substances that are primarily fat-soluble into water-soluble by-products. This complex chemical transformation is performed by enzymes through a process called metabolism. While metabolism can occur at different sites in the body, most of it happens in the liver.

All drugs taken orally pass through the liver before reaching the blood stream. This is referred to as "first pass effect." Because this deactivates some drugs before they can have any effect, they need to be given by another route such as inhalation or injection in order to work.

As a drug becomes progressively less fat-soluble, it loses its ability to enter the brain, and hence loses its psychoactivity. However, it is not always the case that all metabolic action decreases the psychoactivity of all substances. In fact, sometimes the metabolic by-products are as active or more active than the original substance. An example of this is heroin, which is transformed into morphine when it passes through the liver.

Elimination

As a drug is absorbed into the body, bloodstream concentration of the drug starts to fall. This drop reflects first, the movement of the drug from the bloodstream into the tissues (distribution), and later, its metabolism and excretion from the body (elimination). The exact rate of metabolism and elimination is partly genetically determined for each individual, but is also dependent on some of the characteristics of the drug itself.

The rate of excretion of a drug from the body is often described using the concept of elimination "half-life." This is the time required for the drug concentration in the blood to fall by one-half. When this concept is applied, it means that it takes five half-lives for a drug to reach a constant level or steady state in the body (drug intake = drug elimination). Likewise, it takes five half-lives for a drug to be completely eliminated from the system.

Half-life can be used, in part, to determine how frequently a drug should be administered to maintain an expected effect. It can also be a factor in determining the abuse potential of a drug. A drug with a short half-life, such as cocaine, will cause severe withdrawal symptoms, and a client is likely to use it again to get rid of these symptoms. Marijuana, on the other hand, has a very long half-life (partly because it is extremely fat-soluble) and is far less likely to cause withdrawal symptoms.

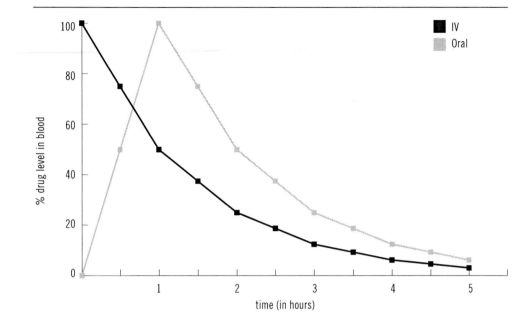

Figure 2.2: Drug with half-life of 1 hour: IV vs. oral administration

Figure 2.2 illustrates the concept of half-life. In this example, the drug has a half-life of 1 hour. Once fully absorbed, it takes 1 hour for the level to fall from 100% to 50%, then 1 hour to fall again from 50% to 25%, 1 hour to drop from 25% to 12.5%, and so on. While, mathematically speaking, the drug concentration does not actually reach zero, in practical terms the drug in this example will be eliminated from the body in 5 hours.

The duration of effect of many drugs increases with the user's age. This could result from increased amounts of body fat (which act as a reservoir for highly fat-soluble drugs) or from impaired liver or kidney function.

There are two major routes of excretion for most drugs:
· in the urine (via the kidneys)
· in the feces (via the liver) through the bile duct and both the small and large intestines.

Certain drugs are also excreted through the lungs. The concentration of the drug in the exhaled air is always directly proportional to the concentration in the blood at that time. Since about 5% of a dose of beverage alcohol is exhaled, this principle can be used to estimate blood alcohol content (BAC). Various roadside screening devices ("breathalyzers") are used for this purpose.

There are also several other minor routes whereby small amounts of a drug may be excreted. These routes include:
· milk (of significance for the infants of nursing mothers)
· saliva (can be used for forensic analysis, [e.g., the alcohol dip stick]);
· other body fluids (sweat, tears, semen, etc.).

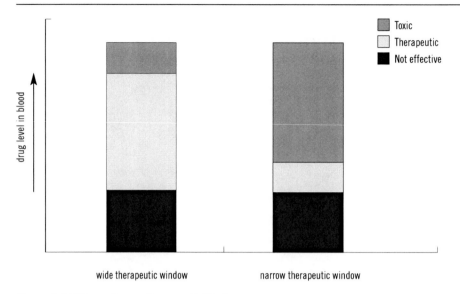

Figure 2 .3 Wide vs. Narrow Therapeutic Window

Therapeutic window, also called therapeutic index, indicates the margin of safety of a drug. This is the blood level at which a drug produces the desired effect without causing toxicity. A drug with a wide therapeutic index, such as diazepam (Valium®), is effective at many doses, and does not usually cause life-threatening toxicity even at very high doses. With a narrow therapeutic index drug such as methadone, however, the difference between an effective dose and a life-threatening, toxic overdose is very small.

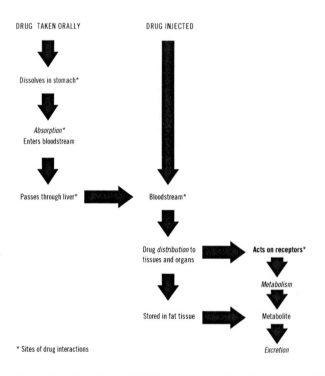

Figure 2 .4 drug effects in the body and potential sites for drug interactions

Drug interactions

A drug interaction occurs when one drug alters the action or effects of another drug present in the body at the same time. Some interactions can be trivial, while others can be dangerous and possibly life-threatening.

· Drugs taken together can act independently of each other. For example, alcohol does not seem to interfere with the action of vitamins or oral contraceptives, or vice versa.

· Drugs taken together can enhance each other's effects. This could happen because of the similarity of their action on the brain or because one drug increases the concentration of the other in the body by interfering with its distribution, metabolism or excretion. For instance, alcohol and antihistamines are both CNS depressants, and are additive in their effects. Therefore, the combination can increase both the desired effects of the drugs (e.g. disinhibition) as well as the side effects (e.g., drowsiness).

· Drugs taken together can have an antagonistic effect. This could occur when one drug "blocks" or prevents another drug from producing its effect. Antagonism could also occur when two drugs have opposite effects on the brain (e.g., alcohol-induced drowsiness versus caffeine-induced alertness) or if one drug alters the absorption or distribution of another.

While interactions can usually be predicted with prescribed medications, the effects can be less predictable with substance users. They may use different kinds of drugs to induce a spectrum of effects or to control extreme effects. For example, LSD and an amphetamine may be taken together to produce both hallucinogenic and stimulant effects simultaneously. Sedatives may be used to counteract the effects of a cocaine "crash." The problem is that a number of variables, such as drug potency, purity and dose cannot be controlled for, and the interactions can lead to toxic reactions.

Other factors influencing drug effects

An individual's response to a drug or a combination of drugs is also affected by body size, gender, nutrition, health status, habituation, state of mind, and social setting. Psychological factors also can play a critical role. Indeed, anticipation of a drug effect is often the most powerful predictor of its occurrence.

2.3.2 EFFECTS OF LONG-TERM USE: THE BODY'S ADAPTATION TO DRUGS

When a person continues to use drugs over an extended period of time, issues become relevant. We refer to the user developing a "tolerance," becoming "dependent," and suffering "withdrawal" when drug use stops. These terms are part of our everyday clinical vocabulary, but they are not always defined clearly nor used consistently, even by the "experts." This problem is compounded when we try to apply them to a young drug user, who has not yet developed the body reactions of a long-time user.

There are many factors that influence a drug's effects and their duration. These include the type of drug, its dose, how it is taken, its absorption and elimination. There is a whole slate of drug, person and environment variables which all come into play. For these reasons, you cannot expect to predict the effects of a drug of unknown quality and dose on a particular user.

Tolerance is defined as the loss of sensitivity to a drug. It can be thought of simply as the body's way of protecting itself from the effects of drug use.

Tolerance

The degree of the body's response to a drug depends not only on the drug concentration, but also on the sensitivity (responsiveness) of target cells and organs. Sometimes the body can adapt to certain effects of a drug, but not others. For example, a drug may initially cause drowsiness which goes away with repeated administration. On the other hand, an effect such as sexual dysfunction may not improve as the drug use continues. Normally, chronic use of a substance leads to loss of sensitivity, or tolerance.

Tolerance is an adaptation of the body to repeated drug exposure, such that drug effects of a particular dose become progressively less intense, and therefore escalation of the dose is required to achieve the initial drug effect.

Normally, tolerance is a gradual process that develops over the course of days, weeks, or months of drug administration. But with some drugs, such as tobacco, it occurs after just a few routine administrations, as in the case of "learning" to smoke, which involves rapid tolerance to initial nausea and dizziness.

FACTS ABOUT TOLERANCE

- Its onset varies from drug to drug.
- In some cases, when tolerance develops to one drug, it can lead to the development of cross-tolerance to another drug.
- The higher the dose taken, the faster tolerance develops.
- It develops faster if a drug is taken in a regular pattern than in a binge pattern.
- It develops faster if the user has a previous history of tolerance to that drug.
- It does not develop equally for all effects of a drug (e.g., the lethal dose may remain constant while the dose necessary to get high may rise).
- It may develop faster with respect to effects like the loss of dexterity and alertness, which interfere with performance on the job, etc.

Drug processes also involve social and emotional dynamics. In the case of tolerance, for example, if a drug is administered in the same room each day, a person learns to expect the substance in that room, and his or her body learns to resist (or tolerate) the drug effects when in that environment. So tolerance is not just a physical process, but a psychological one, as well.

Dependence

Drug dependence is normally described in terms of separate psychological and physical components, but this distinction is not always clear nor useful in practice. It is more likely that "drug-seeking behaviour" is both psychological and physiological in origin.

Psychological dependence is a major cause of the misuse of psychoactive drugs. With certain drugs, such as tobacco and marijuana, which are associated with relatively mild physical withdrawal symptoms, psychological dependence can be the main reason for their continued use.

COUNSELLOR'S TIP

Psychological dependence is a major factor in the continuation of drug use beyond experimentation and consequently, it is an important focus in treatment.

FACTS ABOUT DEPENDENCE

- Physical dependence may not be apparent as long as the drug is being taken.
- The magnitude of physical dependence and the severity of withdrawal vary with the amount, frequency and duration of drug use, as well as the drug's half-life.
- Dependence, in itself, does not mean a substance has abuse potential. Many medical drugs can "cause" dependence (e.g., insulin for diabetes, inhalers for asthma, antidepressants for depression), yet these are not substances of abuse.
- Drugs that are injected (e.g., heroin) or inhaled (e.g., nicotine) are more likely to produce dependence than those that are swallowed.
- The type of withdrawal symptoms manifested tend to be the opposite of the primary drug effect—that is, the withdrawal symptoms reverse the acute effects of the drug. For example, withdrawal from depressants is characterized by hyperactivity of the CNS (irritability, seizures, etc.) while withdrawal from stimulants produces hypoactivity (slowing of CNS activity) and mood depression.
- Tolerance and dependence are separate phenomena and may develop independently of each other.

The degree of physical dependence is indicated by the severity of withdrawal symptoms. For drugs such as alcohol, barbiturates and opioids, the withdrawal symptoms can be so unpleasant and threatening that they contribute enormously to the user's drive to continue taking the drugs

Severity of withdrawal is also determined by half-life. Drugs with a short half-life tend to have severe withdrawal symptoms that dissipate in a shorter period of time, while drugs with longer half-lives have milder withdrawal symptoms that last for a longer period of time.

Psychological dependence is defined as the emotional or mental drive to continue taking a drug because the user feels that its effects are necessary to maintain a sense of well-being. In simple terms, the user "depends" on the drug in order to function or feel comfortable in some situation, for example, at parties. In extreme cases, the user depends on the drug to cope under any circumstances.

Physical dependence is defined as the adjustment of bodily tissues in response to the continued presence of a drug, such that disturbing withdrawal symptoms develop when use of the drug is discontinued.

Cross-dependence refers to the ability of one drug to suppress the withdrawal symptoms from another drug, and therefore to substitute for the other in maintaining the physically dependent state (e.g. benzodiazepines and alcohol). Cross-dependence explains the possibility of methadone maintenance programs for narcotic addicts. The synthetic opioid, methadone, can substitute for other drugs in the same family (heroin, morphine, etc.), but has the advantages of oral administration, longer-lasting effect, lack of euphoric effects and composition control.

The fact that some users do not develop dependence even with heavy use suggests the existence of a predisposing factor in certain people, or in their social circumstances, and challenges our assumption that the power to addict lies in the drugs alone.

Withdrawal

Withdrawal refers to a set of physical symptoms and reactions, sometimes dramatic, which take place when a habituated drug user suddenly stops using. The body's adaptive restructuring (functional tolerance) is unmasked, and the drug user will experience the full extent of oppositional responses the body has developed. This means they will suddenly experience the opposite effect of what they had been achieving with the drug. Thus, stimulant drugs tend to produce "down" withdrawals, while depressant drugs produce "hyper" withdrawals.

There is considerable overlap in the withdrawal symptoms associated with drugs in the same group and even among drugs of different categories, so you cannot accurately infer what drug has been used simply from observing withdrawal. The possibility of confusion is compounded when the user has a multiple drug-use pattern. A recent and accurate drug- use history, including doses and times of administration, is essential for the implementation of appropriate therapeutic procedures.

The duration and severity of withdrawal varies considerably from drug to drug depending on dose, half-life, type of drug taken, duration of use, level of dependency, abruptness of discontinuation and other pharmacological factors.

Serious withdrawal can be a medical event, and may need to be treated where there are life support and drug-testing facilities. Withdrawal from alcohol, barbiturates and benzodiazepines can be life threatening because of the risk of seizures. Withdrawal from opioids, while sometimes extremely unpleasant, is rarely life threatening.

As with dependence, withdrawal is a phenomenon not exclusive to substances of abuse. Withdrawal can occur with many medications. Again, this is a matter of the body suddenly having something taken away after it has adapted to using it.

There is a range of withdrawal symptoms that can include depressed mood, insomnia, restlessness, anxiety, irritability, frustration, anger and difficulty concentrating. These symptoms can mimic psychiatric symptoms and disorders, and can make proper diagnosis very difficult.

Addiction

The term "addiction" appears in a variety of contexts with different implications, and very often carries unnecessary moral overtones. Most experts use it to describe dependent patterns of drug use, including both physical and psychological dimensions. It is best to think of "addiction" in terms or a continuum of escalating use with increasing involvement and dependence, as well as increasing detriment to the user.

COUNSELLOR'S TIP

- For the younger user, the psychological and social aspects of drug dependence may be the most relevant factors to consider during treatment. Looking for dramatic signs of drug "addiction" in terms of physical dependence in a young person could lead to an underestimation of the problem. On the other hand, assessing all drug use as "addiction" may lead to an overestimation of the degree of difficulties being experienced.

- Awareness of the range of drug-using behaviours is particularly important when you are assessing the young drug user, who will not have the more striking physical symptoms of an older client with a long history of use.

2.3.3 DRUGS OF ABUSE AND THEIR EFFECTS

In this section, we provide information on drug identification, classification and abuse potential. Where possible, the information in this section is youth specific. Remember, you don't have to be an expert on individual drugs to work well with young users. Often they are the best informants of how a drug affects them.

Identification and analysis

The accurate identification of drugs is not easy. It cannot reliably be done by sight or street name, and should not be attempted by the untrained. Young drug users can be your best source. They can tell you what substances they are using, and likely are more up-to-date than you about street names, what's "in" and what's "out," what new combinations are being tried, etc. However, since illicit street drugs are uncontrolled, neither you nor your client can be absolutely sure of the composition, potency or purity of the drugs they are using.

Sometimes the Internet can be useful for identification. While it is not always the best place to look for reputable scientific or medical information, there are some reliable sites. And when identifying a substance of abuse, sites that are aimed at users may have some helpful information.

If it becomes necessary to know the precise identity or composition of the substances being used (most often, in relation to health effects and consequences), only laboratory analysis provides certain results.

Don't be intimidated by adolescents' "street knowledge" of drugs. Treat them as a resource, and give them credit for what they know. However, don't assume they know everything.

- -

Drug Classification

There are many different ways of classifying drugs based on dimensions such as source, function and effect. The classification you will probably find most useful is a simple one based on pharmacological effects in the central nervous system (CNS).

CNS depressants

· alcohol

· sedative/hypnotic/anxiolytics such as benzodiazepines (e.g., diazepam [Valium®], lorazepam [Ativan®])

· GHB

· ketamine

· inhalants/solvents

· barbiturates (e.g., Amytal®, Seconal®, Nembutal®).

opioid (narcotic) analgesics

· heroin

· morphine

· codeine

· methadone

· opium

· meperidine (e.g., Demerol®)

· and many others.

hallucinogens

· cannabis (marijuana, hashish)

· MDMA (ecstacy)

· LSD (acid)

· psilocybin (magic mushrooms)

· mescaline

· PCP.

stimulants

· nicotine

· caffeine

- cocaine
- amphetamines (e.g., methylphenidate [Ritalin®], crystal meth)
- and others.

psychotherapeutic agents
- antidepressants
- antipsychotics
- mood stabilizers.

Within any of these principal groups, drugs may be further classified into subgroups, clarifying the particular type of drug dependence possible.

Abuse Potential

A great deal is known about individual drugs and their effects—more than we can easily condense for this chapter. Of course, we cannot predict exactly what pieces of drug information might become useful to you in the process of working with particular young people. In fact, often the most important thing to know for purposes of youth counselling and support is what drug effects the client is expecting. Usually, whatever effects are anticipated are achieved. It is also the case that young drug users might experience unique effects because of their stage in the life cycle. They have not yet reached maturity— physically, psychologically or socially—and the greatest negative effects of use may be to interrupt those developmental processes.

We recommend that you supplement this chapter by obtaining a handbook of drug information for reference purposes such as *Drugs and Drug Abuse, 3rd Ed, CAMH, 1997*. For more information on specific drugs and their effects, you can refer to the *Do You Know...* series published and updated regularly by CAMH, in Appendix C. The series provides descriptions of 14 commonly used drugs or groups of drugs. These publications may also be given to youth and their parents. *Do You Know...* brochures can be ordered from CAMH, marketing@camh.net, or 1 800 661-1111 (416 595-6059 in Toronto).

2.4 STAGES OF CHANGE MODEL

The stages of change model developed by Prochaska, & DiClemente (1982) has become a very important tool for anyone who is trying to help others achieve behavioural change. According to this model, change is a process, and people will move forward– and sometimes back again—through different stages. At times, they may relapse and return to problematic substance use, eventually beginning the process of change all over again. Each stage of change is associated with a distinct set of cognitive, emotional and behavioural characteristics.

[The stages of change model] "has played an integral role in the development of motivational interviewing and brief interventions using a motivational approach" (DiClemente & Velasquez, 2002, 202).

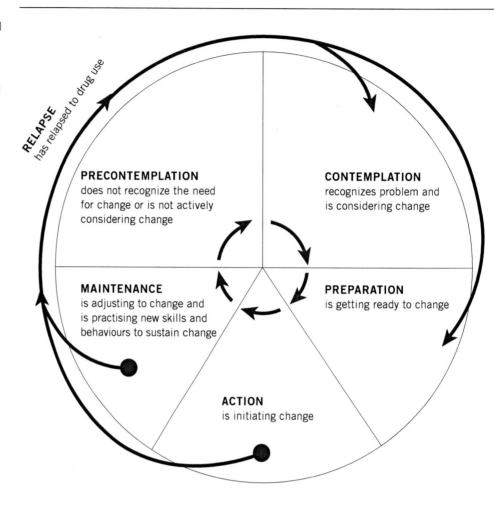

Figure 2.5 Stages of change model. Adapted from Prochaska, J. O., & DiClemente, C. C. (1982)

Precontemplation: not thinking about change

In this stage, young individuals are defensive and resistant to engage in the change process. They typically are unaware of the extent of their use and of the consequences associated with their use.

Contemplation: thinking about change

In this stage, youth express some distress and begin to consider making changes. They are typically ambivalent about whether or not they can make the changes and if it is worth the effort.

Preparation: preparing to change

In this stage, young people express an intention to change. They are prepared to make a firm commitment to follow through on the change process.

Action: making the change

In this stage, young people are actively working on goals to stop or reduce substance use, as well as making changes to their environment (e.g., avoiding certain places or people, developing constructive leisure time activities, etc.).

Maintenance: maintaining the change

In this stage, individuals are working toward sustaining their initial changes, which may include continuing to make other changes that support their goals (e.g., making new friends, getting a part-time job, etc.).

Relapse: back to problem use

Relapse refers to reverting back to a previous, unacceptable level of drug use that the youth has set a goal to change. It varies from a minor slip to a return to previous problematic behaviour. After relapse, a youth may return to any of the previous stages of the model. Relapse is a very common experience in the change process and there are specific approaches to preventing and coping with relapse that are discussed in Chapter 4.

Some important implications for working with substance use clients have emerged from this model:

· There are specific interventions for each stage of change. Therefore, it is important to recognize the client's stage.

· Young clients who are in the pre-contemplative stage may be good candidates for brief interventions (see Chapter 4 and First Contact).

· Young clients who are thinking about change may benefit from looking at the pros and cons of changing or not changing their drug use (see Chapter 4 and First Contact).

· Young clients who are prepared for change may benefit from doing a functional analysis of their drug use, thereby identifying triggers and consequences. (see Chapter 4 and First Contact).

· Many youth are in the precontemplative stage when they are first seen for assessment or counselling, and are not yet prepared to change.

· Youth frequently revert back to a previous stage and therefore, ongoing check-in to identify the stage they are in is important.

· Change is a process, not an event.

· For someone who uses multiple substances, it is not uncommon to be in different stages. For example, a youth may be in precontemplation about alcohol use, in contemplation about cannabis and in action for cocaine.

Young people can be at different points in the change cycle for their substance use problems than for their mental health problems. The young client may be more (or less) aware of the consequences of one or the other problem, and therefore more concerned, and more prepared to take action on the problem of which they are more aware.

You can use the stages of change model to tailor how you work with young people and help them become ready for change. Additional information on tailoring treatment to stages of change is included in Chapter 4. In particular, you can learn how to interact with young people in ways that can enhance their motivation for change.

2.5 MOTIVATIONAL INTERVIEWING (MI)

In this section, we introduce a "way of being" with the client that is particularly helpful for working with youth who are in precontemplation or contemplation stages of change. It is a client-centred approach in that the focus is on the client's concerns, and it is directive in the way you as the counsellor play an active role in moving the client toward change. The therapeutic relationship is a partnership in which the counsellor takes a supporting rather than an authoritarian role, and creates a positive and collaborative interpersonal environment. The counsellor's focus is not on giving information or instilling insight, but rather on eliciting these things from the client. The counsellor respects the client's autonomy and freedom to choose his or her own course of action (Miller & Rollnick, 2002).

Practical information on how to do motivational interviewing (MI) is covered in Chapter 4. The *First Contact* manual is based on motivational interviewing.

You already know that there are young people capable of changing their behaviour and increasing their well-being without your help. In fact, most young people who use substances eventually cut back or stop using substances without any intervention. In other words, they go through a natural process of behaviour change.

When you work with young people, you discover that you cannot push or force them to change. With the right communication style, however, you can help facilitate their change process.

According to Miller and Rollnick, a person's motivation for change involves being "ready, willing and able."
· their readiness to change (the extent to which change is a priority)
· their willingness to change (the extent to which they consider change important)
· their confidence in their ability to change (their sense of self-efficacy) (Miller & Rollnick, 2002, 10–11).

Like most of us, young people are often ambivalent about change. They both want and don't want to change. By using an empathetic, warm and non-judgmental style, you are more likely to be able to guide a young person towards identifying and resolving (or getting "unstuck" from) their own ambivalence. This includes guiding them to examine the costs and the benefits of their situation and to consider what they are motivated to do.

"...motivational interviewing is a method of communication rather than a set of techniques... it is fundamentally a way of being with people and for people — a facilitative approach to communication that evokes natural change" (Miller & Rollnick, 2002, 25).

MI is best defined as "a client centered, directive method for enhancing intrinsic motivation to change by exploring and resolving ambivalence" (Miller & Rollnick, 2002, p. 25).

A young person's motivation is not a fixed characteristic or personality trait (as in, "she or he is not a motivated person") but rather an *interpersonal process* (Miller & Rollnick, 2002, 22). In other words, motivation is influenced by the empathy, trust, understanding, acceptance and commitment between that person and yourself.

When you work with young people, your ability to guide them in exploring and enhancing their motivation for change may be the most important skill you can offer them.

The spirit of motivational interviewing

Fundamental approach of motivational interviewing	Mirror-image opposite approach to counseling
Collaboration: Counseling involves a partnership that honors the client's expertise and perspectives. The counselor provides an atmosphere that is conducive rather than coercive to change.	*Confrontation:* Counseling involves over-riding the client's impaired perspectives by imposing awareness and acceptance of "reality" that the client cannot see or will not admit.
Evocation: The resources and motivation for change are presumed to reside within the client. Intrinsic motivation for change is enhanced by drawing on the client's own perspectives, goals, and values.	*Education:* The client is presumed to lack key knowledge, insight, and/or skills that are necessary for change to occur. The counselor seeks to address these deficits by providing the requisite enlightenment.
Autonomy: The counselor affirms the client's right and capacity for self-direction and facilitates informed choice.	*Authority:* The counselor tells the client what he or she must do.

(Miller & Rollnick 2002, 35)

The following four guiding principles are the foundation of motivational interviewing:

Express empathy

Acceptance facilitates change.

Skillful reflective listening is fundamental.

Ambivalence is normal.

Develop discrepancy

The client rather than the counselor should present the arguments for change.

Change is motivated by a perceived discrepancy between present behaviour and important personal goals or values.

Roll with resistance

Avoid arguing for change.

Resistance is not directly opposed.

New perspectives are invited but not imposed.

The client is a primary resource in finding answers and solutions.

Resistance is a signal to respond differently.

Support self-efficacy

A person's belief in the possibility of change is an important motivator.

The client, not the counselor, is responsible for choosing and carrying out the change.

The counselor's own belief in the person's ability to change becomes a self-fulfilling prophecy.

(Miller & Rollnick, 2002, 37–41)

There are a number of reasons why young people who attend substance use treatment, may be hesitant to change or even resistant. For example, they may:

· have a history of controlling adults in their lives

· have been exposed to exaggerated drug education messages

· have a sense of invulnerability

· have been coerced into treatment by the justice system

· need to establish their identity

· not yet be dependent on substances (Baer & Peterson, 2002).

· feel that the positive effects of using drugs outweigh the negative consequences.

In addition, if young people also have mental health problems, they may:

- have deficits that prevent them from understanding that they have problems and recognizing their impact
- rationalize their use of substances as a way of coping with their mental health problems
- be demoralized and have a sense of futility (Connors et al., 2001)
- have symptoms (depression, mania, etc.) that make it difficult to sustain a stable affect or sense of motivation.

Nonetheless, there are many reasons why motivational interviewing may be a particularly useful style for working with young people. These include:

- Motivational interviewing emphasizes exploring and resolving the ambivalence about identity, roles and behaviours that is so common among young people.
- Motivational interviewing's emphasis on being respectful, acknowledging choices and ambivalence, minimizing arguing and avoiding confrontation are approaches that work well with young people who so often have limited choices and control.
- Motivational interviewing's exploratory approach and emphasis on personal change goals seem to mesh with young people's curious and philosophical nature and desire for autonomy.
- Motivational interviewing is consistent with the harm reduction approach that is appropriate for young people who do not have chronic substance use problems.
- Motivational interviewing is particularly appropriate for prevention programs aimed at young people who have already engaged in substance use.
- Motivational interviewing is helpful as a means of engaging and retaining young people in services, especially those who have often been "forced" to enter treatment by families, schools or courts.
- Motivational interviewing can be delivered in brief formats suitable to use in informal youth settings such as drop-in, recreational and placement centres.

(Baer & Peterson, 2002)

- -

COUNSELLOR'S TIP

Motivational interviewing is an approach that is useful at any stage of change because young people can start to feel ambivalent at any point during the treatment process. Motivational interviewing is, however, particularly helpful for engaging young people with low motivation and/or high ambivalence (and that may be the majority of youth) because, even within one session, it allows you to guide them toward an exploration of a range of needs and issues that may be linked to their substance use.

2.6 HARM REDUCTION

Harm reduction approaches are essentially designed to reduce drug-related harm without requiring a young person to stop using drugs. Rather than judging people who use drugs, harm reduction focuses on meeting young substance users "where they are at" and helping them find humane, pragmatic strategies that reduce the harm they experience.

Young people who use substances take potentially harmful risks while they are under the influence, including:

· having unprotected sex and risking unwanted pregnancy, infection or transmission of hiv or other sexually transmitted diseases

· driving (or riding in a vehicle driven by someone under the influence) and risking injuring or killing themselves or others

· using unclean equipment to inject or snort drugs and risking HIV or hepatitis C infection or transmission

· engaging in other risky behaviours, such as boating or diving, that could injure or kill themselves or others.

The concept of harm reduction accepts the reality that, although abstinence may be the ideal strategy for reducing harm, many individuals may not be ready (in precontemplation or contemplation) or willing to stop using substances altogether. If, however, they are willing to consider alternate goals such as reducing their substance use, using substances more safely or substituting a less harmful substance, they may be able to reduce the harm they or others may experience as a result of substance use. And many individuals who initially adopt harm reduction strategies eventually do move on to abstinence.

Because of its flexibility in terms of treatment goals, its emphasis on reducing stigma, and its integrated focus on substance use and other related high-risk behaviours, harm reduction is a pragmatic, humane approach to making it easier for young substance users to engage in, and remain in treatment.

Outreach strategies such as needle exchanges provide opportunities to connect people who are not willing to participate in formal treatment with services as needed.

Some of the best-known examples of harm reduction strategies include:

· Substance use and mental health treatment services which do not insist on abstinence as the only possible treatment goal (and the prerequisite for receiving treatment), and instead allow flexible treatment goals to be determined by young people

· Needle exchange programs that provide clean needles and syringes

· Methadone maintenance treatment for people who are dependent on opioids

· Provision of free condoms

· Helping drug users access medical care, food, housing and shelter (e.g., one program works with homeless young people to provide services that do not require abstinence).

Harm reduction is increasingly being accepted as an important alternative public health approach. It may be a particularly realistic approach to working with adolescents and young adults.

For an in-depth discussion of harm reduction, we encourage you to consult Marlatt, (1998).

COUNSELLOR'S TIP

Harm reduction approaches could pose some legal and ethical questions. For example, if an underage drinker in your treatment program adopts a goal of moderate drinking, or you provide information about how to use an illicit substance more safely (e.g., switching from injecting to smoking), you run the risk of being seen to aid and abet the committing of an offence. Therefore, your agency should have clear policies and procedures in place regarding harm reduction goals and strategies when working with young people.

2.7 IMPROVING ACCESS: CULTURAL COMPETENCE

Many young people and their families do not feel comfortable seeking help from mainstream services. Consequently, when they are referred to mainstream services, they don't always go. And, if they do show up, they might not return because they assume you cannot be helpful. For youth from specific ethnocultural groups or sexual orientations, part of the problem may stem from the fact that the service providers either don't come from the same background, don't speak their language or lack sensitivity to the norms and values of a particular culture. When working with gay, lesbian, bisexual and transgendered youth, for example, you need to send a clear signal that their sexual orientation is accepted and affirmed. We encourage you to consult the following resource: *Asking the Right Questions: Talking about Sexual Orientation and Gender Identity during Assessment for Drug and Alcohol Concerns* (Barbara, Chaim & Doctor, 2002).

Improving your cultural competence will make you more effective in working with families and young people from different racial, cultural and sexual backgrounds. Components of "cultural competency" include values, self-awareness, knowledge and skills and are briefly described here. (Hansen & Pepitone-Areola-Rockwell, 2000).

Values
· critical self-reflection
· evaluation of personal values
· social justice orientation

- recognition of power issues
- valuing diversity.

Self-awareness
Awareness of how your own culture shapes personal values, assumptions and biases toward identified groups. Specific cultural aspects include:
- cultural heritage
- class
- ethnic-racial identity
- gender
- sexual orientation
- age cohort
- disability.

Knowledge
Knowledge of:
- history and manifestation of oppression, prejudice and discrimination in North America and their psychological consequences
- sociopolitical influences (e.g., poverty, stereotyping, stigmatization and marginalization) that impinge on the lives of identified groups
- issues such as interactional styles and normative values about illness and help-seeking behaviour of identified groups
- culture-specific assessment procedures and tools and their empirical support
- differences in family structures, gender roles, values, beliefs, and worldviews across identified groups, along with their impact on personality formation, developmental outcomes, and manifestations of mental and physical illness.

Skills
Ability to:
- evaluate culture-specific and universal hypotheses related to people from identified groups and to develop accurate clinical conceptualizations including awareness of when clinical issues involve cultural dimensions, and when theoretical orientation needs to be adapted for more effective work with members of identified groups
- assess your own multicultural competence, including knowing when circumstances (e.g., personal biases, stage of ethnic identity, sociopolitical influences, or lack of requisite knowledge, skills or language fluency) are negatively influencing professional activities and adapting accordingly (e.g., obtaining needed information, consultation or supervision or referring the client to a more qualified provider)

- modify assessment tools and qualify conclusions appropriately (including empirical support where available) for use with identified groups
- design and implement unbiased, effective treatment plans and interventions for youth from identified groups
- assess such issues as a young person's degree of acculturation, acculturative stress, and stage of gay or lesbian identity development
- evaluate effects of therapist/client language difference (including use of translators, if necessary) on assessment and intervention
- establish rapport and convey empathy in culturally sensitive ways (e.g., taking into account cultural interpretations of verbal and nonverbal cues, personal space and eye contact)
- initiate and explore issues of therapist/client differences, when appropriate, and incorporate these considerations into effective treatment planning.

2.7.1 OUTREACH STRATEGIES

Outreach means reaching out to young people and respecting them, wherever they are, rather than waiting for them to come (or be sent) to you. Outreach involves:

- making contact with young people in places and at times that fit with their lives, rather than expecting them to access services on their own during regular office hours
- establishing rapport and building trust with young people so you can identify substance use and mental health problems
- establishing ongoing supportive relationships with young people so you can engage or re-engage them in treatment
- building partnerships with providers in other agencies and systems
- actively involving families, where appropriate
- meeting young people's basic and practical needs including their need for safety
- offering creative, non-threatening activities and access points for young people and their families.

Outreach programs can be developed as adjuncts to existing substance use or mental health treatment programs. The following are some examples of these types of initiatives:

Substance Abuse Program for African Canadian and Caribbean Youth (SAPPACY)
This is a treatment and prevention program in Toronto for African Canadian and Caribbean youth, aged 13 to 29, based on an African-centred addiction treatment model. Emphasizing outreach into the community, SAPPACY treatment sessions are informal, with counsellors meeting young people in their communities, parks, coffee shops, and in any other places they feel comfortable.

"...addictions counsellors... are available to students to talk confidentially. The results are often surprising. Adolescents come and talk about friends and families they are worried about who are substance abusing. Counsellors are accessible to youth in schools and can help in developing coping skills" (Schwartz, 1997, 51).

"Other places for outreach are youth hostels, shelters for abused women, community health centres, local community centres and even bus stations. Outreach workers need specialized skills in working with transient youth who cannot access traditional services" (Schwartz, 1997, 52).

Addictions counsellors in schools

Many substance use treatment services have recognized the value of offering in-school programs and have partnered with their local schools to offer drop-in, individual and/or group counselling.

Street outreach programs

Some youth programs employ outreach workers to work on the street. They provide emotional and practical supports including basic necessities and referrals to street-involved young people. These programs usually have a harm-reduction focus and may include strategies such as providing condoms as well as other supplies.

Internet outreach

These strategies build upon young people's use of this technology. There are many Internet resources dealing with drug and alcohol use and smoking cessation. Skinner, Maley, Smith, Chirrey & Morrison (2001) have developed a framework (the seven critical functions model) to help providers adapt these resources for use as brief interventions.

Outreach strategies include virtually any proactive, creative approaches that offer young people and their families easy-to-access opportunities for education, support, practical assistance, recreation, creativity or fun.

2.8 PROMOTING DISCLOSURE ABOUT DRUG USE

When young people come (or are sent) to you, they may be unable or unwilling to tell you about their substance use because they:
· Fear being judged
· Believe they will get in trouble and/or punished (breach of probation, school suspension, loss of privileges in their family or group home).

Punitive policies and procedures discourage disclosure. If, on the other hand, young people know that it is "safe" to tell you about substance use, they are likely to be more open. You need to assure them that what they tell you will be kept confidential. If they tell you about their substance use in an effort to get help, they need to know they will receive assistance rather than punishment. It is important to create an atmosphere in which they feel that it's all right for them to discuss substance use and the problems they are experiencing without having to admit to violating rules.

2.9 MANAGING BEHAVIOUR

There may be times when a young person with whom you are working is disruptive. Rather than confronting the individual, you may be able to prevent or defuse the situation by changing either your own behaviour or the environment. For example:

· Use the motivational interviewing style of communication and "roll with resistance" to avoid confrontation (see section 2.5). Invite new perspectives when you see behaviours that are undesirable.

· Establish reasonable rules or even a formal "contract" clearly indicating the behaviours you expect and the consequences of not following those behaviours. Offer rewards (that are within your power) if the young person fulfils his or her side of the deal.

· Focus on enhancing a young person's autonomy, competence and relatedness, the basic human psychological needs at the core of motivation.

· Arrange the space so that there are no potential weapons or items available that could trigger cravings (scissors, letter openers, glue, corrective fluid, matches, lighters, needles or syringes, etc.), and position yourself closest to the door.

If a young person is intoxicated, it will probably be more helpful to make changes in the environment. For example, if the young person has been using stimulants, reduce stimulation in the environment by:

· dimming the lights (especially fluorescent lights)
· speaking softly
· controlling the noise level in the area
· not offering coffee.

If the young person has been using depressants, you may want to increase stimulation in the environment by serving coffee, for example.

If the young person is experiencing distorted perception, reassure her or him that the feeling is not real but the effect of the substance or a symptom of the mental health problem. Reduce stimulation as much as possible and, if you continue the interview, keep the pace relaxed.

Still, youth under the influence can and need to be held accountable for their behaviour. You can directly acknowledge their behaviour using a non-judgmental tone.

COUNSELLOR'S TIP

It is not a good idea to proceed with counselling or group treatment when a youth arrives for an appointment obviously intoxicated. It does make sense to check up on his or her safety, address any concerns and end the session by making plans for the next appointment.

2.10 LEGAL ISSUES

When you work with young people who use substances, the key legal issues that you need to understand are consent (including when it is required, when it is valid and at what age it is necessary) and confidentiality and its limits.

Consent

Ideally, you want to obtain written consent from young people before you begin treating them. Simply because a person returns for another session, do not assume consent to treatment has been given unless it is in writing. It is important to tell them about treatment alternatives and the pros and cons of treatment versus no treatment in order for them to be fully informed before giving consent.

COUNSELLOR'S TIP

You cannot force a young person to consent to any treatment, even, for example, when the treatment is part of a probation order. You may proceed without consent only in life-threatening situations (e.g., the young person has taken a potentially lethal overdose and is either unconscious, very high or incoherent).

In order to give consent, young people must understand what is involved in the treatment and they must be considered competent. If they are under the influence, they are not considered competent. Generally, if a young person is considered capable of understanding the proposed treatment, then it is her or his choice to consent or not, regardless of age. In Ontario, according to the Family Services Act, the age of consent to treatment is 12, although counsellors are obliged to speak to youth between 12 and 15 years of age about the advisability of involving their parents or guardian in the decision.

Parents, guardians or next of kin may give consent for treatment if the young person, for some reason, is not competent to do so. However, they must exercise this power only "in the young person's best interests", which can sometimes be difficult to determine. Generally, if the action taken improves a young person's quality of life, it is seen to have served their best interests.

Some provincial and federal legislation, as well as codes of ethics of various professions, also require that information obtained from clients remain confidential. This means that you may not release information obtained from a young person even to a parent without the young person's consent.

Confidentiality

Generally, it's good practice to not reveal any information that clients tell you either about themselves, family members or others unless you have their permission. Ideally, there should be a signed consent form specifying to whom the information may be released and what the time limits are. Consent may be renewed if information needs to be disclosed at a later date.

Health care professionals are not required to report a criminal offence that the client reveals during counselling (e.g., possession or trafficking in drugs, prostitution, etc). Under certain circumstances, however, you may be required to disclose information without the young person's consent. For example:

· Reporting child abuse is mandatory.
· If you are a health care professional, you may be required to report a person with a communicable disease to the appropriate health authority.
· A physician is required to report a patient whose condition makes it dangerous for her or him to drive.
· You may be required to disclose information if you or your files are subpoenaed by the courts.

Your obligation to report is less clear in situations where you believe that people who are using substances may be dangerous to themselves or others (e.g., if they are suicidal, violent or planning to drive while intoxicated). However, you do have a clear obligation to take the necessary steps to ensure their own or others' safety by involving the appropriate resources such as emergency services, child protection agencies, etc. Be aware of your agency's policies and procedures in these situations, and be prepared to err on the side of safety.

COUNSELLOR'S TIP

It is important to explain to young clients early on in the relationship what those circumstances might be in which you could be required to disclose information without their consent. This gives them the option not to disclose certain information that could be incriminating if you are subpoenaed.

CHAPTER 3

IDENTIFYING, ASSESSING AND PLANNING TREATMENT FOR SUBSTANCE USE AND MENTAL HEALTH PROBLEMS

3.1 THE IMPORTANCE OF IDENTIFYING SUBSTANCE USE AND MENTAL HEALTH PROBLEMS

Regardless of the setting in which you work, your contact with young people gives you the opportunity to observe and question what is happening in their lives. If you are knowledgeable about what to look for and are prepared to explore issues in an objective and non-judgmental way, you are more likely to establish a rapport with youth, build trust and enhance their motivation for change.

Unfortunately, young people's problems often are ignored and it's not until there is a crisis or they have harmed themselves or others that the problems are recognized. Identifying problems at an early stage increases the chances of engaging a young person in treatment and helping him or her to avoid or reduce later harmful consequences. Also, by intervening early, you increase the likelihood of positive treatment results. This is particularly crucial for young people experiencing both substance use and mental health problems, because they are at even higher risk for poor outcomes.

When you spot potential problems with substance use and mental health, you need to determine whether or not there is cause for concern. If there is:

· Work with youth and/or their family to explore how they perceive the problem.
· Consider with them what action they are prepared to take.

If you do not spot problems, and particularly if you do not spot both types of problems when they co-occur, the assessment and treatment process either may not happen, or may focus on only one side of the story and, therefore, be ineffective.

For example, young people involved in the justice system could be considered high risk due to behaviour that results from their concurrent substance use and mental health issues. It might be more appropriate for them to receive treatment rather than a more intensive level of supervision but, in order for that to happen, someone has to identify the underlying problems (Trupin & Boesky, 2001).

Identifying potential problems is not the same as doing a comprehensive assessment or making a diagnosis. Identification does not require specialized training or formal tools, although in some settings, you will have access to substance use and mental health screening tools, which you may decide to use in addition to more informal approaches. (See Appendix D: Screening tools.) Depending on your setting and what you feel is appropriate for a young person, you might decide to use only one or a variety of methods including observations, questions and formal screening instruments to identify whether or not a young person has problems with substance use and mental health.

For example, you might be more comfortable gathering information about the young person by having conversations, asking questions and making observations. This method can provide you with enough information to determine that the young person's substance use is harmful or problematic and that a more comprehensive assessment is necessary.

Formal screening tests can back up your observations, confirm that there is a problem and provide the young person with concrete feedback on her or his problem. Based on test scores, for example, you can place drug use or mental health symptoms on a scale of "no problem" to "serious problem," based on accepted norms. You may choose to conduct routine screening tests with all of your clients as a quick and easy way of identifying substance use and mental health problems.

- -

COUNSELLOR'S TIP

If you are not already routinely checking for substance use and mental health problems, consider integrating simple screening questions into your intake or assessment process.

- -

3.2 IDENTIFYING SUBSTANCE USE AND MENTAL HEALTH PROBLEMS: APPROACHES AND TOOLS

There are many ways to identify potential substance use and mental health problems in young people. Your work setting and your level of expertise, as well as your time and resources, will determine the specific approaches you use.

You may use one or more of the following approaches to identify substance use and mental health problems among young people that you work with:

APPROACHES TO IDENTIFYING SUBSTANCE USE AND MENTAL HEALTH PROBLEMS

Make observations and use your judgment	Observe their appearance and behaviour. Listen to the thoughts they express
	Remember that what you see may not be related to a substance use or mental health problem. (e.g., It might simply be a young person who is in love!)
	If you have known the young person for a while, you can ask yourself if you think he or she has ever had a drinking or other drug problem in the past. (Definitely? Probably? Not at all?)
	Whenever possible, check your observations with the young person. (e.g., "I've noticed that...")
	Check with others who know the young person(family, friends and/or other providers) or review available records with her or his consent to get corroboration.

During screening:

- Be aware of your own values and attitudes about substance use and mental health.
- Avoid labels.
- Be proactive in asking young people about substance use and mental health issues so you can identify problems early and increase the chances of better outcomes.
- Understand what motivation is and how to enhance it.
- If you identify substance use and mental health problems, both should be prioritized for further assessment and integrated treatment planning.

Ask a few questions	You can ask young people directly about their substance use, in a non-judgmental manner. For example: · Have you ever used alcohol? Cannabis? Cocaine? Tobacco? · When did you last use…? · How often do you use…? (Everyday? 2–3 times per week? Once per week? Once per month? 3–4 times per year? Once per year, or less?) · Can you tell me what a typical day is like when using alcohol or drugs? · In the past month, how many drinks have you typically had when you drank? · Have you had any problems related to your use of…? · Has anyone else, such as a relative, friend or doctor, ever been concerned about your use of…, or suggested that you cut down? · Do you use…on your own or when you are with others? · How does using…make you feel? · Are you at all worried about your use of…? · Have you ever tried to stop using…? · Can you tell me all the good and bad things about using alcohol and/or drugs? You can also ask young people non-judgmental questions about mental health. For example: · How are you feeling? How are you enjoying life? · How are things going in school, with family and friends, etc.? · Have you ever felt depressed or suicidal? · Have you ever harmed yourself or thought about harming yourself? · (If yes) Had you been using alcohol or drugs at the time? · Have you ever been treated for a mental health concern such as anxiety, depression, etc.? · Have you ever been prescribed medication for a mental health issue? · Are you taking any medication now? If yes, what type? · Have you ever been hospitalized for a mental health problem?

Use substance use and mental health screening instruments	Depending on your setting, you may have access to brief screening instruments which can provide an initial measure of problems and provide you and the young clients with more information about whether their substance use and/or mental health issues are problematic. After you use a screening instrument, it's useful to tell them their screening results in an objective, non-judgmental manner and solicit their thoughts and feelings. For information on instruments that screen for substance use and mental health problems see Appendix D.

This table is adapted from Health Canada (2002, 30-39).

Whenever you try to identify substance use and mental health problems among young people, keep in mind that a young person might:

· be in crisis, withdrawal or extremely agitated

· have substance use and mental health problems that are interacting with each other (e.g., using cocaine or methamphetamine could trigger a manic episode in someone with bipolar disorder)

· have a mental health problem that is in remission

· use substances to self-medicate mental distress (e.g., smokes marijuana only when depressed to avoid feeling sad)

· have had other symptoms in the past that differ from current symptoms

· not see her or his substance use or mental health problem as a "problem"

· be motivated to get help for one problem but not others (e.g., wants to stop hearing voices, but unwilling to stop smoking marijuana).

3.2.1 WHAT TO LOOK FOR

There are many, and often similar signs that indicate a young person might be having substance use and/or mental health problems. It is important to keep in mind, however, that changes in a young person's appearance, behaviour or cognitions, the three key indicators of substance use and mental health, could be happening for other reasons.

SIGNS TO LOOK FOR:

Appearance (alertness, affect, anxiety)

· smell of alcohol, drugs or inhalants

· significant changes in self-care or appearance

· inappropriate affect

· change in mood

· emotional distress: depression, suicide ideation or attempts, confusion, mood swings

Behaviour (movements, organization, speech)

· behaviour changes

· unsteady gait

· agitation

· lethargy

· hyperactivity

· faintness, passing out

· accident proneness

· high levels of physical complaints, health problems

· legal problems

· financial problems

· sudden weight loss

· sleep disturbances

· significant changes in friends, school performance, attitude, relationships with significant others

· quitting hobbies

· dropping out of recreational activities

· dropping out of school

· self harm

· suicide attempts

· frequent vandalizing or starting fires

Cognition (orientation, calculation, reasoning, coherence)

· concentration problems

· rapid-fire speech

In some jurisdictions, drug testing may be used to identify substance use. However, the reliability of this approach is questionable due to variance in the way that different substances are metabolized and excreted from the body.

3.3 DETERMINING SEVERITY OF USE AND COURSE OF ACTION

If you know that a young person is using substances and if you suspect a mental health problem, you will need to work with him or her to find out the extent of drug use. You will also need to determine whether or not he or she needs, and is willing to undergo a comprehensive assessment process (and if so, where it will be done).

You can make your own preliminary judgment about what next steps might make sense by considering where the drug use is on the continuum of substance use below.

NON-USE:
Never used a particular substance

EXPERIMENTAL USE:
Has tried a substance once or several times. Use is motivated by
curiosity about the substance's effect.

IRREGULAR USE:
Use is infrequent and irregular, usually confined to special occasions
(holidays, birthdays, etc.) or when opportunities present themselves directly.

HARMFUL USE:
Use has resulted in
harmful consequences.
Use has resulted in
high-risk behaviours.

REGULAR USE:
Use has a predictable pattern, which may entail frequent or infrequent
use. The young person actively seeks to experience the substance effect,
or to participate in the substance using activities of the peer group.
Usually s/he feels in control of the substance use (i.e. s/he can take it
or leave it).

DEPENDENT USE:
Use is regular and predictable and usually frequent. The young person
experiences a physiological and/or psychological need for the substance.
S/he feels out of control vis-à-vis its use, and will continue to use despite
adverse consequences.

Figure 3.1: Continuum of substance use

Most young people begin with experimentation but the vast majority do not progress beyond this stage. Some young people will proceed to ongoing but irregular use, then to regular use and finally to dependent use. Their escalating pattern of substance use may stop at any stage or it may vary depending on the substance. For example, a young person may be an experimental hallucinogen user, irregular cannabis user, regular alcohol user and dependent tobacco user.

Harmful use can occur at any stage of substance use. Even one-time use can result in risk behaviour, such as unprotected sex or driving while under the influence, and can have serious consequences. Harmful use is also use that results in acute consequences such as dropping out of school, street involvement, etc. For young people with mental health issues, even relatively low levels of substance use can create problems.

If the substance use is an issue:
· What are the substance use behaviours and problems?
· Where does the use lie on the continuum?
· Is the youth likely to experience harm from the use?
· Is he or she likely to increase use?

If the young person appears to have mental health problems:
· What are the symptoms?
· How severe do they appear to be?

If the young client appears to have both substance use and mental health problems:
· What does the relationship between these problems appear to be?

Does the young person have any other urgent needs that need to be addressed immediately (e.g. safety, medical treatment, housing, food, clothing, money, or other necessities such as condoms or clean needles)?

Based on your observations and the answers to your questions, you can work with the young person to identify a course of action.

You have a number of options for addressing substance use and mental health problems. The options that make sense will depend on a number of factors including the young person's:
· level of involvement in substance use
· risk of increased involvement in substance use
· risk of experiencing harmful consequences from substance use
· stage of change
· motivation for change.

Where appropriate, consider discussing with the young person the following options:

Ongoing monitoring
Carry out periodic checks to identify any changes in substance use involvement and mental health symptoms. Use your own observations and judgment in addition to asking questions.

Education
Provide facts about substances including their effects on physical and mental health as well as their legal status. Offer information about general well-being and mental health. Emphasize wellness.

Prevention

Reinforce attitudes and behaviours that are incompatible with substance use through discussion, peer counselling, social skills development and other activities.

Harm reduction

Give support and assistance to reduce the potentially harmful effects of substance use (without requiring abstinence).

Comprehensive assessment and integrated treatment planning

When youth have both substance use and mental health problems, refer them and their families, if possible, for a comprehensive assessment followed by integrated treatment. If an integrated treatment service is not available, refer them instead to a substance use treatment program or a mental health service and take on an ongoing case management role to ensure that both the substance use and mental health problems are comprehensively addressed and an integrated treatment plan is developed.

Stage of substance use involvement (with or without mental health symptoms)	Goals	Course of action
Non-use	Prevent initiation of substance use.	Reinforcement of non-use Education Monitoring
Experimental use	Enhance motivation for change. Prevent further involvement in substance use. Reverse involvement in substance use. Reduce harm from substance use.	Education Harm reduction Monitoring
Irregular use	Enhance motivation for change. Prevent further involvement in substance use. Reverse involvement in substance use. Reduce harm from substance use.	Education Harm reduction Monitoring

Stage of substance use involvement (with or without mental health symptoms)	Goals	Course of action
Regular use	Enhance motivation for change. Prevent further involvement in substance use. Reverse involvement in substance use. Reduce harm from substance use.	Education Harm reduction Monitoring Assessment
Dependent use	Enhance motivation for change. Reverse involvement in substance use. Reduce harm from substance use.	Harm reduction Assessment Treatment
Harmful use	Enhance motivation for change. Reverse involvement in substance use. Reduce harm from substance use	Harm reduction Assessment Treatment

If your goal is to *prevent initiation into substance use*, your strategy will include education and prevention activities, as well as ongoing monitoring. Given that many young people receive education and prevention messages about substance use at school, in the community and at home, you may only need to reinforce non-use, and check in with the young person periodically.

If your goal is to *prevent further involvement in substance use* among, for example, young people who are experimental and irregular substance users, it may be appropriate to offer education and prevention activities. With the right approach to exploring the problem, you can encourage young people to recognize the need for change. This can be enough to reverse the course of substance involvement among some young people. Harm reduction strategies may also be needed. It will be important to continue to check in with them on an ongoing basis.

If your goal is to *reverse existing involvement*, your strategy will depend, among other things, on the severity of the problem and the risk of increasing involvement in substance use. With the right approach, you can assist youth in identifying and resolving ambivalence and enhancing motivation to change their behaviour. With young people whose substance use is low and has not had harmful consequences, you may offer education and prevention activities. For young people who have already experienced harmful consequences and who are at risk for increasing involvement in substance use, encourage participation in a comprehensive assessment leading to an integrated treatment plan to reduce the (current and potential) harmful consequences of substance use.

3.3.1 IDENTIFYING OTHER RELATED OR URGENT NEEDS

You may need to respond to young people who are in crisis and have urgent needs.
They may be:

· at risk of being victimized or abused
· experiencing trauma from abuse
· experiencing acute mental health symptoms
· dangerous to themselves or others
· injured or ill
· pregnant
· acutely intoxicated
· experiencing severe withdrawal
· in crisis or experiencing ongoing problems related to housing, employment, school,
  family or other relationships
· involved in the justice system.

Familiarize yourself with the services and resources available in your agency and/or community
so that you can help young people get the support, referral, and follow-up they need.

3.4 THE IMPORTANCE OF COMPREHENSIVE ASSESSMENT

Whenever you identify young people who are using substances regularly or in a way that may
be harmful to themselves or others, encourage them to participate in a comprehensive assessment
process. Even if they are being ordered to participate in an assessment (by parents, school
personnel or the justice system) it's a good idea to explain to them that a comprehensive assessment
process can help them discover more about themselves including their needs, strengths and
options for change.

Inform youth that, depending on their literacy level and language needs, an assessment process
could involve interviews, questionnaires (sometimes computerized) and/or assignments (e.g.,
keeping a journal or diary). Family members or other people they know may also be interviewed.
Sometimes, records (school, treatment, justice system) may be reviewed as part of the information-
gathering process.

The purpose of a comprehensive assessment is to:
· Establish the scope and severity of a young person's substance use and mental health
  problems. In some settings, the primary goal of a comprehensive assessment of
  substance use or severe mental health problems is to confirm diagnosis. This includes
  distinguishing between substance use and dependence using DSM-IV criteria. In these
  settings, mental health evaluation involves an interview conducted by a professionally
  qualified mental health professional (psychiatrist or registered psychologist.)

- Explore their functioning in other areas of life.
- Look at the links between the various issues with which they are dealing, including the relationship between substance use and mental health problems.
- Identify their strengths and resources.
- Identify and enhance their motivation for change.
- Develop a treatment and support plan that addresses their needs in an integrated manner.

Depending on your setting, you may be able to conduct a comprehensive assessment, either on your own, or with the help of your colleagues. Alternatively, you may develop linkages and collaborate with other providers in other settings.

3.5 TIPS ON THE ASSESSMENT PROCESS

- Focus on making young people feel comfortable about disclosing information.
- Establish a good rapport before asking for a lot of information.
- Be sensitive to young people's concerns.
- Use non-judgmental language.
- Be sensitive to diversity issues such as language, culture, and sexual orientation.
- Conduct interviews when the young person is sober and fairly stable emotionally.
- Conduct interviews in private, away from interruptions.
- If possible, have someone with whom the young person is familiar conduct the interview.
- Inform young people at the beginning about how the information will be used.
- Let them know from the start that what they tell you will be kept confidential, except in specific situations where you may have to disclose information.
- Ask simple, direct questions using clearly defined time frames.
- Frame questions in a way that normalizes substance use. (e.g., "Many people have experimented with drugs. Have you every had any experience with…?"
- If young people have trouble recalling events and details of past use, help jog their memories by asking questions about the setting. (e.g., "What grade were you in when…?" or "Who were you with when…?")
- Use information from other sources to verify self-reported information before drawing conclusions.
- Reassess their situation at a later date.

3.6 MOTIVATIONAL INTERVIEWING AT ASSESSMENT

This section contains some suggestions, many of which are based on the principles of motivational interviewing, to help you conduct assessment in a way that engages young people, and enhances their motivation.

To ensure that the assessment process enhances young people's motivation for change, it is best to "begin where they are at" and demonstrate that you are willing to listen, accept their situation and provide help. You can do this by explaining the assessment process, allowing them input and control over the interview and highlighting confidentiality (and its limits). Bear in mind that your actions as well as your words are what will reassure them.

Find out if the young person is in crisis. If young people are in acute states of physical or emotional distress, they may not be able to cope with immediate problems, and in some cases may be dangerous to themselves or others. You will need to respond to young people's urgent needs immediately, before conducting assessments.

Some indicators of extreme stress are:
· physical agitation
· inaccurate verbal "following"
· lack of concentration
· rapid mood swings
· extreme apathy
· disengagement and withdrawal from the interview process.

Ask the young person about his or her state of mind.
Young people often show up for assessment saying that they don't think they have substance use or mental health problems and that it's others (court, family and/or school) who think that they do. They are there undergoing assessment and treatment, not because they want help, but to avoid negative consequences, (e.g., breach of probation, parental punishment or suspension from school). Let them know that you believe compliance in order to avoid negative consequences is a valid starting point, and that you are willing to help them meet those external expectations. If they are angry or resentful about being coerced into assessment, try to acknowledge their feelings and address this issue right away. It could help alleviate their frustration and give them some sense of control if you can offer a range of options from which they can make choices.

Express empathy. This is the first principle of motivational interviewing. Your acceptance of a young person's situation and feelings can help make the change process easier.

Listen. Being a skillful, reflective listener is central to effective communication. This is particularly important when dealing with non-verbal, young people where a slower, quieter pace may be helpful.

Use non-judgmental language. Avoid talking about "problems." Instead, use terms like "choices," "behaviours" or "risks."

Ask the young person about expectations regarding assessment and treatment and address those expectations. Depending on the setting in which you work, young people may not be expecting you to ask them questions about substance use, mental health or other issues. Be

"...motivational interviewing (is) a promising approach for engaging youth in services. Few youth identify their risk behaviour as a problem in need of treatment or other services. Motivational interviewing, with its nonjudgmental, nonconfrontational style may be a useful approach for outreach or initial engagement" (Baer & Peterson, 2002, 323)

"It can be very difficult for young people with mental health problems such as schizophrenia to feel energetic and motivated enough to get up and get going. It may be unrealistic to expect them to keep appointments at 8:30 in the morning" (Jean Addington, personal communication).

prepared to make a case for discussing these issues. Tell them that you want to know as much as possible about them, and about all the things that are affecting their life, including substance use and mental health problems. It's also important to find out if they have any preconceived ideas about what treatment for substance use and mental health problems involves. Many young people, for example, think treatment means entering a medical facility, or involves punitive and coercive approaches. Answer any questions or concerns your clients have.

Explain that assessment is a process in which you and the young person work together to:
· identify her or his unique situation and the problems she or he is facing
· explore his or her strengths in dealing with those problems
· look at what changes she or he is interested in making to improve the situation
· talk about what treatment options are available.

Let your clients know who you are, what they may expect from you, and what you expect of them.
Share information about your area of expertise, your role in your agency and how you and your agency are linked to other services. Tell them where they may go for help if needed between appointments. Describe the assessment process—how long it will take, what topics will be explored (allow for flexibility to include what they want to discuss) and how questions will be asked (verbal, written, etc.). Discuss whether or not other people such as family members will participate and what is involved in giving consent for their participation. Let them know that you will inform them of the results of the assessment. Give them a sense of what next steps may follow an assessment.

Explain to your client that information they provide is confidential, but that there could be situations where you will have to disclose information.

Advise your client of any costs that may be involved.

COUNSELLOR'S TIP
Let your young clients know that they should not use substances for 12 to 24 hours before coming to see you. Explain that this is to avoid having the effects of alcohol or other drugs distort the assessment results. If they are high, it is best to set another appointment and help them plan how to avoid substance use prior to meetings.

Deal first with whatever seems pressing. Ask the young clients why they have come to see you and what they think the problems are. Their perspective will be unique and possibly very different to what others think. They may be concerned about any one of a number of different issues including substance use, school failure, probation orders, debt, suicidal thoughts, family conflict, etc. It's useful to begin by acknowledging and discussing the problem(s) they consider most important. You will have opportunities to explore other issues and the links between them as you move along.

Proceed at your client's pace. Be flexible and sensitive about when and how you use specific assessment tools. Don't be in a hurry to launch into assessment and/or provide feedback. Focus primarily on discussion that builds rapport and proceed according to the young person's level of comfort.

Ask about personal values and attitudes. Young people may believe, for example, that certain substances are "not really dangerous," or that adults are overly moralistic about substance use. They may also have personal goals and values that are not consistent with their substance use or related behaviours. One of the principles of motivational interviewing is to try to help young people see the inconsistency between their present behaviour and their personal goals and values they say they have. It is important, however, that they be the ones that present the arguments for change, rather than you.

Avoid arguing. Another key principle of motivational interviewing is to "roll with resistance." This means that you don't argue with a young person to try to persuade him or her to change. Indeed, it is best to avoid talking about change at all in the initial stages of contact. Even later on in the process, it is advisable not to directly oppose your client if he or she offers resistance. Instead, interpret resistance as a signal that you need to respond differently. You may offer new information and different perspectives, and, of course, invite your client's perspectives, but you must not impose your views. Your young person will be the one to find the answers and solutions.

Explore how the young person uses her or his strengths and resources to cope with problems. The assessment process focuses not just on problems, but also on young people's strengths and abilities. Try to find out as much as possible about how they deal with problems. (Do they handle problems on their own or seek others' help? What has worked well and not so well for them?)

Support self-efficacy. Young people's belief in the possibility of change is a very important influence on their motivation to change. It is important to emphasize that they are the ones who are responsible for making changes in their lives. Encouraging and supporting their confidence in their own ability to make change is critical.

Provide personalized feedback. Give young people individual feedback about their substance use that is relevant to them. Let them know how their pattern of use compares with typical patterns of use for their age and gender and with established guidelines for low-risk use. You can also provide feedback that focuses on other areas including likes and dislikes, involvement in social networks, and short-term (rather than long-term) consequences of substance use. Feedback should be clear and easy to understand. The *First Contact* manual provides you with a step-by-step process and materials for providing feedback at assessment. The graphs allow youth to compare their drug use to use among high school students, and gives them information about the prevalence of substance use and mental health problems.

Delay giving advice about treatment. When using motivational interviewing techniques, be prepared to acknowledge a young person's ambivalence about changing. Delay advising him or her about treatment until a later point, when he or she is in the "preparation" stage of change.

3.7 COMPREHENSIVE ASSESSMENT: APPROACHES AND TOOLS

Comprehensive assessment explores substance use and mental health problems as well as functioning in other life areas. It includes assessment of young people's strengths and their motivation to change. Depending on your setting, you will use various approaches and tools to explore these areas. Appendices E and F provide information on widely used assessment instruments.

When choosing assessment tools you may want to consider the following:
· Are the instruments and the questions in it culturally appropriate?
· If reading is required, are the reading and comprehension levels appropriate for young people?
· What background or training is required to administer the instrument?
· For which specific age group was the instrument developed?

When young people have been or are currently involved with other professionals, as is often the case, it is important that these professionals be consulted, to ensure a co-ordinated and consistent approach to assessment and intervention.

You may decide, with your clients' consent, to obtain copies of written assessment reports or discharge summaries. When you consult written records, however, bear in mind that:
· Problems manifest differently at various stages of development, and may have resulted in multiple, conflicting diagnoses over time.
· Young people may not have been asked about substance use and mental health problems in previous assessments.
· Written records may be incomplete, misleading, or misidentify the cause of a particular symptom.

COUNSELLOR'S TIP
Having appropriate linkages in place with the providers in your community who conduct screening and/or assessment of substance use and mental health problems will help you efficiently share information. This will make it easier for clients, who will then not have to "tell their story" more than once.

"...although tools and instruments are important, they are one of a number of approaches used in the process of assessment. Professional judgment will direct the balance between tools, interviews and relationship building that will best serve an adolescent" (Schwartz, 1997, 47).

3.7.1 ASSESSING SUBSTANCE USE

When you assess a young person's substance use, you are trying to explore the pattern and severity of the problem. This may include gathering information about:

· **Quantity of use**: How much do they consume (number of drinks of alcohol, tokes or joints of marijuana, hits of LSD, etc.)?

· **Frequency of use**: How often did they use substances in the past week or months?

· **Most recent use**: Have they used substances in the last few days? If so, how much? Are they at risk for withdrawal symptoms?

· **Stage of involvement on the *continuum of substance use*** (see section 3.3): Are they at a harmful stage of use?

· **Substances ever used**: The range of substances used over time is one indicator of the seriousness of a young person's involvement.

· **Multiple drugs used**: Does the young person tend to combine certain drugs such as cocaine and alcohol, marijuana and alcohol, opiates and amphetamines, etc.?

· **"Substance of choice"**: This may not be the substance that is most heavily used, but it may be the one that will be the hardest to give up, and it should be emphasized.

· **Problem priority**: What is the substance that causes the most severe problem? It may be a specific substance or an entire pattern of use that is the young person's primary concern.

· **Onset of initial substance use**: What is the age of first use for each substance? The earlier a young person starts using a substance, the greater the potential for problematic use.

· **Onset of regular substance use**: When did weekly or more frequent use for each substance begin? Early onset and rapid progression through stages of use increase risk of developing substance use problems.

· **Duration of use**: How long has the young person been using drugs over his or her lifetime?

· **Pattern of current versus past use**: Is the young person using more or less of some drugs now as compared to the past? The present pattern may not be the primary or prevalent one. For example, a youth who comes for an assessment of cocaine use may have had a problem with cannabis before starting cocaine. The cannabis could resurface as a problem once the cocaine use has stopped.

· **Mode of administration of each substance used**: Does the young person smoke, inhale or inject drugs, and has he or she changed modes of use of any drugs (e.g., from smoking cocaine to injecting cocaine or vice versa)?

· **Circumstances of use**: Does the youth use substances alone or with others? Use in particularly inappropriate settings such as before driving or during school hours is considered problematic. It does not make sense to wait until negative consequences such as arrest or accidents have occurred before dealing with the issue.

- **Periods of abstinence or reduced use**: Have they stopped using before or reduced use? If so, what happened? How long did these periods last? What helped to reduce or quit use? Why was there a relapse and when was the most recent period of abstinence or reduced use?
- **Treatment history**: What has been helpful and what has not been helpful?

COUNSELLOR'S TIP

It is important to screen and assess for nicotine dependence among young people. Tobacco use is very common among young people with mental health problems such as schizophrenia. There is no evidence that addressing nicotine dependence results in relapse to other substance use.

(Myers, Brown & Kelly, 2000).

Readers are encouraged to consult Winters (2001) for a detailed overview of assessment of adolescent substance use and other areas of functioning.

3.7.2 SUBSTANCE USE ASSESSMENT INSTRUMENTS

There are many substance use assessment instruments available. The addiction treatment system in Ontario uses a standard package of assessment tools as part of intake, assessment and treatment planning.

The following substance use assessment instruments from the package are suitable to use with adolescents.
- Psychoactive Drug History Questionnaire (DHQ)
- Adverse Consequences of Substance Use
- Readiness for Change

See Appendices E and F for more information on these and other assessment tools.

3.7.3 ASSESSING MENTAL HEALTH

When you are involved in assessing young people's mental health, the approach you use will vary depending on your setting and qualifications. For example:
- Social workers and child and youth workers in community-based children's mental health centres assess youth and their families in terms of both their problems and their strengths.
- Psychiatrists and registered psychologists do assessments that result in formal psychiatric diagnoses.
- Certified addiction counsellors in addiction programs explore some aspects of mental health in the course of substance use assessments.

"The DSM-IV criteria for (substance use disorders) SUD was developed for adults, and is not always applicable to adolescents" (Bukstein et al 1997). SUD in youth differ from adult forms in that youth often present with more tolerance and less withdrawal symptoms and medical problems. Early onset of substance use, and intense and frequent use may indicate a SUD. The quicker a youth increases the frequency of use and amount of substance used, the greater the risk that he or she will develop a SUD. (Ballon, in press)

Some aspects of a young person's mental health that may be addressed in an assessment include:

· emotional and behavioural problems
· risk of harm to self and others
· history of mental health problems and diagnoses
· current and past mental health treatment
· use of prescription medication (psychotropics)
· symptoms of post-traumatic stress disorder.

The following table outlines the dimensions of mental health that are assessed by the Concurrent Disorders Program within CAMH (Skinner & Toneato, 2001).

Dimensions of mental health	Symptoms
psychosis	· experiencing hallucinations · delusions or distorted perception of reality · verbal behaviour: "weird talk"
anger	· problems with impulsivity, aggression, rage · verbal behaviour: "threat talk" · mind set: "survival mode"
mood (including depression)	· instability of affect such as depression or mania · verbal behaviour: self-critical—"loser," "hopeless," "sad/too happy talk"
anxiety	· problems related to apprehension, distress, panic and inhibited response · verbal behaviour: "fright," "fear," "danger talk"
behavioural problems	· difficulty paying attention, distractibility, self harm, etc.

3.7.4 MENTAL HEALTH ASSESSMENT INSTRUMENTS

There are a number of instruments used to assess the mental health of youth. In Ontario, many of the Ministry of Community, and Social Services/Ministry of Children's Services funded programs are using the Brief Child and Family Phone Interview (BCFPI) as a screener and the Child and Adolescent Functional Assessment Scale (CAFAS), that looks at impairment in day-to-day functioning, due to emotional, behavioural, psychological, psychiatric and substance use problems.

See Appendices E and F for more information on mental health assessment instruments.

"...the duration, timing, frequency and place that symptoms appear are key in assessing the existence of a disorder. In particular, with adolescents, stresses can build and show themselves for short periods of time. This does not indicate a disorder. A minimum of six months of symptoms is standard before considering a diagnosis. How often symptoms appear and how long they last is important as well. And lastly, where they show themselves is very significant. If symptomatic behaviour appears at home, at school, at recreational activities and with peers, there could be a pervasive problem. Where as problems that are at home only would be viewed in a different light. These variables are all indicators of a continuum of problem severity used by professionals in discerning disorders." (Schwartz, 1997, 35).

Sorting out the relationship between substance use and mental health problems requires you to use your 'best guess' for developing a working diagnosis. If necessary, you can modify it later but it's best not to delay treatment for mental health symptoms. You will need to maintain ongoing contact with the young person so that you can continue to reassess over time to refine your understanding of the problems and the relationship among them (Ballon, personal communication).

3.7.5 ASSESSING CONCURRENT SUBSTANCE USE AND MENTAL HEALTH PROBLEMS

When you assess a young person for concurrent substance use and mental health problems, you are conducting a full assessment of both types of problems, including the interaction between the two. It is important to bear in mind that symptoms may have multiple causes A number of common diagnostic dilemmas have been identified by Ballon (in press):

· **"Delinquent" behaviour**: Is it depression? Addictive behaviours? Conduct disorder? Or a combination of them all?

· **Psychotic symptoms**: Are they substance-induced? Is it schizophrenia? Is it hallucinogen persistent perception disorder (HPPD)? Is the fear justified by real threats to the person's safety? Is it a form of post-traumatic stress disorder (PTSD)? Or some combination of them all?

· **Self-harm behaviour**: Is it substance induced? Is it a major depressive disorder? Is it bipolar disorder in a depressive phase? Is it addictive behaviour? Is it conduct disorder or another type of personality disorder? Or a combination of them all?

The following are some examples of how substance use and mental health problems can mimic, mask, cause or worsen each other.

· Psychological distress can be associated with intoxication, substance use or withdrawal.

· Psychotic symptoms can be associated with intoxication from almost every class of substance.

· Anxiety and depressive symptoms can be associated with intoxication or withdrawal from alcohol, cocaine and sedatives.

· High doses and chronic use of stimulants (e.g., methamphetamines) can provoke an episode of psychosis or mania.

· Stimulant withdrawal can produce symptoms of lethargy, depression, agitation and insomnia for months after cessation of use

· Subacute withdrawal symptoms may produce symptoms of hyperactivity, hyperarousal and panic attacks. These symptoms can emerge weeks to months after the youth discontinues use of alcohol, stimulants, benzodiazepines or opioids (Trupin & Boesky, 2001).

· Chronic cannabis use may be misdiagnosed as ADHD because it mimics the inattentiveness associated with ADHD.

· Substance use can cause symptoms of bipolar disorder to appear mixed, or it can create a rapid-cycling effect.

· Psychotic symptoms may be induced by substance use, particularly stimulants such as cocaine or amphetamines (Ballon, in press).

The assessment will focus on the severity of substance use and mental health problems, but in order to explore the relationship, you will also need to examine:

· chronology of the onset of substance use and mental health problems

- presence or absence of mental health symptoms during periods of reduced use or abstinence (e.g., If they had a time when they cut back or stopped using cannabis, did the symptoms decrease or go away?)
- whether there are days when the symptoms are better or worse, and if so, how it relates to their substance use.

3.7.6 ASSESSING FUNCTIONING IN OTHER LIFE AREAS

For many young people, substance use and mental health issues are only part of a whole constellation of problems.

You need to find out as much as possible about how young people are functioning in all aspects of their lives as well as explore how these areas are interacting with their substance use and mental health problems.

The following table lists areas of life, many of which reflect the risk and protective factors discussed in Chapter 1, that you need to explore as part of a comprehensive assessment:

Area of life	Potential issues
Basic needs	Access to: · Food, clothing, money, transportation · Safe housing · Stable and supportive living environment · Protection from immediate danger or threat of victimization or abuse.
Health status	Engagement in high risk behaviours: · Substance use severity (see section 3.7.1) · Sexual activity and unprotected sex · Drinking or drug use and driving · Sharing needles and other drug-taking paraphernalia such as cookers, water, swabs, etc. · Other risk taking behaviours. Overall wellness: · Psychological status (see section 3.7.3) · Current or past pregnancy · Nutritional status · Serious diseases since birth · History of accidents

Area of life	Potential issues (continued)
Health status (continued)	· Occurrences of HIV/AIDS, hepatitis C, other sexually transmitted diseases, and other conditions such as mononucleosis, tuberculosis, etc. · Allergies · Physical disabilities. · Developmental disabilities (including exploring the possibility of FASD) · Illness/disability management · Current medication, if any, and attitudes toward them (use of analgesics could indicate pattern of self-medication) · Serious diseases of family members. · Perception of health status, health problems and risks for future
Family/home environment (see section 3.8)	· Family togetherness · Parenting practices · Parental substance use behaviours and attitudes · Family norms and expectations about substance use · Sibling substance use behaviours · Chronic marital/family dysfunction · Separation/divorce · Family psychiatric history · Other significant adults in the young person's life (e.g., grandparents, family and friends).
Sexual orientation and gender identity	· Coming out · Discrimination · Family issues · Community involvement · Body image · HIV concerns For more information see *Asking the Right Questions: Talking about Sexual Orientation and Gender Identity during Assessment for Drug and Alcohol Concerns* (Barbara et al., 2002)
Abuse and neglect	· Sexual/physical abuse and trauma symptoms · Child maltreatment history · Witnessing violence · Threats that have been experienced · Suicide ideation/attempts

Area of life	Potential issues (continued)
Abuse and neglect (cont.)	· Self-harm (including cutting) · Harm to others · Risky sexual practices · Other risk behaviours · Symptoms of PTSD (e.g., nightmares, flashbacks, numbness or detachment)
Peer environment	· Peer substance use · Peer norms · Abstinent role models · Gang involvement · Social network
School environment	· Learning disabilities and difficulties · Academic standing/achievements · School affiliation · Literacy · Use of drugs at school
Work environment	· Employment status and history · Availability of drugs at work · Use of drugs at work
Leisure/recreation	· Involvement in drug-free activities
Religious affiliation/ spirituality	· Beliefs and values · Involvement in religious/spiritual activities
Delinquency/justice system involvement	· Involvement in delinquent behaviours · Current or past involvement with justice system, upcoming court dates or other legal appointments
Involvement with the child protection system	· Current or past foster care, permanent wardship, etc. (as children or as parents)

COUNSELLOR'S TIP

It is important for you to become "trauma-informed" so that you have the knowledge and skills necessary to help young people deal with any flashbacks, memories, etc., which can emerge in the context of addressing abuse and neglect, or when stopping substance use.

For more information see *Bridging Responses: A front-line worker's guide to supporting women who have post-traumatic stress* (Haskell, 2001)

Parents may feel that if only the young person could be sent home (to their country of origin), things would be better (Charles Senior, personal communication).

Ethnocultural identity

The values, knowledge and skills involved in culturally competent assessments are outlined in Chapter 2. In addition, when dealing with young people from various ethnocultural groups, it is important to ask about specific experiences and situations that affect their lives including, for example:

- When did they (or their parents or earlier generations) come to Canada and how involved are they in their culture?
- What is their cultural identity? What is the cultural identity of their parents?
- How do they value that identity?
- How do they relate to the cultural identity that they see around them?
- What is their level of collective, cultural, racial, and self-esteem?
- How does their ethnocultural group perceive and deal with mental health problems?

Among Aboriginal youth, it is important to find out as much as possible about the following (Peter Menzies, personal communication):

- why and when did they come to an urban centre (and whether or not they came from a reserve)
- their personal history (including parents' experiences of residential schools and involvement with child welfare agencies)
- history of trauma including intergenerational trauma
- whether they are traditional, non-traditional or neo-traditional (e.g., they walk in both worlds) in their practices
- extent of support available in their home community or in the city
- extent of isolation, marginalization, discrimination and racism they experience
- extent of shame and feelings of not belonging
- values
- family involvement
- degree of trust in service provider (you may be seen as an authority or as an oppressor).

Although you may be able to access training that will increase your knowledge and sensitivity in dealing with Aboriginal youth, it is important to recognize and respect the complexity in working with these young people. This involves asking about their lives, listening to their perspective and not making assumptions.

Working in partnership with Aboriginal agencies is essential to ensure that young people are properly assessed, diagnosed and have access to traditional healing practices, if they wish to utilize them.

3.7.7 ASSESSING A YOUNG PERSON'S STRENGTHS AND RESOURCES

Regardless of the number of problems a young person is facing, he or she always has strengths and resources to draw upon for survival. Assume that your client has qualities and abilities that have helped him or her cope with difficulties and contributed to accomplishments. Your interest in identifying a youth's capabilities and supports, and your skills in reflecting these back, can reinforce feelings of self-esteem and self-efficacy.

COUNSELLOR'S TIP

Bear in mind that a young person may be getting criticism and negative feedback from parents, school authorities and others. It can be empowering to focus on her or his strengths. For example, when you are working with a youth who has not been successful in terms of getting good marks in school, ask about other school-related experiences that may have been more positive. These may include non-academic skills such as friendships at school, ongoing efforts to learn despite frustration and difficulties, participation in extracurricular activities or teams, etc.

3.7.8 ASSESSING READINESS FOR CHANGE

The assessment process should include an exploration of those aspects of a young person's thinking that are associated with behaviour change including:

· reasons for substance use (social, coping, psychological, self-medication, etc.)
· expectations about behavioural outcomes (including risk perception)
· Stage of change (see Table below)
· motivation
· self-efficacy (confidence in the ability to achieve personal goals (Winters, 2001).

Assessing a young person's readiness for change is particularly important. If, for example, a young person has reduced his or her use of substances in the past three months, this may be a good indication of readiness for change. Self-initiated behaviour change is also a good predictor of successful treatment outcomes.

Common characteristics of individuals in the *precontemplation* stage of change

Defensive

Resistant to suggestion of problems associated with their drug use

Uncommitted to, or passive in treatment

Consciously or unconsciously avoiding steps to change their behaviour

Lacking awareness of a problem

Often pressured by others to seek treatment

Feeling coerced and "put upon" by significant others

Common characteristics of individuals in the *contemplation* stage of change

Seeking to evaluate and understand their behaviour

Distressed

Desirous of exerting control or mastery

Thinking about making changes

Have not begun taking action and are not yet prepared to do so

Frequently have made attempts to change in the past

Evaluating pros and cons of their behaviour and pros and cons of changing it

Common characteristics of individuals in the *preparation* stage of change

Intending to change their behaviour

Ready for change in terms of both attitude and behaviour

On the verge of taking action

Engaged in the change process

Prepared to make firm commitments to follow through on the action option they choose

Making or having made the decision to change

Common characteristics of individuals in *action* stage of change

Have decided to make change

Have verbalized or otherwise demonstrated a firm commitment to making change

Making efforts to modify behaviour and/or their environment

Presenting motivation and making effort to achieve behavioural change

Have committed to making change and involved in the change process

Willing to follow suggested strategies and activities to change

Common characteristics of individuals in the *maintenance* stage of change

Working to sustain changes achieved to date

Focusing considerable attention on avoiding slips or relapses

Expressing fear or anxiety regarding relapse

Facing less frequent but often intense temptations to use substances

Common characteristics of individuals in the *relapse* stage of change

Reverting back to problem use

Feeling disappointed, guilty or discouraged

Dropping out of treatment

Unsure about changing and reverting back to an earlier stage, such as precontemplation or contemplation

Becoming more determined to change and wanting to learn from the relapse

Looking for support and understanding from the counsellor

This table is adapted from Connors et al. (2001, 13, 19, 22, 25, 30).

In Appendix F you will find an easy-to-use tool called *Readiness for Change*. This tool will help you assess the stage of change your client is in. Once you have an understanding of the young person's motivation level, you can adjust your approach. Working with the young person based on his or her current stage of change will build rapport.

COUNSELLOR'S TIP

Generally, programs and services are set up to work with youth in the action stage of change. The challenge is to help youth who are in precontemplation or contemplation to reach that point. Try to avoid referring to programs that are not flexible in adjusting services to match young people's stage of change.

You can use the *Stages of change* model to tailor how you work with young people and help them become ready for change. Additional information on tailoring treatment to stages of change is included in Chapter 4.

3.8 FAMILY ASSESSMENT

The messages about the role of families in assessment and treatment for young people are mixed. In substance use treatment, while the involvement of families has been identified as a best practice (Health Canada, 1999), in actuality, the extent of family involvement varies. Many programs provide treatment to young people without parental consent or involvement, if necessary.

Within mental health, on the other hand, there has been a much stronger emphasis on the involvement of families. Indeed, parents are considered the primary client if they bring their child for treatment, and are usually given more access to information about the assessment and treatment of their child. There are important issues around what family "involvement" actually means. Among some mental health treatment providers, there is a hesitancy to imply that families need "treatment."

When you are doing a comprehensive assessment, it's important to recognize that the role of the family in a young person's life is very influential. Depending on family history and capacity, family involvement may be a powerful source of support. There are, however, important limitations on this, and there may be situations where family involvement is either not a good idea or the family needs significant support and intervention to play a positive role.

It's important to be cautious about involving family in treatment, particularly in situations where a young person has been victimized by one or more family members. Where families are seen to be part of the problem, it may be helpful to conduct a family assessment.

Where appropriate, family members need to be provided with support, information, insight and understanding in order to contribute to the young person's progress. They may need to be involved in family counselling to modify family dynamics that are dysfunctional for a young person.

It is important to obtain information on the substance use of family members to better understand the context of the youth's use. Problematic use in the family means that the youth is at greater risk, and is a factor in deciding the best treatment approach. In addition, including family members in the assessment process offers a broader picture of the youth's use and functioning, and opens the door to family counselling as a treatment option (Chaim & Shenfeld, in press).

The goals of a family assessment are to:
· Listen to the insights of family members into a young person's problems, including substance use, mental health concerns and be open to hearing an alternative view of what's going on.
· Establish the extent to which the young person's substance use may be related to other family issues that the family has not been able to recognize or deal with, including substance use and mental illness of other family members.
· Assess and harness family resources (strengths and supports) to help a young person overcome her or his substance use and mental health problem and allow the family to play a collaborative role in the management and treatment of the youth.
· Provide feedback to parents regarding assessment findings and inform them of treatment plans.
· Identify the need to reshape family interactions (which may require referral to a family service for long-term marital/family therapy, or individual referrals for family members with specific needs) so that the gains in the young person's treatment are reinforced.
· Identify the need for support for the family in dealing with the effects of their child's substance use and mental health problems such as school failure, legal problems, etc.

It is important to:
· Involve each family member in the assessment process

- Draw out not only family problems but also family strengths
- Build a sense of hopefulness and optimism in the family, even in the face of difficulties
- Clarify problems
- Help the family face difficult issues without blaming, accusing or judging
- Develop a treatment plan with clear goals and strategies not only for the youth, but also for other members of the family
- Provide a referral to a youth and/or family service for longer-term intervention when indicated.

Based on your assessment findings, you can determine the type and level of family involvement that is best for the overall treatment plan for the youth. The table below suggests guidelines for determining the level of family involvement.

Types of Family involvement	Level of Intervention	Goals
Collateral information gathering	Consulting with family members to obtain their insights and input into the young person's life and situation.	To broaden your perspective about the young person's life— and their challenges, strengths and supports.
Family orientation	Orienting the parents/family to the treatment plans for the youth, and providing information about drug use and mental health.	To inform the family about the treatment that the young person is embarking on, and to enlist family supports.
Parent/family Psycho-education or support group	Involving parents and/or families in family life education with special reference to substance use and mental health information.	To inform parents and/or families about family relations issues and how they may be relevant to substance abuse and mental health.
Family counselling	Contracting with the family for interventions aimed at resolving identified problems	To bring about resolution of problematic issues identified by family members and related to the young person's drug use and mental health issues.
Family therapy (myriad approaches)	Contracting with the family for intervention aimed at chronic and systemic family dysfunction.	To bring about change to elusive and intractable areas of systemic family dysfunction identified as directly related

Types of Family involvement	Level of Intervention	Goals
Family therapy (myriad approaches) (continued)		to the young person's substance use. Family interventions may identify substance use or mental health problems among parents or siblings. Intervention and referral for these family members is very important.

(Boudreau, in press)

One of the possible outcomes of a family assessment is that you reframe the substance use and/or mental health issues as being not just a youth's problem, but a family concern that is impacted by, as well as impacting upon the family. The focus will be on helping everyone in the system make changes and thereby taking the pressure off the youth as the only one who needs to make changes. Instead of the youth being seen as "the problem," the family takes it on as "our problem."

Ideally, an overall treatment plan would involve more than just the family and would cast a wider net to include other social systems that influence the young person such as schools, work settings, recreational facilities, health care services, etc. You may want to involve co-workers or superiors, girlfriends or boyfriends, in addition to family members.

Of course, friends and family do not always fit into the "support" category. The youth's problems could affect family members and/or close friends deeply and directly. During the assessment, try to identify and consider people in a young person's social environment who are:
· directly affected by the young person's substance use and mental health
· contributing to the young person's problems
· able to provide support and assistance.

Consider also the possibility of tapping into less obvious sources of insight and support (e.g., grandparents).

3.9 DEVELOPING A TREATMENT PLAN

Once you have completed a comprehensive assessment, you will need to work with the young person and the family, if possible, to tailor a treatment plan that reflects the youth's specific needs, as well as stage of change. A good treatment plan will build upon, and reinforce the young person's and family's strengths and resources.

It is important to keep in mind when making referrals to programs or services in the community, that for young people with both substance use and mental health problems, the treatment plan must address the need for an integrated approach.

With the consent of the young person, family members and/or significant others may be involved in treatment planning or informed of treatment plans that have been formulated.

3.9.1 PRINCIPLES OF TREATMENT PLANNING

The following is a list of some general principles of treatment planning that you may wish to use as a checklist.

· The treatment plan acknowledges and reinforces the young person's personal responsibility for his or her health-related behaviours and for changing those behaviours.

· The treatment plan is tailored to the young person's stage of change and level of motivation.

· The treatment plan maximizes the young person's strengths and support systems while minimizing identified problems.

· The treatment plan is comprehensive and holistic, aiming to take into account all contributing factors identified.

· The treatment plan uses the least intrusive intervention options (e.g., outpatient as opposed to residential treatment) in order to cause as little disruption as possible to positive aspects of the young person's home, job and social life.

· Whenever possible, offer treatment in a single setting, either by an individual practitioner or a team.

· Be familiar with local community resources for youth, including their program goals, intake criteria and other relevant features (e.g., waiting lists).

· When referral is necessary and possible, preference should be given to agencies that provide treatment based on continuing assessment of individual needs, rather than agencies that treat all young persons in one set way.

· The family context is usually the best and most successful basis for treatment planning, and ongoing family involvement is desirable.

3.9.2 USE OF PLACEMENT CRITERIA AND DECISION TREES

Depending on the system and jurisdiction within which you work, you may use standardized placement criteria that help ensure that young people receive the least intrusive yet most appropriate services that meet their needs.

In Ontario, for example, there are admission and discharge criteria with related sets of decision trees that substance use treatment providers use to decide:
· where to admit young persons when they first enter the treatment system
· when to refer them to other services in the system.

The following admission criteria reflect seven categories of strengths and needs that Ontario (Ontario Substance Abuse Bureau & Ontario Addiction Services Advisory Council, 2000, 18-21). recommends you explore when assessing young people's level of functioning:
· **Acute intoxication and withdrawal needs:** the young person's ability to function related to use of, and withdrawal from substances
· **Medical/psychiatric needs:** any signs or symptoms of medical/psychiatric problems
· **Emotional/behavioural needs:** the young person's ability to function in terms of life skills, problem-solving abilities, coping skills and self-management
· **Treatment readiness:** the young person's readiness to change her or his substance use and/or other aspects of her or his life
· **Relapse potential:** the young person's potential to resume substance use (if abstinent) or to relapse from agreed upon treatment goals
· **Recovery environment/supports:** the level of support and safety available to the young person
· **Barriers and resources:** the barriers/commitments that prevent a young person from participating in treatment, and the resources available or needed to attend scheduled treatment.

3.9.3 IDENTIFYING GOALS FOR TREATMENT

The impetus for change must come from the young person. Once he or she is ready and willing to talk about making changes, you can discuss possible treatment goals to pursue.

You and the young person together will negotiate and decide upon what changes he or she is ready to make. Arriving at a "change plan" involves the following steps, adapted from Miller & Rollnick (2002, 133-139):
· **Setting goals:** Start with the goals that the young person is most interested in pursuing and bear in mind that these may be broader goals that deal with more than just substance use. Goals need to be realistic and prioritized. You can suggest additional goals that you think would be helpful for their well-being and efforts to make changes.
· **Considering change options:** There are many different ways to reach goals and you can brainstorm various options with the young person and evaluate different strategies together. In the end, it is the young person's choice.
· **Arriving at a plan:** Ask the young person to describe his or her plan for change. Afterwards, summarize and write down what was said.

· **Getting commitment:** Ask the young person for a commitment. If he or she is not ready to commit, don't force the issue. When ready, it may be helpful for the young person to tell others about the plan.

3.9.4 SEQUENCING OF TREATMENT

There are no hard and fast rules about the sequencing of treatment for substance use and mental health problems. In general, it is best to assess young people for substance use, mental health and other problems, and then treat both substance use and mental health problems at the same time unless there is some compelling reason not to.

Depending on your setting, and on a case-by-case basis, you and a psychiatrist together will need to decide upon the potential risks and benefits of prescribing psychoactive medications for mental health symptoms. Abstinence from substances prior to prescribing medication is preferred, though not always a requirement.

Regardless of your setting, if a young person has both substance use and mental health problems, there needs to be a comprehensive plan in place to address both of these issues, and any other problems that the young person is facing.

3.9.5 IDENTIFYING SETTINGS FOR SUBSTANCE USE AND MENTAL HEALTH TREATMENT

The treatment plan will, in part, be determined by the facilities in your area. It is therefore important that you make yourself familiar with the local services, find out which components of the continuum of care they offer, know their admission criteria and stay up to date.

Look for the least intrusive treatment option that meets a young person's needs yet still provides sufficient support and benefit. Having access to decision trees and/or other tools, as mentioned above, will aid you.

In general, most young people will be treated on an outpatient basis at a community setting. However, if someone is living in an unsafe or unsupported situation, or his or her life is in chaos, he or she may need residential support and/or treatment. Young people who are experiencing serious mental health symptoms may also require in-patient treatment.

It is likely that there will not be many youth-specific treatment services available, and you will probably have to look further afield to find the components of the continuum of care that a young person needs. Another option is to utilize adult-oriented substance use treatment and rehabilitation services that are willing to take on youth. This is less than ideal since youth are best treated in an environment that is geared to them. On the other hand, it may be your only option.

When youth with concurrent disorders begin treatment, various factors need to be considered in choosing the most appropriate and least restrictive environment for therapy. While a withdrawal management service could be best for new clients who present extremely intoxicated or with severe withdrawal symptoms, these young clients may initially be open only to outpatient treatment. Later, once they are more comfortable with therapy, they may be more ready and willing to enter a detoxification program. For youth with concurrent disorders, it is important to take a case management/long-term outlook in order to create the initial therapeutic alliance. (Ballon, in press)

...Many different levels of care are available, and although not all are widely available, it's important to create a spectrum of care. For example, treatment resources may include in-patient psychiatric wards, long- or short-term residential therapy, abstinence-based group homes, day therapy, intensive outpatient individual and group therapy, school programs, self-help group meetings such as Alcoholics or Narcotics Anonymous (AA or NA) or psychiatric groups, and occasional outpatient check-in meetings. (Ballon, in press).

Another possibility is to look for youth-oriented services that are not substance use specific and use these creatively. For example, if there is no residential substance use treatment service for youth in your area, but a young person needs a stable, substance-free living environment in order to benefit from day or outpatient treatment, you may be able to work something out with a group home or halfway house.

Although youth-specific substance use treatment services in Ontario are coeducational, there may be situations where you feel it would be more appropriate to refer a young woman to a females-only treatment program, or you may want to ensure that there are gender-specific components within a coeducational setting.

Culturally appropriate treatment services are another option to be considered.

For further information about the programs and services available in Ontario, please consult the database available at the Ontario Drug and Alcohol Registry of Treatment (DART) at the following website: http://www.dart.on.ca/

3.9.6 IMPLEMENTING THE TREATMENT PLAN AND MAKING REFERRALS

You will either implement the treatment plan in-house, in partnership with another agency or refer a young person for treatment elsewhere.

If you are making referrals, try to find out as much as possible about the service to which you are referring including their requirements. In some cases, people may make their own appointments, but be prepared to provide guidance about the process.

Follow up to ensure that the young person and/or the family have made contact with the treatment service. Also follow up with the treatment service to ensure they are implementing an integrated treatment plan.

- -

3.10 IMPORTANCE OF CASE MANAGEMENT

Case management is central to an integrated response to substance use and mental health problems. Within integrated treatment programs, intensive case management has been shown to increase engagement and retention of clients, reduce hospitalization, reduce substance use behaviour and increase stable remission among clients (Drake & Mueser 2000, 111).

No matter what setting you work in, the importance of taking on a case management role to ensure that young people are receiving integrated treatment and support, cannot be overstressed. Effective case management is a key strategy for ensuring an integrated approach to treatment and support.

Youth often require many interventions and thus having a multidisciplinary team to weave together a concurrent therapy plan is essential. Problems with substance use and mental health are often chronic, and even with treatment, may take years to stabilize. Relapses are common, and the level of need of young clients may increase and decrease repeatedly, requiring ongoing adjustment of degree of support. Providing effective care to youth requires patience, and works best within a comprehensive case management approach that targets not only addiction and mental health issues, but also the many other elements of an adolescent's life, such as family, job, recreation, housing and peer relations.

If you take on the case management role, you will work with various providers in other parts of your agency and often in other systems, to co-ordinate services for young people. You may play the role of case manager on your own, or be part of a multidisciplinary case management team that has combined substance use and mental health treatment expertise.

As a case manager, you will be involved in:

· identification of problems
· outreach strategies
· assessment of a young person's strengths and needs
· treatment planning
· advocating on behalf of young people to ensure access to services they need
· providing practical assistance and linking young people with the services they need
· monitoring young people's progress and providing ongoing support and access to other services as needed. (Bois & Graham, 1997; Drake & Mueser, 2000).

Continuing care

It is important to not end treatment too soon with young clients. This becomes especially important when the mental health symptoms are suggestive of a chronic problem (e.g., mood disorder) or a disorder for which medication may be required (e.g., psychotic disorder). Many mental health disorders first appear during adolescence, and often only a provisional diagnosis can be made. Therefore, it is important that a young client remain connected to a health professional who can continue to monitor progress as well as the emergence of more serious symptoms over time.

Young people can easily fall through the cracks in the system. The case manager acts as an advocate for the youth, and is able to call upon a well-functioning multidisciplinary team to address the myriad issues associated with concurrent disorders. The case management approach aims to build a network of support in the community for the youth, through services, and through family and friends (Ballon, in press).

CHAPTER 4

TREATMENT AND SUPPORT

4.1 INTEGRATED TREATMENT

Although there is very little research on treatment of concurrent disorders in youth, there is best practice information on substance use and mental health treatment for youth, as well as newly developed integrated approaches to concurrent disorders. Information about best practices for treating various mental health problems is extensive and beyond the scope of this resource. For information on treating adolescent mental health problems and disorders, consult the *Diagnostic and Statistical Manual Of Mental Disorders, 4th Edition (DSM-IV)* (American Psychiatric Association, Washington DC., 1994) and *Evidence Based Practice for the Treatment of Depression and Conduct Disorders in Children and Adolescents* (Children's Mental Health Ontario, May, 2001).

Integrated treatment of concurrent disorders requires:
· capacity to treat mental health problems
· capacity to treat substance use problems
· provisions for treating both in a co-ordinated manner within a program or system.

An integrated approach assumes that youth who are assessed as having concurrent substance use and mental health problems will receive appropriate treatment for their mental health problems before, during or after treatment for the drug use, depending on the relationship between the two problem areas.

When developing an integrated care plan, practitioners in the addiction and other fields who lack expertise in treating mental health problems are advised to collaborate with those practitioners who are experienced in dealing with adolescent mental health issues. Basic information on the most commonly occurring mental health problems, their prevalence and potential relationships with substance use is presented in Chapter 1. That, and the tools provided in the *First Contact* manual will enable you to begin to address mental health problems and symptoms as you proceed with substance use treatment. Practitioners who have the expertise to treat mental health problems, but lack experience in addressing substance use, will benefit by using the materials in the *First Contact* manual as well as the cognitive behaviour therapy model for treating substance use in Section 4.8 of this chapter.

4.1.1 PROGRAM AND SYSTEM INTEGRATION

Treatment and support for youth with both substance use and mental health problems is based on four key principles (Drake & Osher, 1997; Health Canada, 1999).

· Address young people's substance use and mental health concerns in an *integrated* manner. This can be done either in one setting or through co-ordination of services in different settings.
· Use *specialized* techniques that address both substance use and mental health problems. This includes having the ability to assess substance use and mental health problems, and understand the interaction between these problems.
· Provide a full range of interventions and supports for young people and their families. This includes developing linkages between programs and services. It also includes providing a *comprehensive* range of services and supports to address multiple issues and needs in addition to substance use and mental health problems.
· Adopt a *long-term* approach when developing a treatment plan and be careful not to terminate treatment early.

It is useful to distinguish between *program integration* and *system integration* as two ways to provide care and support for youth who need treatment for both mental health and substance use.

Program integration means that mental health and substance use treatments are provided by the same workers, or team of workers, within one program. This ensures that youth receive a consistent assessment and treatment, rather than contradictory messages from different providers. The young clients do not have to go to one agency for substance use treatment and another for mental health treatment. At this point in time, that type of ideal situation is rarely available. It, of course, requires that mental health services develop the capacity to treat substance use, and/or that addiction agencies be able to provide treatment for mental health problems. This can be achieved by hiring staff with the needed expertise or by training existing staff. Program integration can be developed in stages, with the first step being the development of integrated screening and assessment procedures followed by the development of a brief intervention such as *First Contact* that addresses drug use in the context of other mental health problems.

System integration: refers to the development of long-term linkages among service providers or treatment agencies within a system, or across multiple systems, to facilitate the provision of services at the local level. Mental health and substance use treatment are co-ordinated by two or more clinicians or support workers who work for different units or agencies to develop and implement an integrated treatment plan (Health Canada, 2002). This option is being implemented in some communities. Some addiction agencies have developed partnerships with psychiatrists to treat mental health concerns in youth in their programs. Other mental health and addiction agencies are running joint programs using staff from both agencies to provide expertise.

4.1.2 CLINICAL ISSUES IN THE TREATMENT OF ADOLESCENT CONCURRENT DISORDERS

Integrated treatment involves understanding the necessity for treating both problems at the same time, either by one counsellor, two or more counsellors in one agency (program integration), or two or more agencies (system integration). To do this successfully, the counsellor(s) need(s) to have the knowledge and skills to address both problems concurrently, as well as the ability to know when one problem needs to be emphasized over the other.

The nature of the relationship between the substance use and mental health problems helps determine your focus in treatment. When symptoms of both a substance use and mental health problem are identified, the counsellor needs to examine how the problems might be connected. Two questions to consider are:

· When are the symptoms of each problem evident (the temporal relationship)?
· Are the substances being used causing the mental health symptoms (the pharmacological relationship)?

THE TEMPORAL RELATIONSHIP
The temporal relationship between the problems can be explored in two ways—long-term and current.

The long-term temporal relationship
· Which problem was experienced first by the client? Did symptoms of a mental health problem exist before substance use began?
· Did the substance use begin before the mental health problem emerged?
· Did both problems begin at about the same time?

The current temporal relationship

· Does a mental health symptom frequently occur just prior to an instance of substance use (e.g., as opposed to being at a party and deciding to use drugs)?

· Does a mental health symptom frequently emerge following an episode of substance use (e.g., feeling depressed following the use of alcohol)?

· Does any other pattern exist?

· Does no pattern exist?

Knowledge of both long-term and current patterns helps you to understand how the two problems might be related. It is important to trace the history of both problems from the time each was first identified. The issue to be considered is whether or not one problem was present in the absence of the other, and if so, why do both problems now exist?

THE PHARMACOLOGICAL RELATIONSHIP

The pharmacological effects of the substance(s) being used by the young person are also relevant. The question to be considered is whether the substance being used is pharmacologically capable of producing the specific mental health symptoms being reported by the youth either due to use or withdrawal. In other words, mental health symptoms can be the result of using a substance or the result of withdrawal from a substance.

In addition to the direct and withdrawal effects, information regarding the quantity and frequency of the substances being used, as well as the duration of their effect(s) helps to identify the relationship.

For example, if a young client reports symptoms of depression for several weeks following the consumption of a moderate amount of alcohol, it is unlikely that the alcohol, in that amount, was "mimicking" depressive symptoms. It is more likely that the alcohol use was "triggering" or "exacerbating" depressive symptoms for which the young client may have been predisposed. On the other hand, if a young client reports symptoms of depression for a few days following prolonged use of excessive amounts of alcohol, it is likely that the alcohol, in that quantity, frequency and duration, was "mimicking" the depressive symptoms.

Clearly, these are guidelines only. However, the point is to try to identify the nature of the relationship when two problems are present. It may be helpful to note that Table 1 in the DSM-IV (American Psychiatric Association, 1994) provides comprehensive information on the direct and withdrawal effects of all drug classes and the mental health problems that each drug class is most strongly related to. In addition, Appendix A in the DSM-IV has a decision tree to assist in identifying substance use and substance–induced problems, which is consistent with the approach described in this section on the relationship between the two problems.

TYPES OF RELATIONSHIPS BETWEEN SUBSTANCE USE AND MENTAL HEALTH PROBLEMS

Once you have identified the *temporal* and *pharmacological* relationships between a young person's substance use and mental health problems, you can develop treatment accordingly. As was discussed in section 1.5, Trupin and Boesky (2001) developed a framework that takes the temporal and pharmacological relationships and subdivides them even more specifically into six possible relationships between the two problems. In five of these, the substance use and mental health problems are related to one another in some way. In the sixth instance, the two problems are independent and unrelated.

Relationship	Implications for treatment
Independent: Each problem has been present without symptoms of the other being present. In other words, the substance use and mental health problems are not related. Each problem exists independent of one another. · There have been times when the youth has used one or more substances on a regular basis for a length of time (e.g., several months) without experiencing the symptoms of a mental health problem. · There have been times when the youth has experienced symptoms of a mental health problem when not using a substance. · Although the two problems may not be related, there could be a common factor underlying them both.	When treating the young person, both problems must be a focus. Otherwise, begin by treating the problem that is present at the time.
Create: The symptoms of a mental health problem emerge after long-term substance use. · No mental health problems are evident before substance use. · The youth reports symptoms of a mental health problem following prolonged use of a substance. · The substance is pharmacologically capable of creating the specific mental health symptoms following prolonged use.	Treat the substance use problem and treat any serious mental health symptoms. Provide continuing care to monitor whether the symptoms of the mental health problem are relieved and do not return.

Relationship	Implications for treatment
Trigger: Symptoms of a mental health problem for which the youth may be predisposed, emerge following an episode of substance use. The young person may have been vulnerable to a mental health problem. · No mental health problems are evident before substance use. · The client reports symptoms of a mental health problem following (short-term) use of a substance. · There is a possible family history of mental health problems which could make the youth vulnerable. · The pharmacological relationship between the substance and the symptoms may be unclear.	Provide personalized feedback and education regarding the youth's vulnerability to substance-induced mental health problems. Treat the substance use problem with a recommendation for abstinence. Treat the mental health problem and relieve any serious mental health symptoms. Provide continuing care and monitoring to determine the need for ongoing treatment for the mental health problem.
Exacerbate: Symptoms of a known mental health problem worsen following one or more episodes of substance use. · There is a previous history of mental health problems. · Mental health symptoms get worse during or shortly after the use of a substance. · Mental health problems improve when not using. · The substance is pharmacologically capable of creating and/or exacerbating the specific mental health symptoms.	Treat the mental health problem, and relieve any serious mental health symptoms. Provide personalized feedback and education regarding the youth's vulnerability to substance-induced mental health problems and treat the substance use problem with a recommendation for abstinence. Provide continuing care and monitoring to determine the need for ongoing treatment for the mental health problem.
Mimic: Symptoms of a mental health problem emerge following an episode of substance use. In other words, the symptoms are induced by the substance use. · There is no previous history of mental health problems. · An episode of heavy substance use precedes the mental health symptoms that emerge during intoxication or withdrawal. · The substance is pharmacologically capable of mimicking the specific mental health symptoms. · The mental health symptoms disappear following abstinence from the substance.	Treat the substance use problem and, if necessary, treat to relieve any serious mental health symptoms.

Relationship	Implications for treatment
Mask: After a youth stops using a substance, symptoms of a mental health problem surface. In other words, the substance hid the symptoms of a mental health problem. · There may have been evidence of a prior mental health problem. · There is no/little evidence of a mental health problem when the youth is using a substance. · There is evidence of a mental health problem when the youth stops using the substance. · The substance is pharmacologically capable of suppressing the specific mental health symptoms.	Make the mental health problem the primary focus of treatment. Provide substance use treatment, depending on the severity of the problem.

Here are three examples of choosing a treatment focus based on the relationship between a substance use and mental health problem.

Example 1: An adolescent with no previous history of depression reports symptoms of depression that emerged only after he or she began using alcohol regularly. The counsellor might hypothesize a "mimicking" relationship and assume the depressive symptoms were induced by the substance (alcohol) use. Because of this relationship, the treatment goal would focus initially on the substance use problem (e.g., reduce or eliminate the substance use), with due regard to any immediate serious mental health symptoms. With this relationship, it would be expected that the depressive symptoms would also reduce in intensity as the substance use is reduced. If the depressive symptoms do not improve, even though the substance use is reduced or eliminated, the counsellor would need to reassess the relationship between the two problems. It could be that the alcohol use "created" the depressive symptoms in a young client who may have been predisposed to depression.

In this example, it is critical that the counsellor is knowledgeable about the pharmacological effects of alcohol, specifically, that long-term use of alcohol can produce depressive symptoms as a withdrawal effect. It is also important that the counsellor is knowledgeable about depression, particularly as it is manifested in adolescents.

Example 2: An adolescent reports being too anxious to go to school following successful treatment for an alcohol and cannabis problem. It is important to note the pattern of mental health symptoms that exists immediately prior to, and following, a specific episode of substance use. In this example, the substance might have been "masking" a social anxiety problem. The treatment goal, which may have focussed initially on substance use treatment, would now focus on the mental health problem—social anxiety. With this sort of relationship, it would be expected that the adolescent would not relapse if the social anxiety improved. However, if the substance use problem did not improve, even though the social anxiety problem improved, the counsellor would need to reassess the relationship between the two problems.

In this example, the counsellor would need to be knowledgeable about the pharmacological effects of cannabis and alcohol, and specifically, that alcohol has anti-anxiety properties. The counsellor also needs to understand social anxiety and its effect on young people.

Example 3: An adolescent reports symptoms of depression even when she or he has not used a substance recently. At other times, the adolescent uses substances excessively, yet does not experience any mental health symptoms either before or after using. In this case, the counsellor would assess the young client as having two independent problems, perhaps due to an underlying, common risk factor. This client would require treatment for both problems.

THE COURSE OF TREATMENT: SHIFTING THE FOCUS

It is important to be flexible, particularly early on in treatment, until both the substance use and mental health problems have stabilized and you are more confident of the relationship between the two. You will likely need to shift the emphasis from one issue to the other during sessions, and between sessions to address both substance use and mental health issues as they present themselves.

It can be helpful to set an agenda that identifies the focus for each session. You can "check-in" with the young person on the status of each problem before determining the agenda for that session. "Checking-in" can be done informally, simply by asking the client to describe any episodes of substance use and to provide a self-rating regarding the mental health problem. You will then need to be prepared to change your focus and respond to the prioritized problem. This becomes more challenging when more than one counsellor is involved in the integrated treatment plan, and highlights the importance of co-ordinating the integrated treatment so that the young person is able to access the appropriate help at the time that he or she needs it.

Sometimes, the counselling will eventually focus on one problem more than the other, for example, when it appears that one problem stems from the other. In this case, effective treatment of the primary problem will also result in the alleviation of the secondary problem.

SELF-MONITORING

Self-monitoring is a technique that is commonly used in substance use counselling. It helps pinpoint a problem, assess the effectiveness of specific interventions, and evaluate progress over time. Self-monitoring can be an especially important tool when working with young clients who may not be complete and accurate reporters of their own experiences. For example, a mood diary can be developed for a young client with symptoms of depression. It can be combined with self-monitoring of substance use to track the relationship between the the mental health problem and substance use problem. These tracking methods can be developed for most problems, including anxiety and anger, two other common concerns for adolescents. In many cases, such self-monitoring instruments already exist. When unavailable, a counsellor can customize a self-monitoring system for their clients.

4.2 HELPING YOUTH THROUGH THE STAGES OF CHANGE

The *Stages of change* model introduced in section 2.4 suggests specific goals and treatment strategies that are appropriate at each stage to help the youth progress through the continuum. Although the strategies discussed below refer to changing substance use, the strategies can be applied to any behaviour change including those that impact on mental health.

PRECONTEMPLATION STAGE

Two basic strategies are helpful in the *precontemplation* stage:

Attempt to establish a therapeutic and trusting relationship with the young client.
The counsellor can do this by:
- expressing empathy, warmth, and understanding of the client's point of view
- emphasizing that the client, rather than the counsellor, is responsible for, and in charge of the change process
- avoiding labels (e.g., alcoholic, addict, etc.)
- using humour, reassurance, and limit-setting to instil a sense of confidence, comfort and safety in the client.

Assist the young client to explore issues.
The counsellor can do this by:
- avoiding judgmental comments
- paying close attention to what the young person sees as his or her problem
- helping the youth determine if problems he or she is experiencing are related to substance use
- examining with the youth, what the perceptions and concerns of significant others (e.g., parents, siblings and friends) are about the client's substance use
- providing harm reduction education about safer and less problematic levels of use or modes of administration

The goal of working with precontemplative clients is to help them connect their substance use with unpleasant consequences, and thereby increase their concern about their use. The transition from precontemplation to contemplation can be difficult, and must be accomplished by the young persons, not the counsellor. Some young clients will seek to please or avoid conflict by agreeing with the counsellor without fully understanding or accepting that there are consequences to their use. However, only when clients begin to express some concern about their use, do they actually begin to move into the contemplation stage of change.

CONTEMPLATION STAGE

The counsellor can assist clients in *contemplation* by:

· continuing the process of building the therapeutic relationship
· continuing the process of identifying and exploring the substance use and the consequences
· helping the youth examine the advantages and disadvantages of working on their substance use behaviour and its consequences
· exploring the clients' ambivalence about making changes
· reviewing possible courses of action including the positive and negative aspects of each.

The goal of working with contemplation stage youth is to help them realize they can solve their problems (self-efficacy) and that the solutions will lead to an overall improvement in their quality of life. When they express interest in making some changes to their substance use behaviour, they are moving into the preparation stage.

PREPARATION STAGE

The counsellor can assist young people in the *preparation* stage by:

· helping the young clients set goals
· helping them select a plan of action that is suited to their personality, needs, cultural background and preferences
· giving them practical support through any barriers to the change process.

The goal of working with preparation stage clients is to help them develop a realistic, firm commitment to change that includes setting goals, and developing a clear plan of action to achieve their goals. When this is accomplished, the client has moved into the action stage.

ACTION STAGE

The counsellor can assist youth in the *action* stage by:

· providing support and encouragement
· helping them develop skills (e.g., assertiveness, cognitive restructuring, dealing with boredom, etc.) for dealing with triggers or cravings for drug use
· helping them develop alternatives to substance use (e.g., non-substance related activities, leisure activities, social skills, etc.).

The goal of working with youth in the action stage is to support the change process by helping them use their problem-solving and coping skills, and helping them develop new skills. When they have achieved their initial goals, they are moving into the maintenance stage.

MAINTENANCE STAGE

The counsellor can assist young clients in *maintenance* by:

· providing support to find different social and recreational activities, friends, and support systems

· identifying additional problem areas that could be a focus of counselling

· focussing on relapse prevention strategies.

The goal of working with clients in the maintenance stage is to help youth assimilate and integrate the strategies and skills developed in the action stage and to help them make lasting lifestyle changes.

RELAPSE STAGE

The counsellor can assist youth in *relapse* by:

· being understanding and supportive

· helping the youth learn from the relapse

· instilling hope and confidence.

The goal of working with youth in relapse is to help them re-enter the process of change.

4.3 KEY TECHNIQUES OF MOTIVATIONAL INTERVIEWING (MI)

COUNSELLOR'S TIP

Motivation is fluid. For young people with substance use and mental health problems, motivation can be highly changeable. Moving back and forth through the stages of change as a result of mental health problems is not uncommon. For example, young people who are in a manic phase experience high confidence and focussed energy. They might also increase party activity (a risk factor for substance use relapse) or be overconfident about their ability to control themselves and just have one additional drink. They can have different levels of motivation for different substances that they use (e.g., they intend to quit drinking alcohol but are unwilling to consider stopping their drug use).

"Within motivational interviewing, the counselor responds in particular ways to change talk in order to reinforce it, and to resistance in order to diminish it, both in the service of resolving ambivalence and promoting behavior change" (Miller & Rollnick, 2002, 51).

This section provides you with an overview of the key techniques involved in motivational interviewing. For further information on learning and implementing these techniques, we encourage you to consult the seminal book on this topic by Miller & Rollnick (2002) entitled *Motivational Interviewing: Preparing People for Change.*

Motivational interviewing strategies are divided into two phases, although it is important to recognize that Phase 1 strategies can continue to be used throughout the process. Phase 1 strategies focus on building a young person's intrinsic motivation for change. Once the young person feels that making change is important, you shift to discussing strategies for change. This marks the beginning of Phase 2 strategies, which focus on strengthening commitment to change and developing a plan to achieve change.

4.3.1 BUILDING INTRINSIC MOTIVATION

The following table outlines some specific MI strategies. By reading through this material and practising these strategies, you can begin to incorporate motivational interviewing into your work with youth.

PHASE 1: STRATEGIES FOR BUILDING INTRINSIC MOTIVATION FOR CHANGE

Early traps to avoid	
Question and answer	You control the session by asking questions but get only "yes" or "no" answers from the youth. Have the youth fill out a pre-counselling questionnaire to get more detailed information. To avoid the question and answer trap, use open-ended questions and reflective listening (see below). As a rule, don't ask three questions in a row.
Taking sides	You argue there is a problem but the young person responds with "there is no problem." This is the most important trap to avoid! Use strategies for responding to resistance (see below).
Expert	You give the impression that you have all the answers and the young person plays a passive role. Expert opinion can play an important role later in enhancing confidence, but early on, the focus is on building the young person's confidence. You must collaborate. Remember that only the young person knows everything about his or her situation, values, goals, concerns and skills, and how change will fit into his or her life.
Labelling	Using a diagnostic label to describe the young person's problem can create resistance. If you encounter resistance around the use of a label, shift the focus away from the label and towards helping the young person discuss his or her substance use pattern. Conveying an accepting and non-judgmental tone is key to building rapport with the young person.

Premature focus	Avoid situations where you want to focus on a particular topic (e.g., what you see as the problem) but the young client has more pressing concerns he or she wants to focus on. The youth may not agree with you at this point as to what the problem is. If you try to focus the discussion too quickly, the young person may become defensive. Begin by listening to his or her concerns and stories. Get a broader understanding of the young person's life. This will often lead back to the area(s) that you are concerned about. The time you spend listening helps build rapport.
Blaming	Blame is irrelevant. If a young person's goal is to blame someone else for the problem, try to reflect and reframe her or his concerns. It may be helpful to offer a brief orientation statement about the purpose of counselling up front so she or he knows it is not about deciding who is at fault. Instead of dealing with blame, move towards building self-efficacy by affirming the youth's strengths and reinforcing the therapeutic alliance.
First Session	The first session is important because it sets the tone and expectations for counselling. Developing rapport at the outset influences whether or not the young person will return.
Opening structure	Start with an orientation which is a simple and brief structuring statement about the first session and counselling, in general. Indicate how much time you have, your role, the goals, the young person's roles and discuss any details that need to be attended to. Ask open-ended questions.
Agenda setting	The obvious topic may not be the only topic or the one to discuss first. Don't assume that you know what the right topic of conversation is. Ask young people about their concerns and priorities for discussion.
Early Methods	The following five methods are useful not only in the first session but also throughout the counselling process.
Ask open-ended questions	Let young people do most of the talking in the early stages. Your job is to listen carefully and encourage expression. You can set the topic of exploration and encourage them to talk to you by asking open-ended questions. Listen reflectively, in addition to using the other methods listed below.

Reflective listening	This is the most important and most challenging mi skill. The crucial element is how you respond. You need to guess what the young person means with a statement, rather than a question. A statement, using the word "you" as the subject, is less likely to evoke resistance. Do not assume that what you think people mean is what they actually mean. Recognize that most statements can have multiple meanings and you have to figure out what is the most likely meaning. Skillful reflection goes beyond what a person has said, but does not jump too far ahead. The purpose of reflection is to encourage personal exploration. It can be useful, particularly with emotional content, to understate slightly what the young person has offered using low-intensity words. Reflection can be directive in that it can reinforce certain aspects of what a young person has said and can alter its meaning slightly. Try to make a large proportion of your responses reflective listening statements in the early stages. Offering two to three reflections per question is appropriate.
Affirm	Direct affirmation and support is a way of building rapport. Notice and appropriately affirm the young person's strengths and efforts.
Summarize	It's good practice to summarize, from time to time, what young people have said to show that you have been listening and to prepare them to elaborate further. Summarizing is a directive technique because you can decide what to reflect and what not to reflect back (e.g., nature of the problem, level of ambivalence, self-motivational statements, etc.). See Miller and Rollnick (2002) for more information about various types of summaries.
Elicit change talk	There are four categories of change talk: · recognizing disadvantages of the status quo · recognizing advantages of change · expressing optimism about change · expressing intention to change. Every one of these types of statements tips the balance further towards change. Evoking change talk is, therefore, a key motivational interviewing skill. Ultimately, the young person is responsible for stating the need to change and you can reinforce this talk.

Methods to evoke change talk	Encouraging change talk is important throughout counselling because ambivalence can surface at any point. Change talk is a constant reminder of the reasons for commitment to change. See Miller and Rollnick (2002) for further information on responding to change talk.
Asking evocative questions	You can encourage change talk from young people by asking open-ended questions about their perceptions and concerns that reflect the four categories of change talk. For example: · what they see as the disadvantages of the status quo · what they see as the advantages of change · what makes them feel optimistic about change · what their intentions are regarding change.
Using the importance ruler	You can ask young people to rate their sense of the importance of change and why they believe they are at a certain point on the scale (and not at zero). You can also ask them what it would take for them to move to a higher rating.
Exploring confidence	You can ask young people how confident they feel about being able to make changes by rating their level of confidence on a scale. You may need to address their confidence if it is low.
Exploring the decisional balance	You can ask young clients to explore the positive and negative aspects of their behaviour. Begin by asking them to list what they like about their behaviour. Then ask them about the downside. It can be useful to have them fill out a decisional balance sheet so they can see the pros and cons at the same time. This also helps them become aware of their ambivalence.
Elaborate	Once a young person has mentioned a reason for changing, ask for elaboration before you move on. You can do this by asking for: · clarification · an example · a description of the last occurrence · anything else regarding change.
Questioning extremes	Ask young people to describe their (or others') biggest concerns and to imagine the worst consequences that could happen. Then reverse it and ask them to imagine what the best consequences of changing might be.

Looking back	Ask the young person to think back to the past before the problem emerged and compare it to the present situation. If things were worse before, ask what has led to the improvement in the situation.
Looking forward	Ask the young person to imagine what things might be like in the future after a change has occurred. Also ask what it might be like if no change occurs. You are trying to get the youth's realistic appraisal of, and hopes for a changed future.
Exploring goals and values	Ask young people to tell you what is most important in their life. What are their goals and values? Ask how the problem fits in or interferes with these? Explore the discrepancy between their goals and values and their current behaviour. Youth's awareness of their own values is a very important aspect of MI.
Affirming change talk	Make positive comments when the young client talks about change.
Responding to resistance using reflective responses	Think of resistance as an opportunity. Client resistance is closely associated with dropout and poor outcome. Resistance is not a personality trait. It is an aspect of the interpersonal relationship between you and the young person. How you respond to resistance makes a difference. You can decrease it by what you say and do. MI focuses on decreasing resistance by rolling with it.
Simple reflection	Respond to resistance with non-resistance using, for example, a simple, reflective listening statement.
Amplified reflection	Reflect back what the young person has said in an amplified or exaggerated form. Do this in an empathetic, straightforward, supportive, matter-of-fact but not sarcastic way.
Double-sided reflection	Capture both sides of their ambivalence in your reflective listening statement.
Other responses to resistance	There are other ways to defuse underlying disagreement and reduce resistance.
Shifting focus	Shift the young person's attention away from whatever seems to be blocking progress. Defuse the initial concern and direct attention to a more workable issue. See labelling (above).
Reframing	Offer them a new meaning or interpretation for what they have said. This may involve communicating new information to shed new light on their situation. Help them to look at things differently.

Agreeing with a twist	Offer initial agreement, but with a slight twist or change of direction. Usually, this is reflection followed by reframing.
Emphasizing personal choice and control	Reassure young people that they will determine what happens in the end.
Coming alongside	If young persons are ambivalent and you make a point of arguing against change, it could have the effect of decreasing their resistance and actually eliciting change talk. Be up front about why you are doing this. Tell them it can be helpful to have a bit of a debate about the value of making changes and that you will take the side of not changing. Ask them to take the side of trying to convince you that there are good reasons to change.

Adapted from Miller & Rollnick (2002, 52–139).

4.3.2 STRENGTHENING COMMITMENT TO CHANGE

Phase 1 strategies are designed to build client motivation for change. Once the client is committed to change, you can move to Phase 2 strategies. Generally speaking, if you develop proficiency with Phase 1 MI strategies, you will be in a good position to learn and use Phase 2 strategies. Bear in mind that the Phase 1 strategies may be needed throughout the counselling process, since ambivalence can re-emerge at any point during the process of change.

PHASE 2: STRATEGIES FOR STRENGTHENING COMMITMENT TO CHANGE

Recognizing readiness	When a young person has developed intrinsic motivation for change, the goal of MI shifts from stressing the importance of change and building confidence (Phase 1 strategies) to strengthening her or his commitment to a change plan. There will be a "window of opportunity" for initiating change. The challenge for you is to be able to recognize when the window has "opened" so you can help the young person move ahead. The signs of readiness to change tend to emerge gradually and subtly.
	See Miller and Rollnick (2002) for information about signs of readiness to change.
Hazards to avoid Underestimating ambivalence	Bear in mind that a young person's ambivalence may not disappear even though the change process has begun.

Overprescription	Don't start telling the young person what to do. The emphasis must remain on the young person's personal responsibility and choice throughout the negotiation of change strategies.
Insufficient direction	If you provide too little help, a young person may lose direction.
Initiating phase 2	This is the time to initiate a change plan.
Recapitulation	Summarize the young person's situation. Explain that you are trying to put together everything you have discussed so far in order to decide what to do next. Come up with as many reasons for change as possible, but also acknowledge any reluctance or ambivalence on the part of the youth.
Key questions	Find out what they want and plan to do. Ask open-ended questions about their next steps. Use reflective listening to encourage further exploration and help them clarify their thoughts. Reinforce change talk and decrease resistance. Emphasize personal responsibility, freedom and choice.
Giving information and advice	You may offer professional advice when young people ask for it, or when they give you permission to do so (which implies that they can take it or leave it). You may want to offer a cluster of options.
Negotiating a change plan	Developing a change plan is a process of shared decision making and negotiation that involves setting goals, considering change options, arriving at a plan and eliciting commitment.
Setting goals	Discrepancy between young people's goals and where they are at now drives motivation. You cannot impose your goals on your clients. Use a shared decision-making process to prioritize goals. Begin with the goals they are most keen to pursue. Their goals may be related to broad life issues rather than specific problems. Ask them to rate their confidence about achieving their goals. Ask them what the consequences of achieving or not achieving them might be. Take more time to talk about issues if they express serious concerns about the importance of these goals or appear to lack confidence.
Considering change options	Involve the young person in brainstorming and evaluating possible change strategies. Formal treatment is only one option, and there are a variety of other approaches that could be used. A young person can also use their own natural resources and social supports to make changes on their own. Offer a menu of possible strategies for change.

Arriving at a plan	Use open-ended questions to have the young person verbalize their plan. Putting the change plans down on paper can also be useful. Summarize the plan that you have developed together and ask whether you have accurately reflected what was discussed.
Eliciting commitment	Ask the young clients if they are committed to following this change plan. They may want to alter it. There may still be reluctance and ambivalence. Making the plan public can reinforce their commitment (if they wish to tell others). Do not press for commitment. If there is reluctance, you may want to come alongside. Maintain contact and follow up on their readiness to commit.
Transition	Some young people will proceed with change on their own once they are committed to a change plan. Others may be helped by action-focussed counselling. You can continue to use the general style of motivational counselling throughout to address ambivalence that may re-emerge.

Adapted from Miller & Rollnick (2002, 126–139). For other examples of motivational interventions, see Sampl & Kadden (2001) and Webb, Scudder, Kaminer & Kadden (2002).

4.4 BRIEF INTERVENTIONS

"Brief intervention" is a general term that includes a number of brief, time-limited treatment models. Most brief interventions build on the principles of motivational interviewing and include other treatment approaches such as cognitive behaviour therapy.

Brief interventions are usually fewer than five sessions and typically contain the following six elements (FRAMES) (Monti, Colby & O'Leary, 2001, 11).

· personalized **F**eedback of assessment results
· emphasis on personal **R**esponsibility for change
· **A**dvice or explicit direction to change
· **M**enu offering a variety of change options
· **E**mpathetic approach (warm, reflective and understanding)
· emphasis on **S**elf-efficacy (optimism about the possibility of change).

Generally non-intrusive, brief interventions are well suited as a first intervention for youth with substance use problems, with or without concurrent mental health problems. For some youth brief interventions are an initial step to more extensive treatment, while for others, they are enough to kick-start them into changing their drug use (see *First Contact*).

Interventions can:

- be planned and structured to be brief (e.g., *First Contact*, a manual detailing a five-session brief intervention program)
- be designed on an individual basis to be brief based on assessment information (e.g., youth with minor problems respond well to brief interventions as opposed to longer-term counselling, particularly if they have effective coping skills)
- become brief due to client preference.

Planned brief interventions can be structured to provide adolescents with a range of treatments that can include psychoeducation, problem identification, feedback, advice, and goal setting over a number of agreed upon sessions. In some cases, an adolescent may agree to attend only one session to satisfy an external demand such as a probation order. In these situations, the goal is usually to provide feedback on the nature of the problem and information on counselling/treatment options that are available should the young person eventually become more concerned about his or her substance use. Adolescents in precontemplation or contemplation are often willing to participate in brief counselling if they know that a commitment to lifelong change is not a requirement. This is consistent with motivational interviewing and could result in the adolescent seeking additional assistance at a later time. In fact, brief interventions are often seen as a "bridge" to more intensive treatment (Myers, Brown, Tate, Abrantes & Tomlinson, 2001).

There is a growing interest in brief interventions because they are a flexible, cost-effective strategy. Brief interventions can be provided in a variety of settings such as schools, outpatient settings and youth justice settings.

RECOMMENDED GOALS FOR BRIEF INTERVENTIONS ACROSS SETTINGS FOR ADOLESCENTS WITH CO-OCCURRING PSYCHIATRIC AND SUBSTANCE-RELATED PROBLEMS

Setting	Major goals of brief intervention
In-patient	Assess for substance use; enhance motivation to change; refer for specialized treatment.
Outpatient	Identify problems; provide feedback; set goals for behaviour change.
Primary care	Screen for substance use and psychopathology; identify problems; provide referrals; enhance motivation to follow through on recommendations.
Juvenile justice	Screen for substance use; refer for more intensive assessment; encourage participation in treatment or support groups following incarceration.
School	Screen for substance use and psychopathology; provide feedback; set goals for change; identify resources for referral.

(Adapted from Table 9.1 in Myers et al., 2001, 285)

Readers are encouraged to consult Monti et al. (2001) for further information on the use of brief interventions with adolescents and young adults. Myers et al. (2001) addresses the use of brief interventions with young people who have substance use and mental health problems.

The principles of brief intervention are applicable to treating adolescents with concurrent mental health and substance use problems. In particular, providing personalized feedback and education regarding the substances that the young person is using, their pharmacological effects, and potential impact on mental health issues such as depression, anxiety and interpersonal conflict, can increase clients' awareness of their problems, as well as their motivation for change. Feedback about substances may include information concerning the short-term and later effects (a few hours later or the next day), and withdrawal effects. Most adolescents are aware of only the immediate effects that are reinforcing and that may in fact have an initial beneficial effect on mental health symptoms (e.g., alcohol use can suppress symptoms of social anxiety). However, they may not be as aware of the later effects that can cause or exacerbate mental health problems (e.g., withdrawal from alcohol can cause anxiety symptoms). Increasing their awareness of the effects of substance use on mental health may motivate them to consider alternative strategies to deal with mental health problems.

"Brevity is by no means a synonym for ineffectiveness. In fact, turning points in life are often brief encounters. What and how we communicate can be more influential than the length of time that we take to do it. It may even be that effective brief interventions are better suited to the nature and needs of adolescents." (Miller, 2001, xii)

"...(the) potential utility of brief interventions lies in identifying substance problems, motivating adolescents in various settings to attend to their substance use behaviors and facilitating behavior change" (Myers et al, 2001, 276).

Brief interventions may be particularly appropriate for working with young people who have mental health problems for the following reasons (Myers et al., 2001, 276–293):

· Many young people with mental health concerns are not being adequately screened for, or educated about substance use.

· Young people are less likely to have developed dependent use because generally, they have not been using substances as long as adults.

· They are suited to treatment goals that focus on moderation or harm reduction, which may be more appealing to young people.

· They are a cost-effective way to increase young people's access to treatment.

· They can be delivered in diverse settings including schools, primary care, in- and outpatient psychiatric facilities and youth justice settings.

First Contact is a brief structured intervention that can be applied as an integrated treatment for substance use and mental health problems, in youth justice and family counselling settings. It can be used in both individual and group formats. Most experienced counsellors will find that they will be able to implement *First Contact* with little or no additional training.

4.5 HARM REDUCTION AND NON-ABSTINENT DRUG USE GOALS

Harm reduction recognizes that not all young clients are prepared to accept abstinence, and that there may be risks (e.g., health, legal, safety, etc.) that can be reduced through counselling, even though the client does not commit to a goal of abstinence.

Marlatt (1998) noted that abstinence can be viewed as the ideal end point along a continuum that ranges from excessively harmful to less harmful consequences. Because lifelong abstinence may be a difficult concept for adolescents to embrace, a harm reduction approach may be more appealing.

Non-abstinent drug use goals focus on using drugs less often or using a lesser quantity of drugs. Young people who use multiple drugs may have different goals for the various drugs that they consume (e.g., abstinence for some drugs and reduced use for others). When discussing non-abstinent drug use goals with youth, it is important that you present all the options, including abstinence, and explore the consequences of each. If you emphasize that it is their personal choice, you are not condoning use.

The harm reduction approach is consistent with the following strategies:

· providing feedback and education in a "co-operative dialogue" (Miller, Turner & Marlatt, 2001)

· stressing self-management and coping skills

· emphasizing reduction of harm associated with substance use at any point along the continuum of risk

- not setting any preconditions (e.g., agreeing to abstinence as the goal) for accessing services ("low threshold access")
- communicating an accepting attitude to reduce stigma for seeking help
- collaborative goal setting and treatment planning
- identifying skills deficits and providing skills training (Parks, Anderson & Marlatt, 2000)
- monitoring the client's motivational state and providing motivational strategies
- preventing any increase in harmful consequences
- pharmacotherapy for substance use including naltrexone to reduce craving for alcohol, methadone for opioid users or nicotine replacement therapy for smokers.

In summary, harm reduction is consistent with the principles of motivational interviewing, the stages of change model and the cognitive behavioural techniques discussed in this chapter. Depending on their views and preferences, the harm reduction approach may be better suited to some young clients. Providing training to improve deficits in coping skills is a further component of this approach.

4.6. SELF-HELP AND 12-STEP APPROACHES

The 12-step (e.g., Alcoholics Anonymous, Narcotics Anonymous) philosophy is rooted in the belief that recovery from addiction is possible only if the individual admits that he or she is unable to use the substance in moderation without having serious psychosocial consequences. Spiritual growth is seen as critical to this process and to later steps, which promote individual responsibility for past behaviour and effort toward building a healthier, more adaptive lifestyle and better interpersonal relationships (Bukstein et al., 1997).

There are 12-step programs in most communities, and some treatment programs incorporate a 12-step model as a program component. It can be very helpful to get advice and encouragement from peers who have experienced similar problems. For example, it can be encouraging to hear from peers (as opposed to counsellors) that a drug-free lifestyle is possible.

However, counsellors who work with youth have expressed the concern that self-help and 12-step approaches are not typically youth oriented. A major limitation of these approaches is that they are abstinence oriented, and many youths are not prepared to accept the premise that they must be abstinent from drugs and alcohol.

"Pressing for a goal of abstinence too soon in the treatment process may overwhelm and alienate the young client and put the therapeutic alliance in jeopardy. With youth, it is often more effective to begin with 'harm reduction' goals that aim to reduce the severity, frequency and adverse effects of substance use. Emphasis on improving functioning and lifestyle, rather than on stopping drug use, is more effective at promoting motivation to change in youth...Having said that, a clinician should promote the benefits of stopping use and finding constructive alternatives to substance use. At the same time, the worker accepts the difficulties and challenges involved in recovery. One strategy that can be helpful is to encourage the client to set substance use goals for specific periods of time, and then review the pros and cons of stopping or reducing substance use in order to set goals for the next period." (Ballon, in press).

4.7 BEST PRACTICE TREATMENTS FOR YOUTH SUBSTANCE USE

Although evidence is somewhat limited, some best practice information about substance use treatment for young people has been identified. In an extensive review of the literature on adolescent drug and alcohol treatment effectiveness, Catalano, Hawkins, Wells, et al., (1991–92) concluded that some treatment was probably better than no treatment. At that time, no particular treatment modality had emerged as superior in terms of effectiveness.

In the past few years, a number of controlled studies have been conducted. Generally, they indicate that three different, but not mutually exclusive psychosocial treatment modalities are effective and possibly superior to other types of treatments for adolescents with substance use problems. They are behavioural approaches, cognitive behavioural approaches and family based interventions. Incorporating all three approaches to address developmental, psychosocial and family issues at the same time may be the most effective approach (Riggs & Whitmore, 1999).

Health Canada's (1999) report on best practices in substance abuse treatment offers a similar perspective: "Adolescents may respond best to flexible approaches which adjust to individual needs. Important program elements include family therapy, behavioural skills counselling, family and peer support, and continuing care" (Health Canada, 1999, 41). The report also underlines the importance of a comprehensive approach: "Ancillary services, such as the availability of school programs for dropouts, vocational counselling, recreational services, psychosocial development, crisis counselling and sexuality counselling, are also important" (Health Canada, 1999, 41).

Cognitive behaviour therapy and family therapy have been identified as best practices in the treatment of adolescent substance use and a treatment model for each will be presented in this chapter.

4.8 A MODEL FOR SUBSTANCE USE TREATMENT USING COGNITIVE BEHAVIOUR THERAPY (CBT)

This section describes how to use CBT to treat substance use problems.

CBT is increasingly being used to treat substance use problems in adolescents (Waldron, 1997). In randomized controlled trials, both group (Kaminer, Burleson & Bouchard, 1998) and individual (Waldron, 1997) CBT approaches have been shown to be more effective than supportive/educational or interactional approaches in treating substance use and in reducing other associated problem behaviours (Riggs & Whitmore, 1999).

Based on social learning theory, CBT is comprised of a wide variety of both behavioural and cognitive strategies. Central to CBT is a person's inner speech ("internal dialogue"). According to CBT, the internal dialogue influences behavioural processes. In other words, the things people say to themselves influence how they behave. CBT involves helping clients to notice how they think, feel, and behave, as a prerequisite to behaviour change. The emphasis in CBT is on acquiring practical coping skills, and on cognitive restructuring, that is, identifying and modifying maladaptive thinking patterns that influence behaviour.

CBT focuses on helping young people identify their thinking patterns that precede and follow episodes of substance use. The CBT process involves:

· identifying situations in which the person is most likely to use
· learning new skills to develop different responses to the situation.

CBT is particularly suited to treating concurrent substance use and mental health problems. It is among the most effective psychotherapy approaches for many mental health problems that occur in childhood and adolescence, including depression (Brent et al., 1997; Lewinsohn et al., 1990), obsessive-compulsive disorder (March and Mulle, 1996) and post-traumatic stress disorder (March, Amaya-Jackson & Murray, 1998).

4.8.1 FUNCTIONAL ANALYSIS (ABC)

A basic technique in CBT is the functional analysis of behaviour. It is based on the notion that substance use serves a "function" for the person. It is also referred to as the "ABC" technique.

The ABC technique involves an examination of:

· the Antecedents that lead to the Behaviour, (substance use) and the Consequences.

Substance use is viewed as a learned behaviour triggered by specific cues and reinforced by specific positive consequences, or "payoffs." The triggers are the *Antecedents*—designated "A" in the ABC analysis. The substance use is the *Behaviour* ("B") that is the focus of change. The reinforcements are the *Consequences* ("C"). According to this model of behaviour, substance use persists because of Antecedent conditions (including internal dialogue) that predispose the adolescent to use a substance for its desired effects, or reinforcing consequences.

This is the key technique in analyzing a young person's substance use pattern and leads to developing interventions specific to the young person's particular pattern of use. The ABC analysis leads to an understanding of:

· the antecedents that "trigger" an episode of substance use ("A")
· the pattern of substance use that resulted in that situation ("B")
· the positive consequences of substance use that maintains the use ("C").

By identifying and modifying maladaptive thinking patterns, adolescents can reduce their negative thoughts, feelings and behaviours, including substance use and associated behaviours. A significant proportion of adolescents report cognitive distortions and negative internalized self-statements (Van Hasselt et al., 1993). Although cognitive therapy has yet to be studied systematically in adolescents with SUDS, cognitive approaches seem to show effects with adolescents treated for depression (Brent et al., 1997; Lewisohn, et al., 1990). Relapse prevention is a cognitive behavioural approach that helps the adolescent develop greater self-control, identify environmental and internal triggers leading to substance use and relapse, and develop strategies for dealing with stressors, triggers and lapses into substance use (Bukstein and Van Hasselt, 1993; Bukstein et al., 1997; Marlatt and Gordon, 1985).

In the following sections, we will show how the ABC technique can be used to:

· analyze specific episodes of substance use
· develop treatment goals
· explore the relationship between substance use and mental health symptoms
· help significant others understand the young person's substance use.

We will then describe the three-step process of conducting the ABC analysis with a client.

USING THE ABC TO ANALYZE EPISODES OF SUBSTANCE USE

Example:

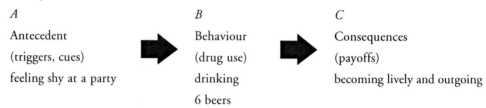

A		B		C
Antecedent		Behaviour		Consequences
(triggers, cues)		(drug use)		(payoffs)
feeling shy at a party		drinking		becoming lively and outgoing
		6 beers		

In this example, the function of the young person's drug use (drinking beer) is to make him or her feel better and more outgoing at parties.

The ABC technique is used first to understand the pattern of substance use, as in the above example. Following that analysis, an individualized treatment plan (goal setting) can be developed.

USING THE ABC FOR SETTING TREATMENT GOALS

The ABC helps most clients to clearly see their patterns at the outset of treatment, and then focus on three specific goals for change in drug use and other life areas.

· *Goals directed towards triggers (Antecedents)*: The objective here is for the youth to avoid or eliminate antecedent conditions that trigger drug use, or respond differently to an antecedent situation by not using drugs.
· *Goals directed toward the substance use Behaviour*: The objective here is to develop strategies to modify the pattern of use (e.g., to low-risk levels) when appropriate, in relation to the client and the substance being used.
· *Goals directed towards payoffs (Consequences)*: The objective here is for the youth to develop alternative ways to achieve the reinforcing consequences of drug use.

In the example above, let us suppose that the youth has a goal to reduce or stop her or his alcohol consumption. Concrete goals which might emerge from an ABC analysis are:

· The youth avoids the Antecedent trigger by leaving the party or not going in the first place.
· The youth makes a non-drug-using response to the trigger by looking for a non-using friend at the party (the new Behaviour).
· The youth develops alternative ways of achieving the desired Consequence (being outgoing at a party) by exploring social skills such as starting and maintaining conversations.

Specific cognitive interventions and practical life skills that can be used to help young clients achieve their goals are presented later in this section.

USING THE ABC TO EXPLORE THE RELATIONSHIP BETWEEN SUBSTANCE USE AND MENTAL HEALTH SYMPTOMS

Symptoms of a mental health problem can act as an antecedent condition to substance use. The ABC model is an effective technique to gather information not only about substance use, but also about mental health symptoms. The triggers to an episode of substance use need to be carefully explored to identify feelings, thoughts and behaviours that could be symptoms of a mental health problem. The question to be asked is whether or not the antecedent feelings, thoughts and behaviours are considered to be within the limits of normal adolescent development or are they perhaps symptoms of a mental health problem.

USING THE ABC TO HELP SIGNIFICANT OTHERS UNDERSTAND YOUTH SUBSTANCE USE

Parents, siblings, spouses, friends and professionals can gain new insight into young people's drug use if they understand its functions. Discussing the ABC analysis with the family (with the clients' permission) is an effective way to involve them in the treatment in terms that are concrete . You can also encourage family members to support youth as they discover and deal with the antecedents and consequences of drug-taking behaviour, and explore constructive alternatives. The ABC may also help significant others see how their own behaviour functions as one of the triggers that sets off and maintains the drug use.

HOW TO DO AN ABC ANALYSIS WITH A CLIENT

When doing an ABC analysis with a young person, explain the reasons for it. In addition, define and describe each of the three components—Antecedent, Behaviour, Consequences.

Write out the analysis on a piece of paper as you do it and give it to the client.
· Establish drug use Behaviour.
· Identify Antecedents of drug use.
· Identify Consequences of drug use.

A	B	C
Peer pressure	Use cannabis	Feel part of the group

Step 1. Establish the drug use *Behaviour*

Begin by establishing the client's drug use pattern according to the following headings:

· type of drug

· mode(s) of administration

· frequency of use

· quantity.

Type of drug: When discussing drug use behaviour, it is important to ask the youth to be as specific as possible about the pattern of use for all drugs, so there are no "secrets" and you know exactly what you are dealing with. Focus on the major drugs used within the past three to six months. Discuss each one separately, in order of priority as the youth sees it.

Mode(s) of administration: For some drugs, there is only one mode of administration (e.g., alcohol is taken orally). For other drugs, there are various modes (e.g., cannabis can be inhaled by smoking or taken orally; cocaine may be smoked, snorted or injected intravenously). See section 2.3.1 for a more thorough discussion of modes of administration.

Frequency: It is necessary to establish how often a drug is taken within a particular time frame. The question can be put in terms of "number of drug-taking occasions" per day, per week, per month or per year. Usually, there is some fluctuation, which can be recorded as a range from minimum to maximum frequency. Note special patterns, such as time of day or fluctuations during the week (e.g., drug use is typically more frequent on the weekend).

Quantity: To discover how much of a particular drug an adolescent uses per drug-using occasion, establish the "typical dose." For example:

alcohol:	standard drink
cannabis:	number of joints, by weight in ounces or grams
pills:	number of pills, noting the strength of each
LSD:	hits or number of units
cocaine:	weight in grams.

By multiplying the frequency of use by the quantity per use, you will establish roughly how much of a particular drug is being used.

- -

COUNSELLOR'S TIP

Questions to ask about drug use behaviour:

· **How much is used?**

· **How often (e.g., days per week, times per day)?**

· **How is the drug administered?**

· **Proportion of use conducted alone and with other people?**

Step 2: Establish the *Antecedents* of drug use

After the pattern of use of a particular drug has been established, identify the Antecedents, or triggers, for its use. Be sure to do this separately for each drug. Antecedents may be found in any area of a youth's life. Here are some typical examples:

- social: parties, hanging out with particular friends
- situational: a drug offer, a fight with parents, boredom, celebrations, getting up in the morning
- physiological: pain, withdrawal symptoms, insomnia
- emotional: anger, depression, confusion, anxiety, happiness
- cognitive: painful memories, lack of confidence, negative thoughts.

Most adolescents have a multitude of antecedents to their drug use. Usually it is sufficient to identify those that are the most frequent and powerful in triggering use. Try to identify about three to five important triggers for each drug used.

It is useful to be as specific as possible. In other words, identify the particular friends that trigger drug use, which celebrations are typically associated with drug use, the specific withdrawal symptoms and/or the nature of the painful memories associated with wanting to use, etc.

COUNSELLOR'S TIP

- The use of one drug may be an antecedent for the use of another drug. This is often the case for youth who use multiple drugs. For example, alcohol use may be triggered by cocaine use when the youth is coming down and wants to "mellow out.
- It is important to look for symptoms of mental health problems or effects of medication, since they may be antecedents for drug use.

A useful tool in identifying a client's trigger risk situations is the Inventory of Drug-Taking Situations (IDTS) (Annis, & Martin, 1985). This 50-item, self-report questionnaire provides a profile of the client's past drug use with reference to eight potential antecedent or trigger situations:

- negative emotions
- physical discomfort
- pleasant emotions
- testing personal control
- urges and temptations to use
- conflict with others
- social pressure to use
- pleasant times with others.

Questions to ask about Antecedents (cues or triggers)

Before you use drugs:

Social:	**Who are you with?**
	How are you relating to people you're with?
Situational:	**What situations are you in (e.g., Where are you? What do you see and hear?)?**
Cognitive:	**What are you thinking about?**
	What are you saying to yourself?
Physiological:	**How do you feel physically (e.g., sensations, aches and pains)?**
Emotional:	**How do you feel emotionally?**

Step 3: Establish the *Consequences of drug use*

Youth who are in the preparation or action stage of change are most likely aware of the negative consequences of use and how they are outweighing the positive consequences. There are many negative consequences of adolescent drug use including parental disapproval, trouble with school and other authorities, and feelings of being out of control. However, if drugs had only negative effects, young people wouldn't use them. At least at the beginning, the payoffs probably have the most impact on youth's life. In the ABC analysis, make your principal focus the discovery of the positive consequences of use, since it is the desirable drug effects that reinforce and maintain drug use.

COUNSELLOR'S TIP

It is often a surprise and refreshing change for an adolescent to find that she or he can talk to an adult about positive drug effects. Most adults deny the reality of those feelings and experiences, and thus discredit themselves in the youth's eyes. The counsellor who explores what a young client likes about drug use, in neutral, non-judgmental language, offers a special understanding by acknowledging and validating the reality of a young person's experience.

Negative consequences are a useful tool in addiction counselling because they can be powerful motivators for youth to change their drug use. Many of the classic negative consequences, such as ill health and debt, are slow to develop and not taken seriously as possibilities that could happen to them. Nevertheless, a listing of negative consequences can be helpful in assisting young clients to see the total "balance sheet" of drug use "pros and cons."

Categories of consequences mirror the categories of triggers. They may be:

· social: (e.g., "All my friends smoke up.")

· situational: (e.g., "It's great to drop acid before going to the movies.")

· cognitive: (e.g., "I'm always going to be stuck in this dead-end job.")

· physiological: (e.g., "A hit of cocaine will pep me up.")

· emotional: (e.g., "A few drinks will calm me down.").

COUNSELLOR'S TIP

Questions to ask about reinforcing Consequences

When you use drugs:

· **What things happen that you like?**

· **What gets better?**

· **What thoughts, feelings and behaviours that you don't like do you get rid of?**

· **What do you think, feel or do differently?**

4.8.2 STRATEGIES FOR ACHIEVING SUBSTANCE USE GOALS

In the preceding section, we described how the ABC technique can be used to:

· analyze the pattern of substance use, which leads to

· setting goals and developing strategies that are related to the antecedents, behaviours and consequences of the client's use.

This is the essence of an individually oriented treatment plan. It is a plan designed specifically to address antecedents, behaviours and consequences of substance use for that individual client.

STRATEGIES FOR DEALING WITH ANTECEDENTS

These strategies are designed to avoid or modify trigger situations so that they do not lead to drug use. Antecedents can be:

· social (e.g., a party)

· situational (e.g., a fight with parents)

· physiological (e.g., pain, withdrawal symptoms, insomnia, etc.)

· emotional (e.g., anxiety, depression, boredom, etc.)

· cognitive (e.g., "I'll have more fun if I'm drinking.").

Most strategies fall into the following categories:

· avoiding high risk situations
· cognitive strategies to deal with unhelpful thoughts
· coping with cravings

Your task is to help youth identify and implement strategies that are most suited to their antecedents.

Avoidance strategies

Youth may not want to avoid all antecedent situations in which there is a high risk of using drugs, but for those situations that definitely need to be avoided, they will likely need to develop skills to do so.

The process of developing strategies to avoid drug use involves the following steps for you and your client to work on together:

· Analyze potential trigger situations.
· Develop possible drug use avoidance strategies.
· Rehearse the strategies.
· Practise the strategies in real life situations.
· Evaluate the outcomes.
· Repeat the steps as necessary.

Once you and your client have identified high risk situations (Antecedents), pinpoint precise triggers. For example, school may be a high risk situation but it does not give you enough information to work with. You need to work on the "how/when/who/where/why?" of the youth's experience at school.

There are several ways to prompt the development of avoidance strategies. One is to talk about typical situations in which drug use has occurred and imagine actions which the client could have taken to avoid it. Another is to ask the youth about actions that were tried in the past to avoid drug use. Most young people have more strengths than they realize, and you can encourage them to recognize and build upon them.

Typically, drug avoidance strategies take one of the following forms:

· a plan for avoiding or eliminating the trigger situation altogether
· a plan for getting out of the situation, should it occur
· a plan for a non-drug-using response to the situation.

You can give youth a valuable head start towards implementing strategies by rehearsing them together in counselling sessions. This could mean talking through what they will do and anticipating any difficulties, or it could mean role-playing the strategy.

Usually, adolescents will be working on several strategies at once in order to deal with the various trigger situations they are facing.

Cognitive strategies

When doing their ABC analysis, most young drug users identify thought patterns that trigger drug use (e.g., "I'll never do well in school, so I might as well spend my time getting high."), but they do not understand their significance. Explain to them that:

· Thinking is "self talk" or inner speech.

· What they say to themselves affects how they feel and act.

· Thoughts come and go so quickly that they often don't pay enough attention to them.

· Thoughts and feelings in the present may be the result of hurtful things that have happened in the past.

· Changing thought patterns really will help make them feel better and change their behaviour.

It's important to explain also that what a person thinks about him or herself and drug use influences how successful he or she will be in controlling it. Cognitive distortion (unhelpful thoughts) often leads to a vicious circle of excuses, guilt, rationalization and drug use.

There are at least 10 commonly held patterns of unhelpful thoughts:

All or nothing thinking: thoughts which are extreme in their implications, or black or white in their categorization (e.g., "Everybody uses so I'll use." "He does not like me so probably no one likes me.")

Overgeneralization: the hasty conclusion that because something happened once, it will always occur (e.g., "Since I haven't suffered in any serious way because of my substance use so far, I never will.")

Mental filter thinking: the preoccupation with one negative detail in a situation (e.g., "It doesn't matter that my grades are up this year, because I just flunked an easy test.")

Disqualifying the positive: the rejection of anything positive, including compliments and one's own efforts, which are seen as merely "good luck"

Jumping to conclusions: the tendency to presume or predict the future, or another person's thoughts and reactions, without cause or fact checking (e.g., "I know my father won't let me take the car tonight." "I know Jane would never go out with me.")

Magnification and minimization: exaggeration (usually of errors, fears and imperfections) or underestimation (usually of strengths, virtues and contributions)

Emotional reasoning: the presumption that feelings are equivalent to reality (e.g., "I feel bad, therefore, I must be a bad person.")

Should statements: an attempt at self-motivation through guilt ("My parents have supported me all my life, I should stop letting them down.")

Labelling and mislabelling: the tendency to measure oneself or others in very narrow and/or stereotypical terms ("I'm nothing but an addict.")

Personalization: the assumption of responsibility or fault for an event when there is no basis for doing so ("My parents are always quarrelling because of me." "My boyfriend is in a bad mood so it must be something I did.")

Once young drug users have identified unhelpful cognitions, they need to learn and practice the following techniques to change their patterns:

Thought stopping: Whenever an unhelpful thought occurs, young people need to tell themselves to stop thinking that thought and substitute something more positive. You might suggest they visualize a stop sign and/or yell the word "stop" internally (or even out loud) to assist in interrupting the thought. Another deterrent is to wear a thick rubber band on the wrist and snap it when an unhelpful thought comes to mind.

Worrying time: The youth sets aside a limited time and particular place to give full vent to negative thoughts. Instruct him or her to make note of any negative thoughts that occur during the day and to save them until the specified time and place.

Blow-up technique: By greatly exaggerating an unhelpful thought, it can be made so ridiculous that it stops being hurtful.

Priming: Priming is a technique to remind young clients of the positive aspects of their lives. Instruct or help them to make a list of positives, and then write each of them onto a "priming" card. The idea is to keep the cards handy and read and reread them throughout the day.

Using cues: Instruct the youth to choose a routine part of everyday life and use it as a signal to generate a positive thought about him or herself (e.g., when stopping at a street light or when eating lunch).

Noticing your accomplishments: Instruct your client to write down the accomplishments of the day as they occur. Even things that seem trivial should be noted (e.g., got up on time, picked a nice place for lunch, etc.).

Positive self-rewarding thoughts: Encourage youth to pat themselves on the back and say rewarding things to themselves. Adolescents often feel such inner speech is boastful and may require further encouragement to overcome this attitude.

Time projection: With this technique, the adolescent acknowledges existing discomfort but breaks its hold by mentally travelling forward and imagining a time when the discomfort no longer exists. Encourage the adolescent to accept some negative feelings as normal.

Coping with cravings

The urgent craving for drugs, which most youth experience during treatment to some extent, presents a particular high risk situation. Withdrawal from drug use is likely to produce particularly strong cravings. Many users are at a loss as to how to endure them, and will need special help in this regard. It is important that youth understand that they can control their cravings, and that they learn how to do this.

- -

COUNSELLOR'S TIP

You can reassure youth that cravings will decrease in frequency and intensity over time, and as they develop alternatives to drug use. The basic idea is to normalize cravings. Explain to them that they won't die, they don't "have to" have the drugs, and they can do something about their problem.

- -

The process for controlling cravings is the same as for avoiding high risk situations:

· learning to recognize cravings for what they are
· identifying trigger situations
· planning strategies to avoid them
· planning strategies to cope with them
· putting strategies into practice
· evaluating outcomes
· repeating this cycle as necessary.

There are two basic strategies for coping with cravings:

· Decrease the frequency of cravings by eliminating triggers.
· Decrease the impact of cravings by engaging in alternative activities that stop the cravings or make it easier to endure them. This strategy usually takes the form of either a cognitive or active "diversion" (e.g., rechannelling thoughts or rechannelling activities).

Encourage youth to be inventive in all their attempts to control their drug use, and to experiment until they find strategies that work for them.

STRATEGIES FOR DEALING WITH BEHAVIOUR

These interventions are designed to help the young client develop a non-drug response to a trigger situation. A specific strategy is drug refusal.

Refusal training

Saying "no" to drug offers is not a simple skill, but it is an important aspect of gaining control over drug use. It involves learning how to refuse something in a manner that doesn't offend other people. It's an important step towards taking full control of their own life. Young people's goal is to know their own mind, and then be pleasant but firm about not taking drugs when they don't want to or doing anything else they don't want to do. This can be difficult and stressful, especially at a time of life when peer influence is strong.

Youth describe the following as typical barriers to refusing drug offers:
· not wanting to offend a friend or acquaintance
· worry about what others will think if they refuse
· concerns about rejection by the peer group
· anticipation of a hassle
· not knowing what to say
· expectations of failure or inadequacy
· fear of losing friends or being lonely
· fear of ridicule.

You need to acknowledge and discuss the negative feelings they will probably have about saying "no," especially to friends. Some additional skills that you can introduce and have them rehearse are:
· sticking to their guns
· looking and sounding determined
· looking people in the eyes when they say "no"
· anticipating reactions of friends and others, and preparing their response
· coping with teasing and rejection
· knowing when to leave a situation where there is too much pressure or conflict.

Rehearsing refusals that are to be used in specific, anticipated situations can also be helpful.

STRATEGIES FOR DEALING WITH CONSEQUENCES

There are usually some immediate positive consequences of the substance use that an adolescent is seeking and expecting, such as having fun, avoiding thinking about problems, feeling more social or relaxed, etc. However, there may be other activities that can provide similar positive reinforcement to that provided by the substance. Finding alternatives to drug use often involves the development of new behaviours and skills. When the youth has a repertoire of alternatives, the substance use can be framed as merely one choice among many available choices for positive reinforcement.

When episodes of substance use are analyzed using the ABC model, it may become evident that the life skills that are typically required to deal with various situations are underdeveloped. This is especially the case for youth who have become reliant on substances to assist them in coping with situations they find particularly challenging.

In the following section, we briefly review some life skill areas in which young clients may be deficient, including:

· social skills
· problem-solving skills
· stress management and relaxation skills
· anger management skills
· leisure skills
· other life skills.

Social skills

The ABC analysis, may indicate that drug use serves social functions as in the following example:

Antecedent	Behaviour	Consequence
feeling shy at a party	drinks 3 beers	initiates conversations

The following is a list of some of the areas of social life where young people may view drugs as being helpful. You need to help young clients learn social skills to cope with these situations in alternative ways without using drugs.

Initiating peer relations: Continuing friendships with other drug users may become less desirable. But it can be difficult to give up old friends unless the youth feels comfortable making new ones.

Conversation skills: Some youth may use drugs in order to be more talkative. They feel more outgoing when they are high, and are more able to express themselves.

Listening skills: Some young people say that using drugs helps them listen to and think about what others say. Conversely, others use drugs so that they can block out or tolerate what is being said to them.

Presenting yourself well: In order to be accepted by non-drug-using peers, some adolescents want to adopt a whole new look so that they aren't seen as drug users.

Expressing positive content: Some young people may view drug use as a way to reward themselves, celebrate an event or just have a good time.

Expressing negative content: Drug use can make it easier to express negative feelings that have been suppressed. Or it can help youth cope with negative feelings, such as anger, sadness, frustration, fear, by relieving the stress that such feelings create.

Conflict resolution: Drug use can offer an escape from conflict or have the opposite effect and enable the youth to confront the conflict head on, but not necessarily in an appropriate way.

Standing up for yourself: Drug use can help adolescents who don't feel confident to act more assertive. Conversely, overly assertive individuals may use drugs to soften their aggressiveness.

Problem-solving skills

During their ABC analysis, young clients often describe a positive relationship between their drug use and problem-solving ability. For example:

· Drug use enables them to concentrate better or to be more analytical.

· The drugs are an excuse for not taking responsibility for poor decisions or for failing to solve a problem (e.g., "I was high, so I just couldn't walk away from that fight at school.").

· Using drugs helps relieve the stress of a nagging problem.

Few young people are deficient in all aspects of the problem-solving process. It is important to identify skills as well as deficits. For the areas that are deficient, there are steps you can teach them to help improve their problem-solving abilities.

Problem solving steps

Step 1:   Identify a problem area (e.g., laziness).

Step 2:   Describe the problem in detail (e.g., no energy to do anything after school including homework assignments).

Step 3:   Generate strategies or potential solutions (at least six) through brainstorming. Do not dismiss any ideas that occur to you just yet. Continuing with the "laziness" example, a list might look like this:

· have a "wake up" shower or go for a brisk walk

· drink coffee or tea

· have a short nap

· think of an enjoyable activity you really want to pursue

· think of the benefits of the activity

· ask someone you like to join you in the activity

· make a commitment to someone to do the activity together

· do homework assignments with other people

· arrange for a work space that would make assignments easier to do.

Step 4:   Eliminate the solutions that look inappropriate or unworkable. Narrow the list down to three choices you are willing to try.

Step 5:   Weigh the advantages and disadvantages of the chosen strategies and choose the one with the fewest disadvantages.

Step 6:   Try the chosen strategy.

Step 7: Evaluate the results, and go back to steps 3 to 5 if the chosen solution did not work. If nothing is working, go back to step 2 and analyze the problem more deeply (e.g., conflict at home interfering with your feelings and your motivation to do anything after school).

Stress management and relaxation skills

Many drugs offer the immediate benefit of inducing a state of relaxation and well-being. For many young people who have not developed alternative ways to cope with stress, drugs offer a quick and effective way of reducing it temporarily. When the drug use is stopped, however, the stress and discomfort that was masked by the use typically returns.

The objectives of focussing on stress management with young drug users are to:
· foster awareness of stress as a normal aspect of life
· provide the youth with effective relaxation skills
· teach alternative stress reduction strategies that may be substituted for drug use
· teach cognitive restructuring
· assist clients in experiencing both the physical and cognitive changes that they can make through their own efforts.

Encourage your young clients to identify the pressures and hassles in their life, and to describe how they respond to them. If they have trouble recognizing that stress is interfering with their life, point out the physical and emotional "flags" such as stomach aches or anger. Recognition is the first step on the way to change.

When working with individuals or groups on stress management techniques, the following topics are useful to include in the sessions:
· understanding the concept of stress
· identifying general and personal stressors
· understanding the alarm response as a normal physiological response
· monitoring stress and developing coping strategies
· identifying the role of emotions in ongoing stress and appropriate ways to deal with emotions
· understanding the role of sleep, posture, diet, breath control and physical activity in reducing stress
· using the techniques of cognitive restructuring as a means of reducing stress.

Relaxation skills

The easiest exercise is the progressive muscular technique, which incorporates the use of slow, controlled breathing and rhythmic, alternate contraction and relaxation of particular muscle groups to induce a state of generalized relaxation.

Other techniques include mindfulness training, guided imagery, and specialized breathing techniques.

Anger management skills

For some youth, drugs are used to suppress feelings of anger, while for others, the drug use leads to aggressive behaviour. Learning anger management skills can be helpful for these individuals.

Anger management focuses on:
· normalizing anger and understanding its physical and emotional components
· identifying the pros and cons of changing how your client deals with anger
· functional analysis (ABC) of anger (antecedents, behaviour, consequences)
· effects of drug use on anger
· self-monitoring
· anger reduction strategies such as relaxation, nutrition, cognitive restructuring and assertiveness.

Leisure skills

For some youth, drug use is an integral part of their leisure time. Leisure activities can provide many of the functions that are often attributed to drug use such as having fun, getting a rush, dealing with boredom, enhancing self esteem, alleviating stress and being with friends.

You can help youth develop new leisure activities by talking about their interests, exploring opportunities for leisure activities, and encouraging them to get involved.

Life skills in other areas

A comprehensive approach to treating youth includes addressing a broad range of life areas that enhance well-being and optimum development. The comprehensive assessment will have identified concerns that need attention. New issues also may arise during the course of treatment. There may be illness that needs medical attention or health concerns related to nutrition, sexuality, birth control or sexually transmitted diseases that require counselling. Youth may also have goals with respect to education, employment, or housing that you can help them to achieve.

4.8.3 RELAPSE PREVENTION AND MANAGEMENT

Relapses both during and after treatment are common and can range from a minor slip to a full return to previous levels of drug use. It is important to discuss with young people how to prevent relapses and how to deal with them if and when they do occur.

Relapse prevention focuses on helping clients anticipate when a relapse might occur. It involves identifying high-risk circumstances for relapse and helping them develop strategies, in much the same way as they have done throughout treatment, so that they can avoid relapse.

Relapse management helps youth prepare themselves for how they will cope with a relapse if and when it occurs. It is a good idea to address the issue soon after youth begin to achieve their drug use goals. It involves thinking about a possible relapse in the future and discussing how it can best be handled so that the negative consequences are minimal. Explore with them how they will deal with feelings of failure or disappointment and how they will end a relapse so that they can get back on track with their drug use goal.

When a relapse occurs, it is important to help young clients deal with it constructively and learn from the experience. This involves developing cognitive strategies to deal with negative thinking about the relapse and can include the following perspectives (Parks et al., 2000):

· it can be framed as an opportunity for insight and new learning
· it represents some backward movement only, not a failure
· it does not negate the progress the client has made to this point
· it signals the need to refine the interventions and skills that the client is using to deal with triggers
· behaviour change is a process that involves both advances and setbacks.

You need to carefully select the words you use in a discussion of relapse prevention since they can be an important determinant of how the client responds to an incident of substance use. For minor, single occasions of substance use, with a return to abstinence soon after, some counsellors find it constructive to use the term "lapse" or "slip."

In a sense, as soon as the initial drug use goal has been achieved, all counselling becomes relapse prevention and management. Relapse prevention and management is not comprised of specialized techniques, nor is it a separate phase of treatment. It simply refers to how the counsellor and client try to prevent or manage any incidents of substance use after the initial goal has been achieved. The important feature of relapse prevention and management is the attitude both the counsellor and youth take toward it. Essentially, it means dealing constructively, and not punitively, with incidents of use.

4.9 FAMILY-FOCUSSED TREATMENT APPROACHES

When treating an adolescent for substance use and mental health problems, it is critical to consider the family therapy as the primary or adjunct treatment with the youth, if you want to achieve the best possible outcomes. Sometimes, there are contraindications to involving the family, such as when there is unresolved violence or sexual abuse, or when the youth or the parents refuse family involvement. Nonetheless, it is still possible to address family issues with the youth through "one-person family counselling," in which the principles of family therapy are used to effect change in the family unit (Szapoznik, Kurtines, Foote, Perez-Vidal, Hervis, 1986).

"Central to the life of adolescents is the family. When family life is disorganized, or worse, and does not provide an anchor for growth and development, the results can be devastating. It is for this reason so many practitioners insist on the family's involvement in therapy when an adolescent substance abuser is in treatment. Research has shown that family involvement enhances the outcome of treatment" (Schwartz, 1997, 21).

4.9.1 GOALS OF FAMILY INVOLVEMENT

Depending on the level of involvement you decide on during the assessment (see section 3.8), the goals of family-focussed approaches may include the following components:

· Psychoeducation about substance use can increase awareness and concern as well as decrease resistance to treatment. It also serves to increase the family's understanding of how family, in addition to the youth, is affected by the drug use.

· Psychoeducation about mental health symptoms, medications and their side effects helps the family understand how the youth's behaviour and emotional states may be affected by his or her mental health problems.

· Information about the stages of change and harm reduction approaches can help the family better understand the process of change. Exploration of what the family can do to support and help the youth succeed in treatment is an important element.

· You will need to help family members deal with such feelings as fear, loss, frustration, guilt and anger as they face the reality that their child's or sibling's life course may be seriously affected by substance use and mental illness.

· Training is usually required to improve parents' behaviour management skills (e.g., monitoring their child's activities and behaviours, setting consistent limits and imposing appropriate consequences).

· It is useful to provide training to improve positive communication within the family that involves learning how to listen and express thoughts and feelings.

· It is important that the family identify, communicate and enforce values and expectations that members have of each other.

4.9.2 INTEGRATIVE MODEL FOR FAMILY THERAPY

While some mental health problems may develop independently from the family context (e.g., biologically based mental disorders), many other mental health problems are related to, and maintained by family dynamics.

Working with the family to modify relationship dynamics and boundaries can be successful in effecting change even when youth themselves are reluctant to engage in treatment. You can focus the family counselling on helping parents change reinforcement contingencies to suppress certain behaviours and reward other, more adaptive behaviours.

Family therapy may be the treatment of choice for younger adolescent clients who do not have the cognitive and behavioural skills to engage in self-directed or counsellor-assisted behaviour change and emotional regulation.

The Centre for Addiction and Mental Health uses an "integrative model" for working with families (Boudreau, Chaim, Pearlman, Shenfeld, Skinner, 1998). The model incorporates key elements of several family therapy approaches such as:

- *Structural therapy*: attending to boundaries and coalitions
- *Strategic therapy*: tracking and attempting to change key interactional patterns
- *Solution-focussed therapy*: focus on strengths, small changes and creating solutions
- *Cognitive behaviour therapy*: use of self-monitoring and a focus on identifying and addressing cognitions and overt, observable behaviour.

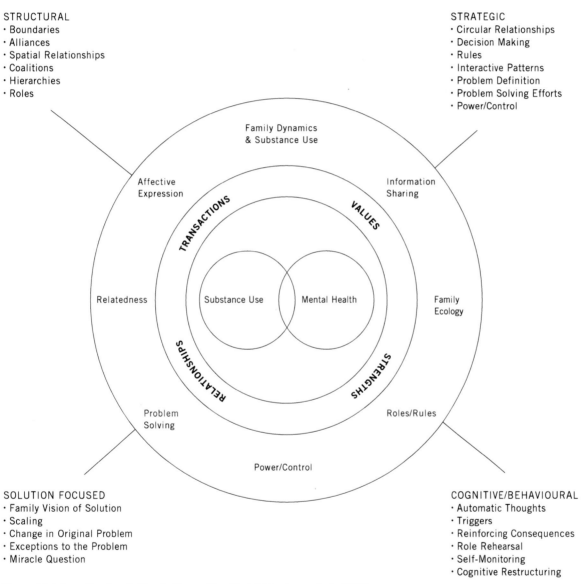

STRUCTURAL
- Boundaries
- Alliances
- Spatial Relationships
- Coalitions
- Hierarchies
- Roles

STRATEGIC
- Circular Relationships
- Decision Making
- Rules
- Interactive Patterns
- Problem Definition
- Problem Solving Efforts
- Power/Control

SOLUTION FOCUSED
- Family Vision of Solution
- Scaling
- Change in Original Problem
- Exceptions to the Problem
- Miracle Question

COGNITIVE/BEHAVIOURAL
- Automatic Thoughts
- Triggers
- Reinforcing Consequences
- Role Rehearsal
- Self-Monitoring
- Cognitive Restructuring

Figure 4.1 Integrative Couple/Family Counselling Model (Boudreau et al., 1998)

The integrative model looks at four key areas of family functioning:

- *Strengths*: to build on when searching for solutions to the presenting problem(s)
- *Values*: the family's unique perspective, beliefs and where they situate themselves in the socio-cultural-political world
- *Relationships*: the depth and quality of the relationships in the family
- *Transactions*: the positive and negative interactions between members.

These four core areas are further specified and translated into more detailed dimensions of functioning. Gathering information in these more specific areas can help refine your understanding of the family system and how it impacts on the youth's substance use and mental health problems (Chaim and Shenfeld, in press).

Impact of substance use and mental health on family dynamics refers to the unique meaning and role that these concerns have in the family. Information about the use patterns of all members, history of use, mental health problems in the family (including extended family), and values around, and cultural context of substance use and mental health problems are all important.

Information sharing refers to patterns of communication among family members (e.g., how and to whom information is passed, family secrets, or whether or not communication is clear, etc.).

Family ecology refers to the external context surrounding the family, such as socio-economic, religious, educational, community and other factors.

Roles and rules address the overt and covert operating patterns of the family, and how they are organized along differing continua (e.g., traditional vs. modern, flexible vs. rigid, etc.).

Power and control can be assessed along such parameters as shared vs. dominant or democratic vs. autocratic. It is critical to determine whether violence or any form of intimidation is used and, if so, to assess for safety, as well.

Problem solving may be flexible or idiosyncratic, and it is important to understand how different family members' styles may be similar or conflicting.

Relatedness refers to how close or distant family members are from one another.

Affective expression refers to ways that closeness, feelings and emotions are all communicated. Whether or not the family is open or closed in this area may be influenced by cultural and historical factors, and it is important to place this area of functioning into a larger context.

The integrative model is non-prescriptive and provides the therapist with a number of intervention options rather than limiting the therapist to a particular technique to be used in specific circumstances. It can be used at any stage of involvement from intake to termination. The interplay of clinician preference, agency factors and client needs and strengths will influence the application of the model (Chaim and Shenfeld, in press).

CHAPTER 5

PHARMACOTHERAPY

5.1 INTRODUCTION

According to Riggs & Whitmore, (1999), pharmacotherapy for adolescent substance use problems is not empirically well-developed, with the protocols taken largely from adult studies. The current status of pharmacotherapy for adolescent substance use treatment includes the following:

· Pharmacotherapy is most commonly considered for detoxification and treatment of withdrawal.

· Anecdotal reports suggest that desipramine may be of help in facilitating abstinence from cocaine.

· Case studies suggest that naltrexone may be useful in the treatment of alcohol use.

· Case studies suggest that supervised naltrexone treatment is also effective in maintaining abstinence in clients with opioid dependence.

· The use of aversive agents like disulfiram is rare because of a lack of empirical research. If it is used, offer it as a component of a more comprehensive treatment approach.

· Current practice guidelines suggest that, until more empirical research supports their use in adolescents with substance use problems, these agents be considered only after behavioural interventions have failed or in conjunction with behavioural interventions.

Section 5.6 in this chapter describes how medications are used to treat substance use.

The use of pharmacotherapy for certain adolescent mental health problems has been well established. You may need to arrange a psychiatric consultation for a diagnostic evaluation and possible medication prescription. Few agencies that treat substance use or mental health issues have psychiatrists on staff. Therefore, agencies need to consider system integration strategies to ensure that clients have access to psychiatric consultation when it is required. Another option, if access to psychiatric consultation is limited, is for counsellors to work with the client's family physician.

This chapter describes medications used to treat mental health problems and provides information on their classification, uses and side effects, as well as how to manage common side effects.

5.2 PSYCHIATRIC MEDICATIONS AND THEIR USE IN THE TREATMENT OF MENTAL HEALTH PROBLEMS

CLASSIFICATIONS

Psychiatric medications are classified into four main groupings based on their originally intended uses: antidepressants, mood stabilizers, anxiolytics/hypnotics/sedatives, and antipsychotics.

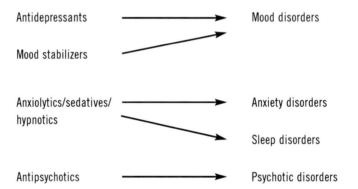

Figure 5.1: Traditional uses for classes of psychiatric medications

Antidepressants

Antidepressants work via a number of different mechanisms, but the end result is to increase the transmission of neurochemicals in the brain. While they were originally used in the treatment of depression, and still are, these medications are also used for many different indications now. They are now first-line treatment for anxiety disorders, replacing traditional anti-anxiety medications such as diazepam (Valium®). Antidepressants take longer to work (usually four to six weeks) and can increase anxiety in the first weeks of treatment. However, in the long run, they can effectively treat a wide range of anxiety disorders, from generalized anxiety disorder and panic disorder to obsessive-compulsive disorder, with less chance of habituation than occurs with the traditional anti-anxiety medications. Other uses for antidepressants include treatment of chronic pain, bulimia, post-traumatic stress disorder, social phobia, premenstrual dysphoric disorder and chronic fatigue syndrome.

Table 1 in Appendix G lists the antidepressants currently available in Canada, along with their generic and trade names, most common side effects and important drug interactions.

Mood stabilizers

Mood stabilizers are used in the treatment of bipolar disorder, formerly known as manic-depressive illness. Lithium was the first mood stabilizer on the market and is still a useful medication. Other medications used as mood stabilizers are often actually anticonvulsants, which are used in the treatment of epilepsy and other seizure disorders. Valproate and carbamazepine were the first anticonvulsants to be tested as mood stabilizers and are commonly used. It is not known how or why they can be used effectively this way, although the theory is that, just as seizures are an "overactivity" of the brain, so is mania. As new anticonvulsants enter the market, generally they also are tested as mood stabilizers. It is therefore important that clients know that their mood stabilizer may not be "officially approved" for use in bipolar disorder, and consequently, much of the information they may find in handouts and on the Internet may only refer to their medication as an anticonvulsant.

Table 2 in Appendix G lists the medications commonly referred to as mood stabilizers, along with their generic and trade names, most common side effects and important drug interactions.

Treatment of bipolar disorder depends on the symptomatology of the individual. Bipolar disorder may also be treated with antidepressants in combination with mood stabilizers. The second generation antipsychotics (Table 4 in Appendix G), which are showing promise in acute mania and other phases of bipolar disorder, may also be used.

Anxiolytics/hypnotics/sedatives

These medications work by enhancing the effects of gamma amino butyric acid (GABA), an inhibitory transmitter in the brain. The main group of medications in this class is the benzodiazepines, such as diazepam (Valium®) and lorazepam (Ativan®). While they do have legitimate uses in the treatment of anxiety and sleep disorders, they do have the potential to be used as substances of abuse. Proper use of benzodiazepines is sometimes difficult, and there is often a lack of education among clinicians about the use of these medications. Ideally, they should be used as a short-term treatment of symptoms, from a few days up to one month. After that time, a client and his or her care team need to address underlying problems and issues contributing to the anxiety and/or insomnia.

Pharmacological treatment of anxiety and panic disorders can also include antidepressants, especially Selective Serotonin Reuptake Inhibitors (SSRI). In fact, antidepressants are considered first-line agents to treat anxiety disorders. Another anti-anxiety agent that can be used longer term is buspirone.

Treatment of insomnia includes treating underlying disorders, such as depression or chronic pain, as well as providing education about proper sleep hygiene.

Table 3 in Appendix G lists the currently available medications in this class, along with their generic and trade names, common side effects and important drug interactions. Some benzodiazepines are classified as anxiolytics, while others are called hypnotics/sedatives. In practice, any benzodiazepine can be used for either anxiety or insomnia. Generally speaking, medications with a quicker onset and shorter half-life are considered hypnotics (e.g., they will help a client get a good night's sleep without any daytime drowsiness), while medications with a longer half-life are considered anxiolytics.

Antipsychotics

Antipsychotics block receptors for the neurotransmitter dopamine, and are traditionally used in the treatment of schizophrenia and other psychotic disorders. With the introduction of the newer, second generation agents, they are now also being tested as mood stabilizers, anti-anxiety agents and even as a treatment for refractory depression. Regardless of the indication for which the antipsychotic is being used, it is important to educate young clients about the real meaning of "psychosis" to help minimize the stigma associated with these terms.

Table 4 in Appendix G lists the currently available medications in this class, along with their generic and trade names, common side effects and important drug interactions.

Despite the terminology of the classes of psychiatric medications, it is important to note that each type of medication can be used for a variety of disorders.

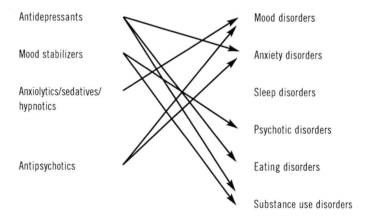

Figure 5.2: Alternative uses for classes of psychiatric medications

5.3 MANAGEMENT OF COMMON MEDICATION SIDE EFFECTS

ANTICHOLINERGIC EFFECTS

Anticholinergic side effects such as dry mouth and eyes, constipation and urinary retention occur because the medication blocks the receptors for the neurotransmitter acetylcholine. They are best described as "drying up" side effects. Because the body adapts to the medication over time, these side effects are often short term.

Dry mouth

· This is common, especially in elderly patients, and with drug combinations.
· Chew sugarless gum or suck on sugarless or sour candy (both dry mouth and excess sugar can increase the risk of tooth decay).
· Ensure good mouth hygiene, including frequent brushing, flossing and use of mouthwashes.
· Have regular dental checkups.
· Use artificial saliva oral lubricants (e.g., MoiStir®).

Dry eyes and/or blurred vision

· Mainly near vision is temporarily affected.
· Read under a bright light while holding the reading material at a distance.
· A physician may prescribe eye drops.

Constipation

· Increase fluid intake (e.g., water, juice and other non-caffeinated, non-alcoholic beverages).
· Increase regular physical activity and exercise.
· Increase dietary fibre (e.g., bran, raw fruits and vegetables).
· Try a bulk laxative (e.g., Metamucil®, Prodiem®) or stool softener (e.g., Surfak®, Colace®).
· Avoid regular use of stronger or stimulant laxatives.

Urinary retention

· If mild, patience and running water while attempting to urinate may be helpful.
· If more severe, a physician can prescribe a medication to help counteract this effect.

CENTRAL NERVOUS SYSTEM EFFECTS

All psychiatric medications act on the brain and can therefore cause central nervous system side effects such as drowsiness, ataxia and headache. Some of these effects are short term, while others can last for the duration of the drug therapy. Because these effects are typical of so many of the psychotropics, they can be additive, or sometimes contradictory (see section 5.5).

Drowsiness

· This is common at the start of therapy with most psychotropic drugs but should decrease with time.
· Try to take most of the dose or the full dose, if possible, at bedtime.
· Use caution when driving or operating machinery.
· The effect will be increased with alcohol or other sedating drugs.
· Confusion, disturbed concentration and disorientation may be signs that the dose is too high.

Ataxia (muscle inco-ordination or weakness)

· Check with a physician since it may be due to an excessive dose.

Headache

· Try over-the-counter headache remedies such as acetaminophen (Tylenol®), aspirin or ibuprofen but first ask a physician or pharmacist to check for any drug interactions.
· With time, headaches should go away, but if they persist, the drug may need to be changed.

EXTRAPYRAMIDAL SIDE EFFECTS (EPS)

These side effects are most commonly seen with the older, typical, first generation antipsychotics, but can also been seen with the newer, second generation antipsychotics in higher doses. Some of these effects, especially the motor restlessness, can also be seen early in treatment with SSRI antidepressants.

· Side effects include tremor, motor restlessness (feel as though can't sit still), muscle stiffness and spasms, gait disturbance and loss of facial expression.
· Dosage adjustment may be required.
· A physician may prescribe antiparkinsonian drugs (e.g., benztropine) but they must be monitored as excessive doses may cause other side effects such as disorientation, confusion and delirium.
· Sometimes propranolol may be prescribed to treat tremor or restlessness, while benzodiazepines (e.g., lorazepam) may be prescribed to treat restlessness.

GASTROINTESTINAL EFFECTS

Gastrointestinal side effects such as nausea and diarrhea are temporary, as the body adjusts to the medication. They commonly occur with antidepressants and mood stabilizers.

Nausea

· Take medications with meals, small snacks or milk.

· Avoid using antacids within two hours of medication dosing time, as they may interfere with drug absorption.

Diarrhea

· Diarrhea should be temporary. Try loperamide (Imodium®) or attapulgite (Kaopectate®) after checking with a physician or pharmacist for any drug interactions.

· Diarrhea with lithium use may be helped by giving smaller doses spread throughout the day or using a slow-release preparation. Sudden diarrhea may indicate lithium toxicity.

CARDIOVASCULAR EFFECTS

Some of these effects are more common early in treatment, and can sometimes be avoided by slowly increasing the dose. Other effects are more serious and may require a change in medications. Cardiovascular effects can happen in each class of psychiatric medication, although they are more common with some specific medications.

Dizziness, fainting

· Referred to as "orthostatic hypotension," this is when blood pressure drops rapidly (e.g., when a person stands up quickly), and causes dizziness and fainting.

· Get up slowly from a lying or sitting position and dangle feet.

· Support hose and calf exercises can reduce blood pooling in the calves.

· Take the drug in smaller, divided doses spread out through the day.

Tachycardia (rapid heartbeat)

· This is usually not a serious problem, but should still be reported to a physician.

Hypertension (high blood pressure)

· Speak to a physician about reducing the dose, changing medication or adding a high blood pressure medication.

WEIGHT EFFECTS

Weight gain is a common side effect of most mood stabilizers and the newer antipsychotics. It is also possible with some antidepressants. The exact cause is not known, but may be due to increased appetite and cravings for carbohydrates, or changes in how the body handles glucose. Sometimes, it may be due to water retention.

· Reduce carbohydrate and sugar intake and consult with a dietician, if possible.
· Increase physical activity and exercise.

SEXUAL SIDE EFFECTS

These side effects include decreased libido, delayed ejaculation, impaired erection, inhibition of orgasm (in both men and women) and menstrual irregularities. Sexual effects are probably the most difficult side effects for people to talk about openly and, as such, they are often under-reported. People usually don't volunteer this information without some prompting from caregivers with whom they have a good rapport and trust.

· Report these side effects to a physician as all the treatments involve prescription medications.
· Sometimes, they may go away with time, but other times, the drug may need to be changed.

ALTERED THERMOREGULATION

This refers to an altered ability to regulate extreme changes in temperature and humidity.

· Be cautious in saunas and on hot humid days due to increased risk of sunstroke.
· Drink plenty of fluids and stay in shade as much as possible. Wear loose-fitting clothing and a wide brimmed hat.
· Avoid overexposure on freezing days due to increased risk of hypothermia.

PHOTOSENSITIVITY

There are medications that can increase the likelihood of sunburn. Some medications, such as the mood stabilizer carbamazepine, can cause a more serious phototoxic reaction that includes a rash and other physicial symptoms such as nausea.

· Avoid prolonged sun exposure. Wear loose-fitting clothing and a wide-brimmed hat.
· Always use sunscreen with SPF 15 or higher.

EXCESSIVE SWEATING

· Daily showering, talcum powder and stronger antiperspirant can increase comfort.
· Dose reduction may be necessary.
· In severe cases, speak to a physician regarding prescription drug treatments.

One of the most important roles for caregivers and/or caseworkers is helping young clients identify and manage the side effects of their medications. This includes creating an open and trusting environment where they feel comfortable describing any undesirable symptoms they are experiencing. It may also include advocating on the patients' behalf to their physicians. While you, as a counsellor or caseworker, cannot make changes in clients' medication regimens, you can help distinguish nuisance side effects from adverse reactions that need to be reported immediately, and help young persons cope with these effects while waiting for a physician to make a change in medication.

- -

5.4 BASIC PRINCIPLES OF MEDICATION MANAGEMENT

SET TREATMENT GOALS IN CONSULTATION WITH THE CLIENT AND FAMILY

Treatment goals need to be realistic. With improvements in psychiatric medications and increased knowledge of how the brain works, the goals of treatment are more ambitious than ever before. Full remission and recovery is attainable, but it must also be recognized that not all youth respond to medications, and there is still a great deal of "trial and error" involved in the process. It is important that youth and family have full input in the decision-making process, as well as full disclosure of benefits and risks of medications.

OPTIMIZE DOSE

It is sometimes surprising how much of a difference even a very small dosage adjustment can make in the response to treatment and/or in the reduction of side effects. The dose may also need to be changed over time. A higher dose may be needed to control an acute episode, but generally, the client can be maintained on a lower dose.

IDENTIFY AND MINIMIZE SIDE EFFECTS

If you can help youth feel comfortable discussing side effects, it can encourage their staying with the medication regimens. It is not uncommon for a young person to stop taking medication after experiencing a side effect and not reporting it to anyone.

ASSESS AND REASSESS RESPONSE

Most psychiatric disorders are lifelong conditions, meaning treatment with medications is often indefinite. Once an acute episode has been successfully treated, it is important to monitor for any signs of possible relapse.

SHORT-TERM VERSUS MAINTENANCE TREATMENT

Youth and their families are often very concerned about how long they will be taking medications. In some situations, the treatment will be short-term, as in the case of a sedative for temporary insomnia. In first-episode depression, the treatment is for at least one year. For bipolar disorder and schizophrenia, the treatment is usually indefinite to prevent recurrence of symptoms. In the case of a first-episode psychosis, it can be difficult to distinguish between a drug-induced psychosis and schizophrenia. Thus, it is important to note that if a youth does not have symptoms for several months, a slow taper and discontinuation of the medication with very close monitoring may be possible.

MEDICATIONS ARE BEST UTILIZED AS A "TOOL" WITHIN A BROADER TREATMENT PROGRAM

Medications are an essential part of many clients' treatment programs, but they are not the only treatment. In many cases, the medication will help stabilize youth and clarify their thinking so they can then engage in other treatments, such as cognitive behaviour therapy, family therapy, group therapy, etc.

General suggestions for users of medications:

· They should know the name and dose of all of their medications, and for what problem each one is being taken.

· Ask them to rank all symptoms on a scale of 1 to 10 and monitor improvement.

· Suggest that they take note of side effects and report any to a health care professional (What are they? How severe are they?).

· Remind them to take medications daily. Educate them about the importance of exercising and eating well.

· Encourage youth to check with a physician and/or pharmacist for drug interactions before taking any new medication (prescription or over-the-counter).

· Remember to encourage young clients to ask any questions they may have about medications.

5.5 INTERACTIONS BETWEEN PSYCHIATRIC MEDICATIONS AND SUBSTANCES OF ABUSE

In this section, we will look at drug interactions between prescribed medications for mental health problems and common substances of abuse. Since there is not much available in the literature, we have to look at ways of anticipating these drug interactions.

ANTICIPATING DRUG INTERACTIONS

It is often difficult to anticipate interactions between psychiatric medications and substances of abuse. Purity, potency (strength), dose and contaminants can be difficult, if not impossible to determine.

Most of the drug interaction information in this area is based on unproven theory, case reports and anecdotal experience. Sometimes an interaction may be anticipated because of experiences with drugs in the same class or drugs with similar effects. Often, theories are based on the receptors and neurotransmitters affected by the individual drugs, or by identifying which liver enzymes metabolize each drug and the pathways common to both drugs. Occasionally, there are single-dose experiments in well-controlled environments with healthy volunteers.

CONSEQUENCES OF DRUG INTERACTIONS

Some drug interactions are considered "not clinically significant," meaning that while the drugs do in fact interact, in reality, the end result does not affect the youth. However, when dealing with substances of abuse, which can have toxic effects on their own, the consequences of drug interactions can be much more serious. The main toxic effects that can occur are:

· central nervous system depression, which, at its mildest, is drowsiness, but in its more severe form, can lead to a coma
· respiratory depression, which can lead to the person to stop breathing altogether
· cardiac effects, such as blood vessels constricting or dilating, or changes in heart rhythm that can lead to the heart stopping
· seizure threshold can be decreased, meaning that the brain can have a seizure more easily
· psychiatric effects, such as psychosis.

SPECIFIC DRUG INTERACTIONS

Because of the lack of data on these interactions, as well as the experimental nature of substance use, it can be difficult to guess what drug interactions a young client might experience. Some combinations, however, are common, and have known effects.

A very useful and youth friendly guide on drug interactions is *Cocktails: Facts for Youth About Mixing Medicine, Booze and Street Drugs* (Collin & Paone, 2002).

Antidepressants and stimulants

If a stimulant, such as cocaine or methylphenidate, is taken with a Monoamine Oxidase Inhibitor (MAOI) antidepressant, a hypertensive reaction can occur. The combination of a stimulant and a tricyclic antidepressant can cause an increased heart rate.

Antipsychotics and marijuana

Marijuana can decrease the effectiveness of antipsychotic drugs and increase the risk of relapse. It can also lead to marked hypotension (low blood pressure) and increased disorientation with certain antipsychotic drugs. Also, there can be additive effects with anticholinergics and other medications that have anticholinergic side effects, leading to increased dry mouth, urinary retention, constipation, etc.

Antipsychotics and tobacco

Smoking decreases the blood concentration level of certain antipsychotics by 20 to 100 per cent, meaning that smokers require higher doses. If a youth on an antipsychotic reduces or quits smoking, the blood concentration levels of the drug will increase, leading to increased side effects and possibly toxicity. Therefore, dose decreases are usually required, but must be monitored closely.

Benzodiazepines and alcohol

Benzodiazepines are used to alleviate symptoms of anxiety. Alcohol is frequently used for the same reason. This combination can lead to additive sedation, confusion, and memory impairment. It can also increase respiratory depression.

Benzodiazepines and tobacco

Some of the substances in tobacco can induce the liver enzymes that metabolize diazepam and chlordiazepoxide. This causes them to clear from the body more quickly, leading to a need for higher doses.

Lithium and caffeine

Caffeine acts as diuretic, which can worsen incontinence. This affects water balance and can therefore affect lithium levels. Caffeine also can increase renal excretion of lithium and lithium tremor. Young clients who are taking lithium may still have some caffeine in their diet, but it is important that they do not drastically vary their intake from day to day.

5.6 MEDICATIONS FOR TREATMENT OF SUBSTANCE USE

In this section, we will discuss the medications that are prescribed to treat substance use. It is important to remember that they are only an adjunct, and *must* be accompanied by other non-pharmacological therapies and support programs.

TREATMENT GOALS AND STRATEGIES

The goals of treating substance use are to reduce the use and effect of the substance, reduce the frequency and severity of relapse, and improve psychological and social functioning. Pharmacological treatment of substance use must be considered only as an adjunct to other behavioural and psychological treatments. Medications are mostly used to treat an underlying psychiatric disorder or the medical complications of substance use. As we learn more about the biological effects of substances on the brain, the effectiveness of medications in the treatment of substance use will become clearer.

The currently available pharmacological treatment strategies include:
· treatment of withdrawal symptoms and associated complications
· substitution therapy in which the substance is replaced with medication less likely to be abused
· antagonist therapy to block effects of the substance
· aversive therapy to discourage use of the substance.

Treatment of withdrawal and associated complications

Treatment of substance withdrawal focuses mostly on alleviating symptoms (e.g., the specific withdrawal symptoms are treated as they emerge). Examples of this include:
· antiemetic for nausea and vomiting (e.g., dimenhydrinate [Gravol®])
· non steroidal anti-inflammatory drugs (NSAID) for muscle, joint and back pain (e.g., ibuprofen [Advil®], naproxen)
· antidiarrheal agent for diarrhea (e.g., loperamide [Imodium®])
· non-benzodiazepine sedative for insomnia (e.g., low-dose sedating antidepressant such as trazodone)
· clonidine for hyperadrenergic symptoms such as increased heart rate, blood pressure and sweating.

Benzodiazepines such as diazepam (Valium®) or lorazepam (Ativan®) have an important role in reducing the symptoms and incidence of delirium and seizures from alcohol withdrawal. Clients are started on large loading doses that are titrated to their symptoms based on a checklist. The doses are then gradually tapered over a few days.

Thiamine (Vitamin B1) is used in acute ethanol (EtOH) withdrawal to prevent neurological complications such as Wernicke's encephalopathy, which can occur in people with chronic alcoholic problems due to thiamine deficiency. Symptoms include disturbances in ocular motility, papillary alterations, nystagmus, and ataxia with tremors.

Substitution therapy

An example of substitution therapy is the use of methadone, a synthetic opioid, in the treatment of opioid dependence, including prescription narcotics and heroin. It suppresses withdrawal symptoms of other opioids as well as the chronic craving, without developing tolerance or euphoria.

To prevent IV administration and mask its bitter taste, methadone is administered mixed in orange juice. It is rapidly absorbed after oral administration, and has a long half-life, varying from 13 to 55 hours, with an average half-life of 35 hours. Its duration of action increases with long-term administration. Methadone, itself, also has dependence liability, and therefore must be tapered very slowly to prevent symptoms and relapse

The side effects of methadone include:
· *Central nervous system (CNS)*: drowsiness, insomnia, dysphoria, weakness, dizziness, lightheadedness and nervousness
· *Gastrointestinal (GI)*: nausea, vomiting, chronic constipation, decreased appetite and dry mouth
· *Other*: sweating, flushing, impotence and ejaculatory problems.

The prescribing and dispensing of methadone in Canada is a carefully regulated process. Patients and physicians must be registered with their provincial licensing authority or the Bureau of Drug Surveillance. The pharmacist does not need special registration, but not all pharmacies are involved in the dispensing of methadone. Usually the pharmacist will observe the clients taking their dose, but after they have been in the program for a while and are doing well, they may get some take home doses called "carries." They must keep these doses out of reach of children and other adults, since even one dose can be fatal to someone other than the client. The clients typically also have regular urine drug screens, and attend individual or group counselling.

Antagonist therapy

Prescribing naltrexone (Revia®) is an example of an antagonist therapy that blocks the effects of opioids. It has a high affinity for the sigma receptor and is used as an adjunct treatment for maintaining abstinence following detoxification from opioids or alcohol. It is most useful in highly motivated clients.

Naltrexone *can precipitate withdrawal* if the client has not been completely detoxified from opioids and, as such, it must be started no earlier than seven to 10 days after the last use of opioids. It has a quick onset and a long duration of action, and can sometimes be given every three days. Naltrexone is contraindicated in people with acute hepatitis or liver failure. The opioid blockade can be reversed with very large doses of opioids, which can lead to life-threatening opioid overdose.

The side effects of naltrexone include:
- *CNS*: insomnia, anxiety, nervousness, dysphoria, depression, lethargy, fatigue, confusion and headache
- *GI*: abdominal cramps, nausea, vomiting and weight loss
- *Other*: joint and muscle pain.

Aversive therapy

Disulfiram (formerly marketed under the trade name Antabuse® is an example of aversive therapy to discourage alcohol use. It blocks breakdown of the toxic metabolites of alcohol (acetaldehyde), causing an accumulation in the body. The symptoms that result when disulfiram is combined with alcohol include nausea, flushing, dry mouth, sweating, throbbing head and palpitations. Although Antabuse® is no longer made commercially in Canada, compounding pharmacies can make capsules using disulfiram powder. It is not recommended for youth.

New pharmacological treatment options

Buprenorphine, which is currently available only in Canada through the Special Access Program, is an alternative to methadone in the treatment of opioid dependence. The advantages of buprenorphine are a much lower risk of death from overdose, milder withdrawal during tapering, and the relative ease of finding the optimal dose (within a few days as opposed to weeks with methadone). Buprenorphine has been found to be as effective as lower doses of methadone (20 to 60 milligrams), which is part of the reason it may be a better option for adolescent clients than methadone.

Buprenorphine is a partial agonist at the μ-opioid receptor, and an antagonist at the κ-receptor. This means it has a mechanism slightly different from methadone. Because it can partially block the effects of other opioids, it can precipitate withdrawal in individuals still taking opioids.

The drug is administered sublingually since it has poor oral bioavailability (e.g., not enough active drug makes it to the bloodstream and sites of action). A client must keep the tablet under the tongue for a few minutes until it dissolves and can be absorbed directly into the bloodstream. As with methadone, this process is usually observed by the pharmacist. The peak level in the blood is reached in 60 to 90 minutes, and the duration of action is 24 hours, at minimum. The side effects are similar to other opioids (e.g., sedation, constipation, nausea, etc.), although it is less likely to cause severe respiratory depression in overdose.

APPENDIX A: RISK AND PROTECTIVE FACTORS FOR POTENTIAL SUBSTANCE USE AND MENTAL HEALTH PROBLEMS

RISK FACTORS	POTENTIAL SUBSTANCE USE AND MENTAL HEALTH PROBLEMS AMONG YOUNG PEOPLE	PROTECTIVE FACTORS
Prenatal experience: Inadequate nutrition and exposure to injury, infection, or toxins including substances such as tobacco, alcohol and drugs (in utero or after birth)	• Biologic and brain abnormalities, fetal alcohol syndrome/effects (now called fetal alcohol syndrome disorder [FASD]) and associated behavioural abnormalities; low birth weight and subsequent developmental challenges. • Behaviourally inhibited infants may display excessively shy and avoidant behaviour in early childhood, and may later experience social phobia and anxiety (Patterson, 2002). • Prenatal alcohol use is associated with substance use disorder in youth (Ballon, in press).	
Family situation	• The family is the "most critical environment influencing children's mental health" (Patterson, 2002).	• Strong family bonds (NIDA, 1997) • Positive connections with extended family members.
Ineffective parenting skills	• Ineffective parenting skills, particularly with children who have difficult temperaments or conduct disorders are associated with substance use problems among youth (National Institute on Drug Abuse [NIDA], 1997).	• Age-appropriate discipline and limit-setting (authoritative parenting).
Single parent family	• Young people from single-parent families have a higher likelihood of experiencing internalizing problems such as depression or anxiety (Adlaf et al., 2002).	• Stable, two-parent family.
Lack of mutual attachments and nurturing in the family	• Associated with substance use problems among youth (NIDA, 1997).	• A high quality infant-caregiver relationship (secure attachment is the foundation for mental health throughout life) and strong parent-child relationship as the child develops (closeness, warmth, trust, open communication).
Quality of the parent-child relationship	• Associated with the presence of both internalizing and externalizing problems among young people. Students who report having a poor relationship with their parents are more likely to report low self-esteem, depressive symptoms, psychological distress, and thoughts about suicide. They are also more likely to report having a pathological gambling problem, and using illicit drugs (Adlaf et al., 2002).	• Good parent-child communication and strong bonding.

APPENDIX A: RISK AND PROTECTIVE FACTORS FOR POTENTIAL SUBSTANCE USE AND MENTAL HEALTH PROBLEMS

RISK FACTORS	POTENTIAL SUBSTANCE USE AND MENTAL HEALTH PROBLEMS AMONG YOUNG PEOPLE	PROTECTIVE FACTORS
Family situation (continued)		
Parental monitoring	• Level of parental monitoring is linked to the presence of both internalizing and externalizing problems. Students who report that their parents do not usually know their whereabouts are more likely to report elevated psychological distress, suicide ideation, delinquency, hazardous drinking and illicit drug use (Adlaf et al., 2002).	• Parental monitoring, clear rules for behaviour within the family, and parental involvement in children's lives (NIDA, 1997).
Turbulent family life, family dysfunction	• Turbulent family life is associated with substance use problems among youth (Schwartz, 1997). Family dysfunction is a signifi-cant independent predictor of psychiatric disorders among children (Offord et al., 1989).	
Exposure to violence in the home	• Exposure to violence, in particular violence directed toward the mother, could place girls at higher risk of becoming victimized within their own intimate relationships and could place boys at higher risk of becoming perpetrators within their own intimate relationships (Department of Justice Canada, 2000). • Children may model the violence they see, and they may become involved in the conflict. Exposure could result in behavioural problems, associations with antisocial peers, school failure and early delinquent behaviour (Patterson, 2002). Exposure to violence predicts long-term problems including criminality and mental health problems (Schwartz, 1997).	
Permissive family attitudes toward drug use	• Associated with substance use problems among youth (Ballon, in press).	
Parental (genetic or adoptive) substance use or mental health problems	• Home environments that are chaotic due to parental substance use or mental health problems are linked to substance use problems in youth (Ballon, in press; NIDA, 1997). Parent(s) with anti-social personality disorder and mothers with depression are associated with substance use problems among youth (Ballon, in press). Parents who are depressed or have other psychopathology are associated.	

APPENDIX A: RISK AND PROTECTIVE FACTORS FOR POTENTIAL SUBSTANCE USE AND MENTAL HEALTH PROBLEMS

RISK FACTORS	POTENTIAL SUBSTANCE USE AND MENTAL HEALTH PROBLEMS AMONG YOUNG PEOPLE	PROTECTIVE FACTORS
Family situation (continued)	with mental health problems among their children. These parents tend to have poorer caregiving skills, less effective discipline and monitoring, and are more likely to be excessively irritable and critical. They also tend to be neglectful and model poor coping skills (Patterson, 2002).	
Physical, sexual or psychological abuse	• Physical or sexual abuse increases a child's risk for psychiatric disorders such as PTSD, conduct disorders, depression and impaired social functioning (Patterson, 2002). Physical and sexual abuse is associated with substance use problems among youth (Ballon, in press). Psychological maltreatment is associated with a range of mental health issues (Patterson, 2002). High levels of criticism and contempt (expressed emotion) increase the likelihood of mental health problems (Patterson, 2002).	
Stressful life events in the family	• Parental death or divorce increases risk for mental health problems. Outcomes are influenced by child's age, extent of permanent life changes and access to resources for coping (Patterson, 2002).	
Individual situation Genetic inheritance	• Genetic factors are linked to autism, bipolar disorder, schizophrenia and attention-deficit/hyperactivity disorder (Patterson, 2002).	• Innate intelligence (genetic inheritance combined with early environmental stimulation and experience).
Temperament and biological factors including thrill-seeking behaviour, emotion/affect dysregulation, problems with behavioural self-regulation (e.g., deficits in planning, attention, reasoning, judgment, motor control, and anger control/aggressive behaviour)	• Associated with substance use disorders among youth (Ballon, in press).	• Outgoing temperament.

APPENDIX A: RISK AND PROTECTIVE FACTORS FOR POTENTIAL SUBSTANCE USE AND MENTAL HEALTH PROBLEMS

RISK FACTORS	POTENTIAL SUBSTANCE USE AND MENTAL HEALTH PROBLEMS AMONG YOUNG PEOPLE	PROTECTIVE FACTORS
Individual situation (contd.) Low resilience, poor self-esteem, affect dysregulation and poor social skills	• Associated with substance use disorders among youth (Ballon, in press).	• Self-efficacy.
Psychiatric disorders including ADHD, conduct disorders, learning disorders, mood disorders, schizophrenia, eating disorders, anxiety disorders and somatoform disorders	• ADHD, conduct disorder and learning disorders tend to emerge in childhood and can later increase the risk of substance use problems (Ballon, in press).	
Anti-social behaviour or inappropriately shy or aggressive behaviour in the classroom	• Associated with substance use problems (NIDA, 1997; Schwartz, 1997).	• Academic achievement/success in school (NIDA, 1997).
Chronic illness or disability	• Increased stress and developmental challenges heighten the risk for emotional and social problems. Risk increases when parents experience problems with adjustment or have difficulty accessing health and education resources (Patterson, 2002).	
Poor social skills/poor interpersonal coping skills	• Associated with substance use problems among youth (Ballon, in press; NIDA, 1997; Schwartz, 1997).	• Good social skills.
Substance use/early substance use	• Substance use can cause psychiatric symptoms (Trupin & Boesky, 2001). • Starting to use substances at a young age is associated with substance use problems (Schwartz, 1997).	• Adoption of conventional substance use norms (NIDA, 1997).
Use of "gateway" substances	• Using "gateway" substances such as cigarettes, alcohol and cannabis is associated with substance use disorder among youth (Ballon, in press).	
Age (and grade transitions)	• Prevalence of mental health problems increases with grade level during adolescence. For example, the transition from grade 7 to 8 (young people aged 12 or 13) is associated with an increased likelihood of experiencing suicide ideation, delinquency, and hazardous drinking (Adlaf et al., 2002).	

APPENDIX A: RISK AND PROTECTIVE FACTORS FOR POTENTIAL SUBSTANCE USE AND MENTAL HEALTH PROBLEMS

RISK FACTORS	POTENTIAL SUBSTANCE USE AND MENTAL HEALTH PROBLEMS AMONG YOUNG PEOPLE	PROTECTIVE FACTORS
Individual situation (contd.)		
	Prevalence of mental health problems peaks in grades 10 and 11 (among young people aged 15 or 16). Between grades 10 and 11, the likelihood of low self-esteem, psychological distress and hazardous drinking increases. Youth in Grade 13 are more likely to engage in pathological gambling and hazardous drinking than those in Grade 12 (Adlaf et al., 2002).	
	• The likelihood of hazardous drinking and illicit drug use (including cannabis) increases between grades 8 and 9 (young people aged 13 and 14). Young people in Grade 10 (age 15) are more likely to engage in hazardous drinking than those in Grade 9 (Adlaf et al., 2002).	
Peer relationships:		
Peer teasing, harassment and rejection	• May alienate youth, contribute to conduct disorders and violence and lead to school and social phobia (Patterson, 2002).	• Affiliation with peer groups that encourage academic achievement and school engagement contribute to youth competence and mental health.
Violent acts by peers in schools	• Traumatizes students and contributes to anxiety and other disorders (Patterson, 2002).	
Negative peer pressure, modeling of deviant, unhealthy behaviours	• Could adversely affect mental health, particularly during critical transitions such as going through puberty or changing schools (Patterson, 2002).	
Lack of positive role models or idealization of poor role models	• Associated with substance use problems among youth (Ballon, in press).	
Associating with peers engaged in deviant behaviours or peers with conduct and/or substance use problems	• Associated with substance use problems among youth (Ballon, in press, NIDA, 1997).	
Culture of thinness among young women	• Eating disorders may flourish among girls who are strongly influenced by peers who promote a "culture of thinness" (Patterson, 2002).	

APPENDIX A: RISK AND PROTECTIVE FACTORS FOR POTENTIAL SUBSTANCE USE AND MENTAL HEALTH PROBLEMS

RISK FACTORS	POTENTIAL SUBSTANCE USE AND MENTAL HEALTH PROBLEMS AMONG YOUNG PEOPLE	PROTECTIVE FACTORS
School and community environment/societal conditions Perceived approval of substance use among peer, school and community environments	• Associated with substance use problems among youth (NIDA, 1997).	• Strong affiliation with prosocial institutions including family, school, and religious organizations (NIDA, 1997).
Lack of academic achievement	• Young people who do not do well in school are more likely to engage in risky behaviours. Students who report a C average or below are more likely to report low self-esteem. They are also more likely to report externalizing problems such as delinquency, pathological gambling, hazardous drinking, any illicit drug use (Adlaf et al., 2002). Failure in school is associated with substance use problems (NIDA, 1997).	
Lack of attachment to school	• Young people who do not feel attached or connected to their school are more likely to experience internalizing problems such as low self-esteem, depression and suicide ideation. They are also more likely to report illicit drug use (excluding cannabis) (Adlaf et al., 2002).	• Supportive relationships with adult community members including religious leaders or teachers.
Feeling unsafe at school	• Young people, who feel that their safety at school is threatened, are more likely to report internalizing problems including low self-esteem, depressive symptoms, psychological distress and suicide ideation. They are less likely, however, to use illicit drugs (Adlaf et al., 2002).	• Positive, proactive linkages between families and schools involving two-way communication and parent involvement.
Poor quality schools	• Schools that have only low levels of academic achievement, problematic relationships between teachers, parents and the school, and lack effective leadership increase the likelihood of behaviour problems and depression among young people (Patterson, 2002).	• Positive linkages and balance between parents' home and work environments, and work environments that support the work-family balance.

APPENDIX A: RISK AND PROTECTIVE FACTORS FOR POTENTIAL SUBSTANCE USE AND MENTAL HEALTH PROBLEMS

RISK FACTORS	POTENTIAL SUBSTANCE USE AND MENTAL HEALTH PROBLEMS AMONG YOUNG PEOPLE	PROTECTIVE FACTORS
School and community environment/societal conditions (contd.)		
Low income/low socioeconomic status	• Poverty and deprivation are predictors of long-term problems such as criminality, mental health issues and reliance on state care (Schwartz, 1997). Low income is a significant independent predictor of psychiatric disorder among children (Offord et al., 1989). Economic stress on families impacts upon children's mental health, particularly in the context of problems such as family conflict, mental health problems and alcohol abuse that can emerge (Patterson, 2002). Low socioeconomic status is associated with substance use problems among youth (Ballon, in press).	• Public social policies that ensure adequate income for families, provide community resources to support family life, and empower parents to nurture their children, and foster healthy child development and mental health.
Community or neighbourhood problems	• Criminal gang activity and lack of community safety are associated with substance use problems among youth (Ballon, in press). • Prolonged economic hardship affects family relationships and increases the likelihood that young people will experience other community problems that threaten their well-being including violence, drug trafficking, aggressive peers, gang involvement, alcohol and drug use, school truancy and failure, and involvement with the criminal justice system. Poor communities tend to have social disorder, incivility, high residential mobility and weak social ties. Experiencing sustained fear of crime is associated with deteriorating mental health. Children in impoverished communities may grow up angry and without hope (Patterson, 2002). • Both availability of drugs and trafficking patterns are associated with substance use problems (NIDA, 1997).	• Social capital, including connections between neighbours and a sense of community belonging. Social capital is associated with a sense of collective efficacy, community organization, collective socialization, more neighbourhood resources, and information about, and access to social resources (Patterson, 2002). • Co-ordinated, comprehensive, affordable, high quality health and education resources. • Availability of age-relevant community resources, such as high quality childcare, libraries, parks, recreation facilities, etc.
Discrimination and racism	• Discrimination and racism compound the risks experienced by marginalized groups of young people.	

Adapted from Adlaf et al. (2002); Ballon (in press); National Institute on Drug Abuse (NIDA) (1997); Offord et al. (1989); Patterson (2002); Schwartz (1997) and Trupin & Boesky (2001). Please note that this information is neither exhaustive nor presented in order of priority.

APPENDIX B: SUBSTANCE USE AND MENTAL HEALTH SERVICES FOR YOUTH IN ONTARIO: A COMPARATIVE OVERVIEW

COMPARATIVE OVERVIEW	SUBSTANCE USE SERVICES FOR YOUTH	MENTAL HEALTH SERVICES FOR YOUTH
Funding and mandate	The Ontario Ministry of Health and Long-Term Care funds most addiction services in Ontario. Services vary in terms of age criteria for admission. Some services, including most assessment and referral services accept clients up to 99 years of age. Youth outpatient programs that have age criteria generally accept youth from 12 years and up. Residential programs vary. Some serve young adults only (e.g., approximately 16 – 24 years old), while others serve adolescents only.	There are two types of specialized mental health services for youth in Ontario: • Hospital-based services (either designated psychiatric or general hospital beds in general hospitals or specialized psychiatric facilities) are funded by the Ontario Ministry of Health and Long-Term Care. The availability of psychiatric services varies widely across the province. While some communities have very specialized services, others have only general hospital services, and still others do not have any psychiatric services at all. In some cases, young people are put in adult psychiatric beds. • Community-based, multidisciplinary children's mental health services are funded by the Ontario Ministry of Community and Social Services/Ministry of Children's Services. Children's mental health is a distinct sector that is linked to, but separate from medical interventions for children's mental health. There is some crossover funding, and centres in some communities have developed protocols with the hospital-based services. In many communities, there is no formal linkage between the children's mental health centre and the hospital. In practice, however, hospitals may contact centres when young patients are being discharged. Centres could require the assistance of the hospital in situations of crises (e.g., when a young person needs hospitalization for an eating disorder or suicide). Each of the 85 children's mental health centres in Ontario serves a specific age group, which varies by centre. Some serve children up to 6 years of age; others serve young people up to the age of 16 or 18; still others serve young people who are in their twenties. Some centres specialize in treating specific disorders.
Providers and services	Staff of addiction services have a variety of professional backgrounds and training. They include: • certified addiction counsellors • nurses • social workers • psychologists • psychiatrists.	Depending on the setting, mental health treatment services for young people may be provided by: • psychiatrists • nurses • psychologists • social workers • child and youth workers.

APPENDIX B: SUBSTANCE USE AND MENTAL HEALTH SERVICES FOR YOUTH IN ONTARIO: A COMPARATIVE OVERVIEW

COMPARATIVE OVERVIEW	SUBSTANCE USE SERVICES FOR YOUTH	MENTAL HEALTH SERVICES FOR YOUTH
Providers and services (Continued)	Assessment/referral centres provide entry services (initial inquiry, intake, screening) and assessment and referral services. They offer short-term counselling (up to 4 sessions) only. However, in larger communities, other community addiction services also provide an assessment/referral function. Clients requiring other care are referred to community (or outpatient) services, day/evening treatment or residential care.	Social workers and child and youth workers are the primary staff in children's mental health centres. They may also have access to psychiatric consultation (via telepsychiatry or a psychiatrist who spends some days per week on site).
	The vast majority of specialized substance use treatment services for youth are community based (outpatient services). Community (or outpatient) treatment programs are less intensive programs in which young people attend weekly (individual or group) treatment sessions.	The vast majority of children's mental health services are outpatient services.
	There are some day (or evening) programs, which offer more intensive treatment on a daily basis. These may include a school component (under Section 19 of the Education Act.)	There are some day-treatment programs, which include a school component (Section 19 under the Education Act). In these programs, class size is kept small and the teacher works closely with a youth worker who provides behavioural/emotional support. The classrooms may be located at the children's mental health centre, in a local school or in a community centre. The goal is to help young people reintegrate into the regular school system.
	Short-or long-term residential treatment is not readily available in many parts of the province. A small number of addiction programs in Ontario are operated by hospitals, a few are youth specific, while others accept young people aged 16 and older. In some cases, young people may be referred to: • short- and long-term programs such as recovery homes, halfway houses, three quarter way houses and therapeutic communities, although most are not intended for youth.	The availability of residential treatment varies, depending on the community. There are also intensive in-home services and crisis services. Many children's mental health services are involved in wrap-around services for young people and families in communities. Hospital-based mental health services for young people include in-patient and out-patient services (or young people are referred to the children's mental health centre for treatment).

APPENDIX B: SUBSTANCE USE AND MENTAL HEALTH SERVICES FOR YOUTH IN ONTARIO: A COMPARATIVE OVERVIEW

COMPARATIVE OVERVIEW	SUBSTANCE USE SERVICES FOR YOUTH	MENTAL HEALTH SERVICES FOR YOUTH
Providers and services (continued)	• existing residential services in other sectors in conjunction with an addictions day treatment program. (e.g. young people may reside in open custody, children's mental health centres or group homes, and attend day/evening treatment in the community) (Schwartz, 1997). There are no youth-specific withdrawal management services available in Ontario. Usually, young people will receive support in the community rather than entering adult detox facilities. Various models of community-based withdrawal management are being piloted in the province. Some young people also attend mutual-aid groups (e.g., Alcoholics Anonymous [AA] or Narcotics Anonymous [NA]). In some communities, youth-specific, mutual-aid groups may be developed, depending on local need and resources. Programs may also provide outreach services to young people in other settings including schools, youth agencies and correctional facilities. Older youth may also access adult substance use treatment services. Family support is an important component of addiction services for young people. In addition to treatment provided by specialized addiction services, young people and their families may also receive substance use counselling and other related services from: • school system (guidance counsellors, social workers or psychologists) • children's mental health services • community health and social service agencies (including child welfare services)	Beyond the community and hospital-based children's mental health centres, young people can receive treatment and support for mental health problems through a wide range of other services including: • school board programs for children with special needs • child protection services • young offender services. A report on the status of mental health services for school-aged children and youth in Ontario emphasized that many different services play a supportive role. These include: • school and community-based programs such as after-school recreation programs • mental health workers working on-site in schools • parks and recreation programs

COMPARATIVE OVERVIEW	SUBSTANCE USE SERVICES FOR YOUTH	MENTAL HEALTH SERVICES FOR YOUTH
Providers and services (continued)	• primary health care settings (doctors' and other health care providers working in physician's offices, health clinics, emergency departments, etc.) • young offenders' services (correctional system personnel).	• programs offered by non-profit organizations such as Boys and Girls clubs, Big Sister and Big Brother • peer-based programs • wraparound services • case management • in-patient treatment facilities (Browne, et al., 2001).
Substance use/mental health focus	Some substance use services have developed close links with medical/psychiatric services in their community to serve young people with concurrent disorders. Alternatively, as in the case of Youth Addiction Services (CAMH), the program team provides treatment for substance use and mental health within the same program.	The extent to which hospital-based or community-based children's mental health services are providing treatment for substance use is not clear. There is recognition that substance use is a problem that requires resolution, and some community-based centres have group programs that address substance use. At this time, however, there are no children's mental health accreditation standards related to substance use treatment, and many children's mental health providers have somewhat limited knowledge about how to address substance use. In terms of identifying substance use problems, however, both children's mental health centres and hospitals are now using standardized protocols including a standardized intake tool called Brief Child Family Phone Interview (BCFPI), which asks about substance use. The BCFPI is a computerized screening tool, which develops a profile of problem clustering. The Child & Adolescent Functional Assessment Scale (CAFAS) is also being implemented as a tool to assess functioning.

APPENDIX B: SUBSTANCE USE AND MENTAL HEALTH SERVICES FOR YOUTH IN ONTARIO: A COMPARATIVE OVERVIEW

COMPARATIVE OVERVIEW	SUBSTANCE USE SERVICES FOR YOUTH	MENTAL HEALTH SERVICES FOR YOUTH
How young people enter services	Few young people present for treatment on their own initiative. Most are referred by adults (most often parents) when they: • are found using drugs • display behaviours that could indicate substance use (e.g., they appear intoxicated, have poor academic performance, become withdrawn or socially isolated, have peers who use substances, or experience conflict with family members). Once referred, most young people enter treatment "voluntarily" as a result of pressure from parents, school authorities, youth counsellors or probation officers.	Few young people present for treatment at children's mental health centres on their own initiative. Most are referred by adults (parents, teachers or child welfare workers) who become concerned about their behaviour. For example, they may be displaying symptoms such as aggression, anger, depression, self-injury, or social withdrawal. Once referred, most young people enter treatment "voluntarily."
Substance use/mental health focus (continued)	Some young people are mandated to attend treatment by the courts.	Some young people may be court-ordered to seek, residential treatment, for example. Within the hospital-based mental health system, a psychiatrist can sign a form to have a young person admitted to hospital. Young people who are suicidal are usually hospitalized. In general, hospitals tend to serve young people with internalizing disorders (major depression, severe anxiety, eating disorders), while children's mental health centres more often work with young people with disruptive behaviour disorders (conduct disorders, oppositional defiant disorder or youth who have assaulted others). However, some young people who assault others enter the young offenders' system.
Philosophy and trends	Within most addiction services, there is an emphasis on: • youth-specific treatment • the bio-psychosocial model of treatment • least intrusive treatment • involvement of family members or other significant people in the young person's life	There are some secure custody treatment facilities, such as the Syl Apps Youth Centre at Kinark Child and Family Services in Oakville, Ontario but the admission process is very stringent and highly scrutinized. These facilities provide very specialized services for young people who have committed serious offences such as murder.

APPENDIX B: SUBSTANCE USE AND MENTAL HEALTH SERVICES FOR YOUTH IN ONTARIO: A COMPARATIVE OVERVIEW

COMPARATIVE OVERVIEW	SUBSTANCE USE SERVICES FOR YOUTH	MENTAL HEALTH SERVICES FOR YOUTH
Philosophy and trends (continued)	• evidence-based interventions and best practices • permitting young people to choose non-abstinent treatment goals, although the ultimate or preferred goal of treatment might eventually be abstinence • harm reduction approaches (see section 2.6), particularly for young people who are hard to reach and serve, including those who inject drugs or are living on the streets • assessing young people's readiness for change and tailoring interventions accordingly (see section 3.7.8) • using motivational interviewing techniques (see section 4.3) • using cognitive behaviour strategies (see section 4.7) • case management to provide young people and their families with support and access throughout treatment (see section 3.10) • standardized assessment tools (see Appendix F) and admission and discharge criteria • integrated service delivery • flexible hours and locations • outreach.	Children's mental health services emphasize the same list as for substance use treatment. However: • Children's mental health services do not use a medical model. Most are highly strengths-focussed and client- and family-centred (encourage client and family input into the goals and methods of treatment). • Centres are striving to balance the strengths-based, family- and client-centred focus with evidence-based best practice information for treating specific disorders. • Children's mental health centres may or may not have access to diagnostic services, but many of the young people they work with would already have diagnoses. • Youth-specific treatment is very important because children and youth display emotional problems differently than adults. • Multi-modal interventions are very important to address multiple domains in young people's lives. Most young people have multiple co-morbid problems such as conduct disorders plus depression and/or substance use. Appropriate interventions depend on each individual's strengths and needs. • Family involvement is a central focus within children's mental health. • There is a big movement to find alternatives to residential treatment (e.g., providing intensive in-home services [which may be called family or home preservation]). • Multisystemic therapy (MST) is an evidence-based alternative for youth with multiple problems. • Although there is a belief in including preventive strategies, there are limited resources available to do this.

APPENDIX B: SUBSTANCE USE AND MENTAL HEALTH SERVICES FOR YOUTH IN ONTARIO: A COMPARATIVE OVERVIEW

COMPARATIVE OVERVIEW	SUBSTANCE USE SERVICES FOR YOUTH	MENTAL HEALTH SERVICES FOR YOUTH
Philosophy and trends (continued)		• Efforts to make contact with difficult-to-reach youth and parents include drop-in centres, school services (e.g., mental health workers in schools, evening appointments, 24/7 crisis support, weekend counselling services and residential satellite programs in high-risk neighbourhoods). • There is a big emphasis on co-ordination and integration of services and community partnerships. Within hospital-based mental health services, the medical model is used. There is an emphasis on formal diagnosis and medically oriented treatment (including medication). Usually, youth are admitted by physicians and are under the care of psychiatrists. The approach is to stabilize and then discharge them as quickly as possible so they can return either to their families, substitute families or residential treatment services. Long-term hospitalization is extremely rare. The duration of residential treatment averages only about one year and often is much shorter. Typically, during a hospital stay, young persons and their families will be assessed and directions for treatment will be developed. Often, children's mental health centres implement the treatment plan.
Treatment approaches	Individual, group and/or family therapy is provided in all treatment structures. Group formats are central, particularly in day and residential programs, since young people may be more responsive to peers than adult influence. Most programs use a range of models and approaches including bio-psychosocial, cognitive behavioural, harm reduction, 12-Step, stages of change and motivational interviewing. Specific treatment interventions include: • brief interventions (e.g., *First Contact* • social skills training (group) • recreational or leisure counselling (group)	Children's mental health centres offer multi-modal interventions delivered in individual and group formats. Family interventions are very important and may occur on several levels including family therapy (myriad models), parent education and training in dealing with behaviour, and intensive in-home support services for families. In-school support interventions are also provided through partnerships between children's mental health centres and the education system in Ontario. Intensive, therapeutic, after-school or day programs are also offered. Treatment consists of specific interventions for specific problem areas (e.g., treatment for young people who have experienced abuse-based trauma such as sexual abuse. Treatment may encompass individual, family and group therapy, play therapy, art therapy, education, parent training, behaviour management, life skills training, social skills training, health education and problem-solving groups.

APPENDIX B: SUBSTANCE USE AND MENTAL HEALTH SERVICES FOR YOUTH IN ONTARIO: A COMPARATIVE OVERVIEW

COMPARATIVE OVERVIEW	SUBSTANCE USE SERVICES FOR YOUTH	MENTAL HEALTH SERVICES FOR YOUTH
Treatment approaches (continued)	• problem solving (group) • social support development (group) • relapse prevention • family therapy, including parent education and training • pharmacotherapy (providing medication when needed) • other psychosocial rehabilitation and supports (including crisis management).	Motivational interviewing and assessment of stages of change are not formally used in mental health. Cognitive behaviour therapy is a valuable component of mental health treatment and is a recommended practice for conduct disorders and depression. However, there is still some concern that it's not a panacea, and thus is not emphasized, although it is gaining support and interest in the literature.

(Adapted from Browne et al. (2001); Carver, Virginia (personal communication); Johnston, Joanne (personal communication); Ontario Substance Abuse Bureau and Ontario Addiction Services Advisory Council (2000); Schwartz (1997) and Tupker, Elsbeth (personal communication).

ALCOHOL

STREET NAMES
booze, sauce, drink

WHAT IS IT?
Alcohol is a "depressant" drug. That means it slows down the parts of your brain that affect your thinking and behaviour, as well as your breathing and heart rate. The use of alcohol has been traced as far back as 8000 BC, and is common in many cultures today.

WHERE DOES ALCOHOL COME FROM?
Alcohol is produced by fermenting, and sometimes distilling, various fruits, vegetables or grains. Fermented beverages include beer and wine, which have a maximum alcohol content of about 15 per cent. Distilled beverages, often called "hard liquor" or "spirits," such as rum, whiskey and vodka, have a higher alcohol content.

Although alcohol comes in different forms, it has the same effect. In the following table, each "standard" drink contains 13.6 grams of alcohol.

WHAT DOES IT LOOK LIKE?
Pure (ethyl) alcohol is a clear, colourless liquid. Alcoholic beverages get their distinctive colours from their other ingredients, and from the process of fermentation.

WHO USES ALCOHOL?
Research reports that alcohol use among Ontarians age 18 and older was 87 per cent in 1992 and 79 per cent in 1999. Even though our laws restrict alcohol use to those 19 years of age and over, a 2001 survey of Ontario students in grades 7 to OAC found that 66 per cent reported using alcohol in the past year, and 27 per cent had been drunk at least once in the past four weeks.

In general, men drink more than women do, and are almost twice as likely to have drinking problems.

HOW DOES ALCOHOL MAKE YOU FEEL?
The way alcohol affects you depends on many factors, including:
- your age, sex and body weight
- how sensitive you are to alcohol
- the type and amount of food in your stomach
- how much and how often you drink
- how long you've been drinking
- the environment you're in
- how you expect the alcohol to make you feel
- whether you've taken any other drugs (illicit, prescription, over-the-counter or herbal).

For many people, a single drink of alcohol releases tension and reduces inhibition, making them feel more at ease and outgoing. Some people feel happy or excited when they drink, while others become depressed or hostile. Suicide and violent crimes often involve alcohol.

Women are generally more sensitive to the effects of alcohol than men, and all adults become increasingly sensitive to alcohol's effects as they age. When someone is more sensitive, it takes less alcohol to cause intoxication, and more time for the body to eliminate the alcohol consumed.

Early signs of alcohol intoxication include flushed skin, impaired judgment and reduced inhibition. Continued drinking increases these effects, and causes other effects, such as impaired attention, reduced muscle control, slowed reflexes, staggering gait, slurred speech and double or blurred vision. A severely intoxicated person may "black out," and have no memory of what was said or done while drinking. Effects of extreme intoxication include inability to stand, vomiting, stupor, coma and death.

HOW LONG DOES THE FEELING LAST?
It takes about one hour for the liver of a person weighing 70 kg (154 lbs.) to process and eliminate eight to 10 grams of alcohol, or about two-thirds of the alcohol contained in a standard drink. This rate is constant, no matter how much alcohol has been consumed, or what food or non-alcoholic beverages are taken.

Drinking heavily usually results in a "hangover," beginning eight to 12 hours after the last drink. Symptoms can include headache, nausea, diarrhea, shakiness and vomiting. A hangover is caused in part by acetaldehyde, a toxic chemical that is created as alcohol is processed by your liver. Other causes include dehydration and changes in hormone levels.

Some people think that having a drink before bed helps them to get to sleep. While alcohol does bring on sleep more quickly, it disturbs sleep patterns, and causes wakefulness in the night.

IS ALCOHOL DANGEROUS?
Yes, alcohol can be dangerous in a number of ways.

APPENDIX C: DO YOU KNOW...

The impact of alcohol's effect on judgment, behaviour, attitude and reflexes can range from embarrassment, to unwanted or high-risk sexual contact, to violence, injury or death. Alcohol is involved in more regrettable moments, crimes and traffic fatalities than all other drugs of abuse combined. Young people, who are less familiar with the effects of alcohol, may be especially prone to act in an impulsive or dangerous manner while intoxicated.

Extreme intoxication can kill, often as the result of the person "passing out," vomiting and choking. A person who has been drinking heavily and is unconscious should be laid on his or her side and watched closely. Clammy skin, low body temperature, slow and laboured breathing and incontinence are signs of acute alcohol poisoning, which can be fatal. Seek emergency medical care.

Women who drink during pregnancy risk giving birth to a baby with behaviour problems, growth deficiency, developmental disability, head and facial deformities, joint and limb abnormalities and heart defects. The risk of bearing a child with these birth defects increases with the amount of alcohol consumed. The first trimester may be a time of greatest risk for the fetus, although there is no time during pregnancy when it is known to be safe to drink alcohol.

Mixing alcohol with other drugs—prescribed or recreational—can have unpredictable results. Alcohol may either block the absorption of the other drug, making it less effective, or it may increase the effect of the other drug, to the point of danger. The general rule is to never mix alcohol with any other drugs; for exceptions, ask your doctor.

IS THERE A SAFE LEVEL OF DRINKING?
While there is no precise "safe" level of drinking, there are guidelines for adults who wish to lower the risks of drinking. People who are pregnant, who have certain medical conditions such as liver disease or mental illness, or who will be driving a vehicle or operating machinery, should avoid alcohol.

The "low-risk drinking" guidelines suggest spacing drinks an hour apart, and drinking no more than two standard drinks per drinking occasion. Men should have no more than 14 drinks a week, and women no more than nine.

IS ALCOHOL ADDICTIVE?
It can be.

Most alcohol-related illnesses, social problems, accidents and deaths are caused by "problem drinking." This term describes alcohol use that causes problems in a person's life, but does not include physical dependence. Problem drinking is four times as common as severe alcohol dependence.

Physical dependence involves tolerance to alcohol's effects, and withdrawal symptoms when drinking is stopped. As people develop tolerance, they need more and more alcohol to produce the desired effect. People who are physically dependent on alcohol can develop withdrawal symptoms, such as sleeplessness, tremors, nausea and seizures, within a few hours after their last drink. These symptoms can last from two to seven days and range from mild to severe, depending on the amount of alcohol consumed and the period of time over which it was used. Some people experience *delirium tremens*, or "the DTs," five to six days after drinking stops. This dangerous syndrome consists of frightening hallucinations, extreme confusion, fever and racing heart. If left untreated, severe alcohol withdrawal can result in death.

Treatment for alcohol dependence usually begins by treating withdrawal symptoms, but most people will need additional treatments to help them stop drinking. Even after long periods of abstinence, a person may continue to crave alcohol, and may begin to drink again. Treatment may include residential or outpatient treatment, individual or group therapy, self-help or mutual help groups, such as Alcoholics Anonymous, and certain medications, such as naltrexone. Some people respond well to one form of treatment, while others do not. There is no single most effective treatment approach.

WHAT ARE THE LONG-TERM EFFECTS OF DRINKING ALCOHOL?
How alcohol affects you in the long term depends on how much and how often you drink.

For middle-aged and older adults, as little as one drink of alcohol every other day can help protect against heart disease. On the other hand, heavy drinking raises blood pressure and puts people at risk of stroke and heart failure.

Heavy alcohol use can result in appetite loss, sexual impotence or menstrual irregularities, vitamin deficiencies and infections. Alcohol irritates the lining of the stomach, which can be painful and is potentially fatal. Alcoholic liver disease is a major cause of illness and death in North America. Alcohol also increases the risk of liver, throat, breast and other cancers.

APPENDIX C: DO YOU KNOW...

Chronic use of alcohol can damage the brain, which can lead to dementia, difficulties with co-ordination and motor control, and loss of feeling or painful burning in the feet. Alcohol dependence often results in clinical depression, and the rate of suicide among people who are alcohol-dependent is six times that of the general population.

Although women's average lifetime alcohol intake is less than half that of men, women are just as likely as men to develop alcohol-related diseases, and are twice as likely to die from these conditions.

ALCOHOL AND THE LAW
Provincial and federal laws regulate the manufacture, distribution, importation, advertising, possession and consumption of alcohol.

In Ontario it is illegal for anyone under 19 years of age to possess, consume or purchase alcohol; it is also illegal to sell or supply alcohol to anyone known to be or appearing to be (unless that person has proof otherwise) under the age of 19, or to sell or supply alcohol to anyone who appears to be intoxicated. Anyone who sells or supplies alcohol to others may be held civilly liable if people (including patrons of a tavern or restaurant and guests in a private home) injure themselves or others while intoxicated.

Federal criminal law sets out a range of drinking and driving offences. For more information, see "Do You Know...Alcohol, Other Drugs and Driving."

ALCOHOL, OTHER DRUGS AND DRIVING

HOW DO ALCOHOL AND OTHER DRUGS AFFECT DRIVING?
When you drive, your hands, eyes and feet control the vehicle, and your brain controls your hands, eyes and feet. To drive safely, you need to be alert, aware and able to make quick decisions in response to a rapidly changing environment.

Alcohol and other drugs alter the normal function of the brain and body, and interfere with even the most skilled and experienced driver's ability to drive safely. While different drugs can have different effects on driving, any drug that slows you down, speeds you up or changes the way you see things can affect your driving— too often with tragic consequences.

ALCOHOL AND OTHER DEPRESSANT DRUGS
Alcohol blunts alertness and reduces motor co-ordination. People who drive after using alcohol can't react as quickly when they need to. Their vision is affected, and may be blurred or doubled.

Alcohol alters depth perception, making it hard to tell whether other vehicles, pedestrians or objects are close or far away. And because alcohol affects judgment, people who drive after drinking may feel overconfident and not recognize that their driving skills are reduced. Their driving is more likely to be careless or reckless— weaving, speeding, driving off the road and, too often, crashing.

Alcohol is a depressant drug, which means it slows down your brain and body. Other depressant drugs, including some prescription drugs such as sedatives and painkillers, affect a person's ability to drive safely, in a way similar to alcohol. Any drug that causes drowsiness, including some cough, cold or allergy medications, can also affect a person's ability to drive safely. When alcohol and another depressant drug are combined, the effect is more intense and dangerous than the effect of either drug on its own. When taking prescription or over-the-counter medications, it is wise to consult with your doctor or pharmacist before driving.

STIMULANTS
Stimulant drugs, such as caffeine, amphetamines and cocaine, may increase alertness, but this does not mean they improve driving skills. The tired driver who drinks coffee to stay awake on the road should be aware that the stimulant effect can wear off suddenly, and that the only remedy for fatigue is to pull off the road, and sleep. Amphetamines do not seem to affect driving skills when taken at medical doses, but they do make some people over-confident, which can lead to risky driving. Higher doses of amphetamines often make people hostile and aggressive.

People who use cocaine are also likely to feel confident about their driving ability. But cocaine use affects vision, causing blurring, glare and hallucinations. "Snow lights"—weak flashes or movements of light in the peripheral field of vision—tend to make drivers swerve toward or away from the lights. People who use cocaine may also hear sounds that aren't there, such as bells ringing, or smell scents that aren't there, such as smoke or gas, which distract them from their driving.

CANNABIS AND OTHER HALLUCINOGENS
Cannabis impairs depth perception, attention span and concentration, slows reaction time, and decreases muscle strength and hand steadiness—all of which can affect a person's ability to drive safely.

The effects of hallucinogenic drugs, such as LSD, ecstasy, mescaline and psilocybin, distort perception and mood. Driving while under the influence of any of these drugs is extremely dangerous.

APPENDIX C: DO YOU KNOW...

WHAT IS BLOOD ALCOHOL CONTENT?

When you drink alcohol, it goes directly from your stomach into your bloodstream. Blood alcohol content (BAC), or percentage of alcohol in your blood, can be measured by police with a breathalyzer or blood test. Under provincial laws in the Ontario Highway Traffic Act, a .05 BAC can result in a 12-hour licence suspension. The Criminal Code of Canada sets the "legal limit" for drinking and driving at .08 BAC. Ontario drivers with a level one or two graduated licence must maintain a zero BAC.

Because people react differently to the effects of alcohol, it is very difficult for a person to judge his or her own BAC. A person may not feel "drunk," but may still be legally impaired.

IS THERE SOME WAY I CAN QUICKLY "SOBER UP" IF I'VE BEEN DRINKING AND NEED TO DRIVE HOME?

No. Once a person consumes alcohol, it enters the bloodstream, and only time can reduce the concentration of alcohol in the blood. It takes about an hour for the average human body to process and eliminate two-thirds of the alcohol in one standard drink. This rate is constant, meaning that the more you drink, the longer time you need to wait before driving. Drinking coffee or other caffeinated beverages might make you more alert, but your ability to drive will still be impaired.

HOW MANY ACCIDENTS INVOLVE DRIVERS WHO HAVE BEEN DRINKING ALCOHOL OR USING OTHER DRUGS?

About 1,350 people die each year in Canada in motor vehicle crashes involving a drinking driver, and many more are seriously injured or disabled. In Ontario in 1997, alcohol was involved in 39 per cent of motor vehicle fatalities, 45 per cent of marine vehicle fatalities and 64 per cent of snowmobile and all-terrain vehicle fatalities. Drinking and driving is the largest single criminal cause of death and injury in Canada.

The role of other drugs, used on their own or in combination with alcohol, is not routinely assessed in traffic accidents, but is known to be an important factor in many road deaths. When people involved in traffic accidents were tested for the presence of drugs in a 1992 study, the drug found most often was alcohol. However, the total number of positive test results for all drugs other than alcohol was greater than the number of positive test results for alcohol alone. After alcohol, the most commonly detected drugs were cannabis, benzodiazepines and cocaine.

Young people who drink and drive may be particularly at risk for being involved in a motor vehicle accident because they have less experience with driving, and are more likely to engage in risk-taking behaviour.

WHO ARE THE PEOPLE WHO DRINK AND DRIVE?

Studies have found that people who have been convicted of impaired driving offenses come from many different backgrounds, age and income groups. Such studies have also identified certain characteristics of people who drink and drive. Looking at convicted drinking drivers, we see that:

· most are male
· a high proportion are "heavy" drinkers
· many have an "antisocial attitude," meaning they lack respect for the law and the safety of others, and
· of those who are convicted of drinking and driving, almost all report having driven while under the influence many times before.

WHAT ARE WE DOING TO REDUCE IMPAIRED DRIVING?

Impaired driving of any vehicle is a criminal offense with strict penalties under federal and provincial law. Such penalties include suspension of the driver's licence, fines, jail sentences, treatment and education.

The term "impaired" refers to not only the effects of alcohol, but also other drugs. More charges are laid for impaired driving offenses, and more court resources are devoted to the prosecution of these charges, than any other offense in Ontario.

Drivers who either fail or refuse a breathalyser test can be charged. In Ontario, a charge of driving with a BAC over .08 or refusing to provide a breath sample brings an automatic 90-day suspension of the driver's licence.

Penalties for impaired driving convictions vary depending on the number of times a person has been convicted of that offense. A first conviction results in the suspension of the driver's licence for one year and a $600 fine; a second conviction results in a three-year suspension of the driver's licence, plus a 14-day jail sentence; and a third conviction results in a lifetime suspension of the driver's licence (which can be reduced to 10 years if certain conditions are met) and 90 days in jail. With a fourth conviction, there is no possibility of that person ever having an Ontario driver's licence again, plus he or she must spend another 90 days in jail. People who are caught driving while their licence is suspended will have the

APPENDIX C: DO YOU KNOW...

vehicle impounded (whether or not they are the actual owner) and face stiff fines.

In addition to these penalties, any person convicted of impaired driving in Ontario, and who wishes to have his or her driver's licence reinstated, must pay for and complete the remedial measures program "Back on Track." Components of the program include assessment, education or treatment and follow-up.

Some laws regarding impaired driving apply to people who serve alcohol, whether it's in a public place, such as a restaurant or bar, or in a private home. For example, if you had a party, and one of your guests drove away after drinking too much and caused an accident, you could be sued for damages. Everyone who serves alcohol has the responsibility to ensure that his or her patrons or guests do not get behind the wheel after drinking too much.

Other measures to prevent and control drinking and driving include widespread public awareness campaigns and the RIDE (Reduce Impaired Driving Everywhere) program, which allows police to stop drivers to check for alcohol use.

Physicians who have reason to believe that a patient may not be able to drive safely due to a medical condition—such as a serious alcohol problem or alcohol dependence—must, by law, notify the Ministry of Transportation. The Ministry may suspend the driver's licence indefinitely, pending a review by a substance-use professional.

ARE PEOPLE MORE CAUTIOUS ABOUT DRINKING AND DRIVING THAN THEY USED TO BE?

Statistics show a steady decline over the years in the number of crashes involving drinking drivers in Ontario. More people are taking the role of "designated driver" and choosing not to drink alcohol when they know they will be driving. Others prefer leaving the car at home, and taking a cab or public transit.

In 1988, there were 17,995 crashes involving drinking drivers in Ontario, and by 1997, that figure declined by 46 per cent to 9,757. While this trend seems to reflect the positive effect of increased public awareness and stricter laws, drinking and driving continues be a major cause of injury and death.

AMPHETAMINES

TYPES OF AMPHETAMINES
amphetamine, methamphetamine, dextroamphetamine

STREET NAMES
speed, bennies, glass, crystal, crank, pep pills and uppers

See also *Do You Know...Methamphetamine* and *Do You Know...Ecstasy*

WHAT ARE AMPHETAMINES?
The different types of amphetamines—and related drugs such as methylphenidate (e.g., Ritalin®)—are *stimulant* drugs. Stimulants speed up the central nervous system. They act like adrenaline, a hormone that is one of the body's natural stimulants. Other drugs with similar effects include cocaine, ecstasy, ephedrine, caffeine and many others.

WHERE DO AMPHETAMINES COME FROM?
Amphetamines were first introduced in the 1930s as a remedy for nasal congestion, and marketed over-the-counter as an inhaler named Benzedrine. These drugs were also used medically to treat obesity and depression. Different types of amphetamines were available from the 1930s until the 1970s. People eventually found, however, that the medical value of amphetamines is offset by their dangerous effects and high abuse potential (the chance a drug will be abused, cause addiction or be otherwise harmful).

In the 1970s, new laws restricted the medical use of these drugs. Today, only dextroamphetamine (Dexedrine®) and methylphenidate are made for medical use. All other amphetamines are made in illicit laboratories.

WHAT DO AMPHETAMINES LOOK LIKE AND HOW ARE THEY USED?
Pure amphetamines are white, odourless, bitter-tasting crystalline powders. Illicitly prepared amphetamines vary in purity. They may be whitish with traces of gray or pink and may be a coarse powder, or in crystals or chunks. They may smell "fishy" or like ammonia. Methamphetamine resembles shaved glass slivers or clear rock salt.

Amphetamines are injected, smoked, sniffed or taken as pills.

WHO USES AMPHETAMINES?
When amphetamines were easy to get, many people used them to stay awake and to have more energy. Truck drivers, students

APPENDIX C: DO YOU KNOW...

and athletes were especially likely to abuse amphetamines. Even recently, soldiers have been given amphetamines for endurance in battle. People with eating disorders may use these drugs to try to lose weight.

A 2001 survey of Ontario students in grades 7 to OAC found that 4.8 per cent of male and eight per cent of female students reported non-medical use of stimulant drugs (other than cocaine) at least once in the past year.

Medically, dextroamphetamine is used to treat narcolepsy (uncontrolled attacks of sleep) and hyperactivity. Methylphenidate is also commonly used to treat hyperactivity in adults and children. It is less potent than the amphetamines.

HOW DO AMPHETAMINES MAKE YOU FEEL?

How amphetamines make you feel depends on:

- how much you use
- how often and how long you use them
- how you use them (by injection, orally, etc.)
- your mood, expectation and environment
- your age
- whether you have certain pre-existing medical or psychiatric conditions
- whether you've taken any alcohol or other drugs (illicit, prescription, over-the-counter or herbal).

When amphetamines are injected or smoked, they reach the brain quickly, and produce a "rush," or surge of euphoria, immediately.

The effects of amphetamines are often different from person to person. Amphetamines can make people:

- alert, confident and energetic
- talkative, restless and excited
- feel a sense of power and superiority
- tense and nervous
- hostile and aggressive.

In children who are hyperactive, however, amphetamines and related drugs, in the correct doses, can have a calming effect.

Amphetamines reduce hunger and increase breathing, heart rate and blood pressure. Larger doses may cause fever, sweating, headache, nausea, blurred vision, very fast or irregular heartbeat, tremors, loss of co-ordination and collapse.

HOW LONG DOES THE FEELING LAST?

The initial rush after injecting or smoking lasts only a minute. With some types of amphetamines, the stimulant effects can last up to 12 hours. Some people may use amphetamines repeatedly over a period of several days to try to stay high.

ARE AMPHETAMINES DANGEROUS?

Yes.

- Overdose can cause seizures, coma and death due to burst blood vessels in the brain, heart failure or very high fever.
- Amphetamines are linked to risky and violent behaviours, and increased injury and sexually transmitted disease.
- Amphetamines may cause bizarre or repetitive behaviour, paranoia and hallucinations.
- Injecting any drug can cause infections from used needles or impurities in the drug; sharing needles with others can transmit hepatitis or HIV.

ARE AMPHETAMINES ADDICTIVE?

When taken as prescribed, amphetamines and related drugs do not cause dependence. However, these drugs can cause dependence if they are misused. Methylphenidate is less likely to cause dependence than other amphetamines.

Regular non-medical use of amphetamines can lead to *tolerance*. This means that the person needs to take more and more of the drug to get the desired effect. Regular use of amphetamines, especially when the drug is smoked or injected, can quickly cause psychological and physical *dependence*.

Dependence means that cravings and compulsive use of the drug become very important to a person. If drug use is stopped, the person usually goes through *withdrawal*, also called "the crash." Symptoms of withdrawal can include fatigue, restless sleep, irritability, intense hunger, depression, suicidal behaviour and fits of violence.

People who use amphetamines often also use other drugs, such as alcohol, cannabis or benzodiazepines, to help them relax and sleep. This increases the risk for dependence on these other drugs.

WHAT ARE THE LONG-TERM EFFECTS OF TAKING AMPHETAMINES?

Chronic use of amphetamines can lead to serious physical and mental health problems. Because amphetamines reduce appetite and fatigue, they can cause vitamin and sleep deficiencies and malnutrition, and make people more prone to illness.

Regular use of amphetamines can also cause *amphetamine psychosis*. Symptoms include hallucinations, delusions, paranoia, and bizarre and violent behaviour. These symptoms usually disappear a few days or weeks after the drug use has stopped.

Longer-term studies support the efficacy and safety of methylphenidate when taken as prescribed to treat hyperactivity, but more information is needed to evaluate its long-term effects.

ANABOLIC STEROIDS

GENERIC AND TRADE NAMES

oxymotholone (Anadrol®), methandrostenolone (Dianobol®), stanozolol (Winstrol®), nandrolone decanoate (Deca-Durabolin®), testosterone cypionate (Depo-Testosterone®), boldenone undecylenate (Equipoise®) and others

STREET NAMES

the juice, the white stuff, roids

WHAT ARE THEY?

Many kinds of steroids occur naturally in various hormones and vitamins. Drugs known as "anabolic steroids" are made in laboratories and have the same chemical structure as the steroids found in the male sex hormone, testosterone. The muscle-building (anabolic) and masculinizing (androgenic) effects of these drugs make them appealing to athletes and bodybuilders.

Anabolic steroids have few medical uses. Their primary use is to promote weight gain and muscle development in farm animals. They are rarely prescribed to humans; however, they are sometimes used to treat delayed puberty, some types of impotence, and wasting of the body caused by AIDS and other diseases.

Steroidal "supplements," such as dehydroepiandrosterone (DHEA), are converted into testosterone or a similar compound in the body. Although little research has been done on steroidal supplements, if taken in large quantities, they likely produce the same effects, and the same side-effects, as anabolic steroids. DHEA is not available in Canada, but is sold in health food stores and on the Internet in the United States.

WHERE DO STEROIDS COME FROM?

Anabolic steroids manufactured by pharmaceutical companies are available legally only by prescription. Most steroids used by athletes are smuggled, stolen or made in clandestine laboratories. Veterinary drugs are often used.

Although trafficking these drugs is illegal, the penalties imposed tend to be minor. Possession of steroids is legal.

WHAT DO STEROIDS LOOK LIKE, AND HOW ARE THEY USED?

Anabolic steroids come in the form of tablets, capsules, a solution for injection and a cream or gel to rub into the skin. Weightlifters and bodybuilders who use steroids often take doses that are up to 100 times greater than those used to treat medical conditions.

Regimented methods of taking steroids are believed to enhance the effects of these drugs and lessen harm to the body. However, there is no scientific evidence to back up these claims. Such methods include the following:

- Cycling: a period of taking and then not taking the drugs in the belief that the drug-free cycle allows the body to recover normal hormone levels
- Pyramiding: taking doses in cycles of six to 12 weeks, starting with a low dose, then slowly increasing it, and then decreasing the amount to zero, believing this allows the body time to adjust to the high doses
- Stacking: taking two or more types of steroids, mixing oral and injectable forms, believing the different drugs interact to have greater effect.

WHO USES STEROIDS?

Most non-medical use of steroids is by athletes who believe that these drugs will help them to win, and by bodybuilders and young men who think they will look better with bigger muscles.

People who use steroids to improve athletic performance and build muscles are mostly men; however, the highest increase in use is among young women. U.S. studies have also noted a disturbing increase in use among adolescents concerned about body image. Some people take steroids because they have a distorted body image where they believe their muscles are small or that they have too much body fat, even when they are lean and muscular. Steroid use has also been found among people with a history of abuse or assault who wish to build muscles in order to protect themselves better.

APPENDIX C: DO YOU KNOW...

Steroid use is banned by the International Olympic Committee and many other amateur and professional sports organizations. But because drug testing is costly, tests of professional athletes are generally "random," and are often preceded by a warning. Regular mandatory testing is standard only at the international level of competition.

Successful prevention of steroid abuse focuses on teaching people about how to refuse drugs and about other ways to build muscle bulk and strength.

HOW DO STEROIDS MAKE YOU FEEL?
Steroids can produce a variety of psychological effects ranging from euphoria to hostility. Some people who take steroids say the drugs make them feel powerful and energetic. However, steroids are also known to increase irritability, anxiety and aggression and cause mood swings, manic symptoms and paranoia, particularly when taken in high doses.

Variations in how people respond to steroids may be due in part to individual differences, or depend on which type of steroid was taken. Scientific understanding of the effects of non-medical anabolic steroid use is limited.

High doses, especially when taken orally, cause nausea, vomiting and gastric irritation. Other effects include fluid retention and trembling.

ARE STEROIDS DANGEROUS?
Yes. Taking high doses of steroids increases risk of:
- enlargement and abnormalities of the heart, blood clots, high blood pressure, heart attack and stroke. Steroid-related heart failure has occurred in athletes younger than 30.
- aggression and violence ("roid rage"), negative personality change, mania and depression, which may lead to suicide. Depression may persist for a year after drug use is stopped.
- hepatitis, liver enlargement and liver cancer
- reduced fertility in both women and men
- tendon ruptures, cessation of growth in adolescents
- hepatitis or HIV if steroids are injected using shared needles, and infections if steroids are injected with dirty needles.

ARE STEROIDS ADDICTIVE?
Yes, they can be.

Addiction to steroids differs from many other drugs in that tolerance to the effects does not develop. However, some people who abuse steroids meet criteria for drug dependence in that they:

- continue to take steroids, even when they experience negative physical or emotional effects
- spend large amounts of time and money obtaining the drugs
- experience withdrawal symptoms such as mood swings, fatigue, restlessness, depression, loss of appetite, insomnia, reduced sex drive and the desire to take more steroids.

WHAT ARE THE LONG-TERM EFFECTS OF TAKING STEROIDS?
Some of the effects of steroids disappear when drug use is stopped, but others are permanent. The effects of long-term use include:
- acne, cysts, oily hair and skin, and thinning scalp hair in both sexes
- feminization in men, including permanent breast development
- testicle shrinking, difficulty or pain urinating and increased risk of prostate cancer in men
- masculinization in women, including breast size and body fat reduction, coarsening of the skin, enlargement of the clitoris, deepening of the voice, excessive growth of body hair, loss of scalp hair and changes or cessation of the menstrual cycle; with long-term use, some of these effects may be permanent
- in children or adolescents, the high levels of testosterone stop bone growth, preventing them from *ever* growing to full height
- and violence; personality changes revert when drug use is stopped.

BENZODIAZEPINES

GENERIC AND TRADE NAMES
alprazolam (Xanax®), clonazepam (Rivotril®), diazepam (Valium®), flurazepam (Dalmane®), lorazepam (Ativan®), temazepam (Restoril®), triazolam (Halcion®) and others

STREET NAMES
benzos, tranks, downers

WHAT ARE THEY?
Benzodiazepines are a family of prescription drugs that are used mainly to relieve anxiety and to help people sleep. These are sedative drugs, which reduce activity in certain parts of your brain, resulting in a calming effect.

Other uses of benzodiazepines include:
- inducing sedation for surgical and other medical procedures
- treatment of alcohol withdrawal
- controlling seizures
- relaxation of skeletal muscles, such as the back and neck.

APPENDIX C: DO YOU KNOW...

Because they are safer and equally effective, benzodiazepines have replaced older drugs with similar effects, such as barbiturates. There are currently over 50 benzodiazepines in use throughout the world; 14 of these are available in Canada.

In Canada and the United States, benzodiazepines are available legally only by prescription.

WHERE DO BENZODIAZEPINES COME FROM?
All drugs in this family are chemical compounds that are made in the laboratories of pharmaceutical companies.

WHAT DO BENZODIAZEPINES LOOK LIKE?
Benzodiazepines are usually in the form of tablets or capsules, in various colours, which are taken orally. A few of them are also prepared as a solution for injection.

WHO USES BENZODIAZEPINES?
Approximately 10 percent of Canadians report using a benzodiazepine at least once a year, with one in 10 of these people continuing use regularly for more than a year. Although use of these drugs has declined in recent years, they are still one of the most widely prescribed drugs in Canada. Women are prescribed benzodiazepines twice as often as men, and a large proportion of these drugs are prescribed to older adults.

Non-medical use of benzodiazepines does occur, especially among people who abuse other drugs. Some people who abuse other drugs use benzodiazepines to enhance the effect of other sedative drugs, such as opioids and alcohol, or to ease the agitation of drugs that have stimulant effects, such as ecstasy or cocaine. Taking benzodiazepines in combination with other drugs can be dangerous.

Even though women are prescribed benzodiazepines more often than men, an equal number of women and men are treated for misuse of benzodiazepines.

HOW DO BENZODIAZEPINES MAKE YOU FEEL?
Low to moderate doses of benzodiazepines can relieve mild to moderate anxiety and make you feel relaxed and calm. Higher doses can relieve insomnia and severe states of emotional distress, and may make you feel drowsy and possibly clumsy.

Benzodiazepines can impair the ability to learn and remember new information, as well as interfere with the ability to perform certain physical and mental tasks. Learning, memory and performance return to normal once the effect of the drug has worn off.

Side-effects such as confusion, disorientation, amnesia, depression and dizziness may be experienced by some people who take benzodiazepines. Other possible effects, which are extremely rare, include agitation and hallucinations.

The way benzodiazepines affect you depends on many factors, including:
- what condition the medication was prescribed to treat, and the severity of the condition
- the type of benzodiazepine you take
- how much you take and how often you take it
- how long you've been taking it
- if you've taken any alcohol or other drugs (illicit, prescription, over-the-counter or herbal).

HOW LONG DOES THE FEELING LAST?
When taken by mouth, the effects of benzodiazepines may be felt within 30 to 40 minutes or within two to four hours, depending on the type taken. Most benzodiazepines have effects that are felt for several hours. The time it takes to eliminate these drugs from the body also varies depending on the type taken, and ranges from days to weeks.

ARE BENZODIAZEPINES DANGEROUS?
When taken as prescribed, for only a few weeks or months, benzodiazepines are safe. However, as with any other medications, there can be dangers associated with the use of these drugs:
- Benzodiazepines can affect your ability to drive a vehicle or operate equipment safely, and increase the risk of collision, especially if taken in combination with alcohol or certain other drugs.
- When used to induce sleep, benzodiazepines may have some "hangover" effects, such as morning and daytime drowsiness, which may impair your ability to perform tasks requiring alertness.
- Sensitivity to the effects of benzodiazepines increases with age. When older adults take these drugs, they may become confused and have reduced muscle co-ordination, putting them at greater risk of falls, hip fractures and automobile accidents.
- Regular use of benzodiazepines should be reduced gradually. When high doses have been used, medical help may be required. Stopping high-dose use abruptly may cause severe withdrawal symptoms.

APPENDIX C: DO YOU KNOW...

- Dying from an overdose of benzodiazepines alone is rare. Risk of overdose increases when benzodiazepines are combined with other sedatives, such as alcohol or barbiturates, or with medications containing codeine or other opioid drugs. Possible overdose symptoms include slurred speech, confusion, severe drowsiness, weakness and staggering, slow heartbeat, breathing problems and unconsciousness.
- Combined use of benzodiazepines and methadone is particularly dangerous, and may be fatal.
- The risk of birth defects from taking benzodiazepines while pregnant has not been well established. If benzodiazepines are used regularly during pregnancy and particularly close to delivery date, there may be withdrawal symptoms in the newborn.
- Benzodiazepines are excreted through breast milk, which means they are passed on to the baby.
- Certain benzodiazepines have been associated with the facilitation of sexual assault, or "date rape." For more information, see *Do You Know...Rohypnol.*

ARE BENZODIAZEPINES ADDICTIVE?

Psychological and/or physical dependence may develop with the use of benzodiazepines in some people in certain circumstances. The risk of dependence increases when benzodiazepines are taken regularly for more than a few months, especially when they are taken in higher than normal doses.

People who use benzodiazepines may develop *tolerance* to some of their effects. This means that the same dose taken over time no longer has the desired effect. Some people who develop tolerance may take higher and higher doses to feel the same intensity of effect as when they started taking the drug.

People who use benzodiazepines for insomnia often develop tolerance to the sleep-inducing effects within a few weeks of regular use; however, tolerance does not usually develop with occasional use. People who use benzodiazepines for anxiety rarely develop tolerance to the anxiety-relieving effects, and rarely increase their dose or lose control over their use of the drug. Tolerance to the effects of one type of benzodiazepine leads to tolerance to other benzodiazepines, and to other drugs with similar effects, including alcohol.

People are said to be psychologically dependent when they have a strong craving for the effects of the drug, and feel compelled to take it, even when the drug does not produce the desired effects. Stopping use of benzodiazepines can be difficult for these people.

People who are psychologically dependent may or may not also be physically dependent. People who are physically dependent will experience withdrawal symptoms if they stop using the drug abruptly.

The severity of withdrawal symptoms depends on the type of benzodiazepine used, the amount used and length of time it is used, and on whether the drug is stopped abruptly. Withdrawal symptoms can include headache, insomnia, tension, sweating, difficulty concentrating, tremor, sensory disturbances, fear and fatigue, stomach upset and loss of appetite. Severe withdrawal symptoms from regular use of benzodiazepines in high doses may include agitation, paranoia, delirium and seizures. Long-term regular use of benzodiazepines should be reduced gradually, with medical supervision.

WHAT ARE THE LONG-TERM EFFECTS OF TAKING BENZODIAZEPINES?

If prescribed by your physician, taken at recommended doses for periods of only weeks or months, and not taken with alcohol or certain other medications, benzodiazepines are safe medications.

CAFFEINE

WHAT IS IT?

Caffeine is a stimulant that speeds up your central nervous system, and is the world's most popular drug. Caffeine occurs naturally in products such as coffee, tea, chocolate and cola soft drinks and is added to a variety of prescription and over-the-counter medications, including cough, cold and pain remedies.

The following are typical amounts of caffeine in products you may use regularly. (A cup refers to an average serving—about 200 mL.)

- cup of brewed/percolated coffee: 100 mg
- cup of instant coffee: 65 mg
- cup of decaffeinated coffee: about 1 mg
- cup of tea: 30 mg
- soft drink containing caffeine (280 mL): 35 mg (Some soft drinks are now available that contain twice this amount of caffeine.)
- chocolate bar (50 g): 20 mg
- cup of hot cocoa: 50 mg
- stay-awake pills: 100 mg

APPENDIX C: DO YOU KNOW...

To find out the amount of caffeine in headache and cold medicines, check the label of over-the-counter medication, or ask your pharmacist about caffeine in prescription drugs.

WHERE DOES CAFFEINE COME FROM?

Both words, caffeine and coffee, are derived from the Arabic word *qahweh* (pronounced "kahveh" in Turkish). The origins of the words reflect the spread of coffee into Europe via Arabia and Turkey from northeast Africa, where coffee trees were cultivated in the 6th century. Coffee began to be popular in Europe in the 17th century. By the 18th century, plantations had been established in Indonesia and the West Indies, and by the 20th century, coffee had become the biggest cash crop on earth.

Caffeine was first isolated from coffee in 1819. It is also found in tea; in cacao pods, and hence in cocoa and chocolate products; in kola nuts, used in the preparation of cola drinks; in the ilex plant, from whose leaves the popular South American beverage *yerba mate* is prepared; and in guarana seeds, an ingredient in some soft drinks.

The caffeine content of coffee beans varies according to the species of the coffee plant. Beans from *Coffea arabica*, grown mostly in Central and South America, contain about 1.1 per cent caffeine. Beans from *Coffea robusta*, grown mostly in Indonesia and Africa, contain about 2.2 per cent caffeine.

WHAT DOES CAFFEINE LOOK LIKE?

In its pure form, caffeine is a white, bitter-tasting powder.

WHO USES CAFFEINE?

Caffeine is the most widely used psychoactive substance in the world. In North America, more than 80 per cent of adults regularly consume caffeine. Worldwide per-capita caffeine consumption (including that of children) is estimated to be 70 mg per day, equivalent to approximately one cup of coffee.

In Canada, coffee consumption increased from 96 litres per person in 1990 to 101 litres per person in 2000. Consumption of tea has also increased, up from 42 litres per person in 1990 to 70 litres per person in 2000.

HOW DOES CAFFEINE MAKE YOU FEEL?

Caffeine stimulates the brain, elevates the mood and postpones fatigue. It also enhances performance at simple intellectual tasks, and at physical work that involves endurance, but not fine motor co-ordination. (Caffeine-caused tremor can reduce hand steadiness.)

If you consume caffeine before bedtime, you will likely take longer to get to sleep, sleep for a shorter time and sleep less deeply.

Contrary to popular belief, drinking coffee will not help you to "sober up" if you've had too much alcohol. The caffeine will make you more alert, but your co-ordination and concentration will still be impaired.

Too much caffeine can give you a headache, upset your stomach, make you nervous and jittery and leave you unable to sleep. Some people feel these effects even with a very small amount. Larger doses of caffeine, especially when consumed by people who don't usually take caffeine, can cause rapid heartbeat, convulsions and even delirium.

HOW LONG DOES THE FEELING LAST?

When taken in beverage form, caffeine begins to take effect within five minutes, and reaches its peak effect in about 30 minutes. It takes about four hours for half of a given dose of caffeine to be metabolized by the body. Normally, almost all ingested caffeine is metabolized, and there is no day-to-day accumulation of the drug in the body.

IS CAFFEINE DANGEROUS?

Moderate amounts of caffeine—up to about 300 mg a day (e.g., three to four average cups of coffee)—will rarely harm an otherwise healthy adult.

But if you regularly drink more than six to eight cups of coffee— or your daily dose of caffeine, from various caffeine-containing products, is higher than 600 mg—you may have trouble sleeping, feel anxious, restless and depressed and develop stomach ulcers. Higher amounts can cause extreme agitation, tremors and a very rapid and irregular heartbeat.

Small amounts of caffeine have a greater effect on children because of their smaller body size. It is wise to be aware of how much caffeine your children consume in chocolate products, soft drinks and medications.

Although caffeine has not been proven to cause birth defects, pregnant women are advised to take as little of it as possible to reduce possible risks to their baby's health. Nursing mothers should be aware that caffeine is excreted in breast milk.

An adult can die from orally consuming more than 5,000 mg—the equivalent of 40 strong cups of coffee—over a very short time.

IS CAFFEINE ADDICTIVE?

Regular use of caffeine can make you physically dependent on caffeine. That means that if you abruptly stop using caffeine-containing products, you may feel edgy and tired and have a bad headache. These symptoms usually appear 18 to 24 hours after the last use of caffeine, and gradually fade over the following week.

WHAT ARE THE LONG-TERM EFFECTS OF TAKING CAFFEINE?

Healthy adults do not appear to suffer any long-term effects from consuming moderate doses of caffeine daily. Larger daily doses (in some individuals as little as 250 mg, or three cups of coffee a day) may produce restlessness, nervousness, insomnia, flushed face, increased urination, muscle twitching, stomach upset and agitation.

Caffeine use appears to be associated with irregular heartbeat and may raise cholesterol levels, but there is no firm evidence that caffeine causes heart disease.

Although caffeine is suspected to be a cause of cancer, the evidence is contradictory and does not allow a clear conclusion. Some studies indicate that caffeine can cause changes in the cells of the body and in the way these cells reproduce themselves.

Lifelong use of coffee and other forms of caffeine may be associated with loss of bone density in women, increasing the risk of osteoporosis.

CANNABIS

Street names: marijuana (grass, weed, pot, dope, ganja and others), hashish (hash), hash oil (weed oil, honey oil)

WHAT IS IT?

Cannabis sativa, also known as the hemp plant, has been cultivated for centuries for industrial and medical use, and for its "psychoactive," or mind-altering, effects. Marijuana, hashish and hashish oil all derive from the cannabis plant.

More than sixty-one chemicals, called cannabinoids, have been identified as specific to the cannabis plant. THC (delta-9-tetrahydrocannabinol) is the main psychoactive cannabinoid, and is most responsible for the "high" associated with marijuana smoke.

Hemp grown for industrial use has very low levels of THC. Hemp fibres are used to make rope, fabric and paper. Hemp seeds are high in protein and yield an oil with nutritional and industrial value.

Many claims about the medical uses of marijuana have not been scientifically proven; however, research has shown that THC and other pure cannabinoids can relieve nausea and vomiting and stimulate appetite. This can help people who have AIDS or who take drugs used to treat cancer. Further research is needed to establish the medical value of marijuana in relieving pain, reducing muscle spasms and controlling some types of epileptic seizure.

WHERE DOES CANNABIS COME FROM?

Cannabis is native to tropical and temperate climates, but is cultivated around the world. Modern illicit growing operations use sophisticated methods to produce high potency marijuana.

People with a medical exemption from Health Canada may grow their own supply or designate someone to grow it for them. Research-grade cannabis is grown by a producer appointed by the federal government.

WHAT DOES CANNABIS LOOK LIKE?

Marijuana is the dried flower buds and leaves of the cannabis plant. It ranges in colour from grayish green to greenish brown and may contain seeds and stems. Hashish is the dried, compressed resin of cannabis flowertops. It ranges in colour from brown to black, and is sold in chunks. Hash oil is made by boiling cannabis flowertops or resin in an organic solvent, which produces a sticky reddish-brown or green substance. The THC content of each variety of cannabis varies, although hash is generally more potent than marijuana, and hash oil is usually the most potent form.

Marijuana, hash or hash oil are sometimes mixed with tobacco, and are most often rolled into a cigarette called a joint, or smoked in a pipe. Cannabis is sometimes cooked in foods, such as brownies, or made into a drink.

Synthetic THC (dronabinol) is produced under the trade name Marinol®. A related synthetic cannabinoid (nabilone) is sold as Cesamet®. Both are prescribed to people who have cancer or AIDS.

WHO USES CANNABIS?

Cannabis is the most commonly used illicit drug in Canada (after alcohol and tobacco use by minors). However, most cannabis use is infrequent and experimental.

A 2000 study reported that 35 per cent of Ontarians over the age of 18 had used cannabis at some point in their life, and 11 per cent of those who had used it did so in the past year. A 1994 Canadian study reported that about two per cent of the people surveyed used cannabis once a week or more.

Rates of cannabis use among Ontario students have risen in recent years and are currently similar to the peak rates of the late 70s and early 80s. A 2001 survey found that about 30 per cent of Ontario students in Grade 7 to OAC had used marijuana at least once in the previous year, with about three per cent reporting daily use in the past four weeks. These rates of use were significantly higher among males than females.

HOW DOES CANNABIS MAKE YOU FEEL?
How cannabis affects you depends on:
- how much you use
- how often and how long you've used it
- whether you smoke it or swallow it
- your mood, your expectations and the environment you're in
- your age
- whether you have certain pre-existing medical or psychiatric conditions
- whether you've taken any alcohol or other drugs (illicit, prescription, over-the-counter or herbal).

When people first try cannabis, they often feel no psychoactive effect. With repeated use, however, these effects are felt.

People can have very different experiences with cannabis. Some may feel relaxed, lively, talkative and giggly, while others feel tense, anxious, fearful and confused. What's more, the kind of high a person has can vary from one drug-taking episode to another. People who are familiar with the drug learn to stop when they've had enough, and have more control of the effects, than do people who are new to the drug.

At low doses, cannabis mildly distorts perception and the senses. People who use the drug say that it makes music sound better, colours appear brighter and moments seem longer. They say that it enhances taste, touch and smell and makes them feel more aware of their body. Some enjoy these effects, but others find them uncomfortable.

Smoking larger amounts may intensify some of the desired effects but is also more likely to produce an unpleasant reaction. Too high a dose may result in feelings of losing control, confusion, agitation, paranoia and panic. Pseudohallucinations (seeing things such as pattern and colour that you know are not real) or true hallucinations (where you lose touch with reality) can occur.

The physical effects of cannabis include red eyes, dry mouth and throat, irritated respiratory system (from smoking) and bronchodilation (expansion of breathing passages). Appetite and heart rate increase, while blood pressure, balance and stability decrease. Cannabis may cause drowsiness or restlessness, depending on the amount taken and individual response to the drug.

HOW LONG DOES THE FEELING LAST?
When cannabis is smoked, the effect is almost immediate and may last several hours, depending on how much is taken. When swallowed, the effect is felt in about an hour, and lasts longer than when smoked. Although the high lasts only a few hours after smoking, THC is stored in fat cells and expelled from the body over a period of days or weeks, depending on the frequency of use and the amount used. This is why drug tests for cannabis use can give a positive result long after the effect of the drug has worn off.

IS CANNABIS DANGEROUS?
While no one has ever died of a cannabis overdose, those who use cannabis should be aware of the following possible dangers, and take measures to avoid them:
- Cannabis impairs depth perception, attention span and concentration, slows reaction time, and decreases muscle strength and hand steadiness—all of which may affect a person's ability to drive safely.
- Cannabis and alcohol, when taken together, intensify each other's effects and can cause severe impairment.
- Cannabis intoxication affects thinking and short-term memory. Using cannabis while at school or work may interfere with learning or work performance.
- Unless you have a medical exemption, it is illegal to grow, possess or sell cannabis.
- Illicit cannabis products are not subject to any health and safety standards, and may be contaminated with other drugs, pesticides or toxic fungi.
- Large doses of potent cannabis, especially when swallowed, can cause "toxic psychosis." Symptoms include auditory and visual hallucinations, paranoid delusions, confusion and amnesia. When cannabis use is stopped, these symptoms usually disappear within a week.

APPENDIX C: DO YOU KNOW...

- Cannabis use raises the heart rate and lowers blood pressure. People with angina or other coronary artery disease may increase their risk of heart attack if they use cannabis.
- Using cannabis during pregnancy may affect the baby. Research suggests there may be a link between cannabis use during pregnancy and subtle cognitive problems in children. Cannabis smoke contains many of the same chemicals found in cigarette smoke, which are dangerous to the fetus.

IS CANNABIS ADDICTIVE?
It can be.

People who use cannabis regularly can develop psychological and/or mild physical dependence. People with psychological dependence crave the high. The drug becomes overly important to them, they may feel they need it, and if they can't get it, they feel anxious. Long-term frequent use can lead to physical dependence. People who develop physical dependence may experience a mild withdrawal syndrome if they suddenly stop using cannabis. Symptoms can include irritability, anxiety, upset stomach, loss of appetite, sweating and disturbed sleep. These symptoms generally last for a week or so, although sleep problems may continue longer.

WHAT ARE THE LONG-TERM EFFECTS OF USING CANNABIS?
Healthy adults who occasionally use cannabis in low doses are not likely to have any harmful long-term effects. However, people who use cannabis heavily or regularly, or people with certain medical or psychiatric conditions, risk the following possible long-term effects:

- Cannabis smoke contains tar and other known cancer-causing agents. People who smoke cannabis often hold unfiltered smoke in their lungs for maximum effect. This adds to the risk of cancer.
- Smoking cannabis irritates the respiratory system. Chronic marijuana smoking has been linked to bronchitis. One study estimated that three to four joints per day causes the same damage as smoking 20 or more tobacco cigarettes.
- The constant intoxication associated with heavy cannabis use often reduces motivation for work and study, although this usually returns when drug use is stopped.
- There is a possible association between heavy regular cannabis use and the onset of schizophrenia. It is not clear, however, whether cannabis use releases latent symptoms of schizophrenia, or whether people use cannabis to help them cope with the symptoms of an emerging psychosis. Evidence suggests that continued cannabis use in people with schizophrenia accentuates psychotic symptoms and worsens the course of the illness.
- Chronic, heavy use of cannabis may impair people's attention, memory and the ability to process complex information for weeks, months and even years after they have stopped using cannabis.

CANNABIS AND THE LAW
A first-time conviction for possession of 30 grams or less of marijuana can result in a six-month jail sentence or a $1,000 fine (or both)—and a criminal record, which limits employment and travel. Subsequent convictions and possession of larger amounts can result in more severe penalties. A first offence of possession of small amounts of cannabis usually results in a fine or discharge. In 1995, 31,299 people were arrested for possession of small amounts of marijuana; this was about half of all drug arrests in Canada for that year.

In an ongoing debate lasting many years, various government, health, police, policy and legal groups have suggested that criminal punishment for the possession of cannabis is too severe, and that our laws do not reflect the practice of our police and legal system.

One option to current laws is to "decriminalize," which would reduce the legal penalty for possession of cannabis, and another is to "regulate," giving cannabis a legal status similar to alcohol, with a legal but restricted source of supply available to adults.

Canada's Controlled Drugs and Substances Act was changed to permit the cultivation of industrial hemp in 1998, and to provide access to marijuana for medical use in 2001.

COCAINE

STREET NAMES
blow, C, coke, crack, flake, freebase, rock, snow

WHAT IS COCAINE?
Cocaine is a *stimulant drug*. Stimulants make people feel more alert and energetic. Cocaine can also make people feel euphoric, or "high."

Pure cocaine was first isolated from the leaves of the coca bush in 1860. Researchers soon discovered that cocaine numbs whatever tissues it touches, leading to its use as a local anesthetic. Today, we mostly use synthetic anesthetics, rather than cocaine.

APPENDIX C: DO YOU KNOW...

In the 1880s, psychiatrist Sigmund Freud wrote scientific papers that praised cocaine as a treatment for many ailments, including depression and alcohol and opioid addiction. After this, cocaine became widely and legally available in patent medicines and soft drinks.

As cocaine use increased, people began to discover its dangers. In 1911, Canada passed laws restricting the importation, manufacture, sale and possession of cocaine. The use of cocaine declined until the 1970s, when it became known for its high cost, and for the rich and glamorous people who used it. Cheaper "crack" cocaine became available in the 1980s.

WHERE DOES COCAINE COME FROM?

Cocaine is contained in small amounts in the leaves of several species of the *erythroxylum* (coca) bush, which grow on the slopes of the Andes Mountains in South America. For at least 4,500 years, people in Peru and Bolivia have chewed coca leaves to lessen hunger and fatigue. Today, most of the world's supply of coca is grown and refined into cocaine in Columbia. Criminal networks control the lucrative cocaine trade.

WHAT DOES COCAINE LOOK LIKE AND HOW IS IT USED?

Cocaine hydrochloride—the form in which cocaine is snorted or injected—is a white crystalline powder. It is sometimes "cut," or mixed, with things that look like it, such as cornstarch or talcum powder, or with other drugs, such as local anesthetics or amphetamines.

Powder cocaine can be chemically changed to create forms of cocaine that can be smoked. These forms, known as "freebase" and "crack," look like crystals or rocks.

Cocaine is often used with other drugs, especially alcohol and marijuana. Cocaine and heroin, mixed and dissolved for injection, is called a "speedball."

WHO USES COCAINE?

A 2001 survey of Ontario students in grades 7 to OAC reported that:
- 4.3 per cent had used cocaine at least once.
- Two per cent had used crack cocaine at least once in the past year.

A 2000 survey of Ontario adults reported that:
- 6.4 per cent had used cocaine at least once.
- 1.2 per cent had used it in the past year.

HOW DOES COCAINE MAKE YOU FEEL?

How cocaine makes you feel depends on:
- how much you use
- how often and how long you use
- how you use it (by injection, orally, etc.)
- your mood, expectation and environment
- your age
- whether you have certain medical or psychiatric conditions
- whether you've taken any alcohol or other drugs (illicit, prescription, over-the-counter or herbal).

Cocaine makes people feel energetic, talkative, alert and euphoric. They feel more aware of their senses: sound, touch, sight and sexuality seem heightened. Hunger and the need for sleep are reduced. Although cocaine is a stimulant, some people find it calming, and feel increased self-control, confidence and ease with others. Other people may feel nervous and agitated, and can't relax.

Taking high doses of cocaine for a long time can lead to:
- panic attacks
- psychotic symptoms, such as paranoia (feeling overly suspicious, jealous, or persecuted), hallucinations (seeing, hearing, smelling, etc., things that aren't real) and delusions (false beliefs)
- erratic, bizarre and sometimes violent behaviour.

With regular use, people may become *tolerant* to the euphoric effects of cocaine. This means they need to take more and more of the drug to get the same desired effect. At the same time, people who use the drug regularly may also become more sensitive to its negative effects, such as anxiety, psychosis (hallucinations, loss of contact with reality) and seizures.

Cocaine also makes the heartbeat and breathing faster, and raises blood pressure and body temperature.

HOW LONG DOES THE FEELING LAST?

Not long. Cocaine is both fast- and short-acting.
- Intranasal use, or "snorting," takes effect within a few minutes, and lasts 60 to 90 minutes.
- Injecting produces a "rush" that is felt within minutes, and lasts 20 to 60 minutes.
- Smoking causes a high within seconds, which lasts only five to 10 minutes.

APPENDIX C: DO YOU KNOW...

When the cocaine high fades, the person may begin to feel anxious and depressed, and have intense craving for more of the drug. Some people stay high by "binging," or continually using the drug, for hours or days.

IS COCAINE DANGEROUS?
Yes.

While many people use cocaine on occasion without harm, the drug can be very dangerous, whether it's used once or often.

- Cocaine causes the blood vessels to thicken and constrict, reducing the flow of oxygen to the heart. At the same time, cocaine causes the heart muscle to work harder, leading to heart attack or stroke, even in healthy people.
- Cocaine raises blood pressure, which can explode weakened blood vessels in the brain.
- A person can overdose on even a small amount of cocaine. Overdose can cause seizures and heart failure. It can cause breathing to become weak or stop altogether. There is no antidote to cocaine overdose.
- Snorting cocaine can cause sinus infections and loss of smell. It can damage tissues in the nose and cause holes in the bony separation between the nostrils inside the nose.
- Smoking cocaine can damage the lungs and cause "crack lung." Symptoms include severe chest pains, breathing problems and high temperatures. Crack lung can be fatal.
- Injection can cause infections from used needles or impurities in the drug. Sharing needles can also cause hepatitis or HIV infection.
- Cocaine use in pregnancy may increase risk of miscarriage and premature delivery. It also increases the chance that the baby will be born underweight. Because women who use cocaine during pregnancy often also use alcohol, nicotine and other drugs, we do not fully know the extent of the effects of cocaine use on the baby.
- Cocaine use while breastfeeding transmits cocaine to the nursing child. This exposes the baby to all the effects and risks of cocaine use.
- Cocaine use is linked with risk-taking and violent behaviours. It is also linked to poor concentration and judgment, increasing risk of injury and sexually transmitted disease.
- Chronic use can cause severe psychiatric symptoms, including psychosis, anxiety, depression and paranoia.
- Chronic use can also cause weight loss, malnutrition, poor health, sexual problems, infertility and loss of social and financial supports.

IS COCAINE ADDICTIVE?
It can be.

Not everyone who uses cocaine becomes addicted, but if they do, it can be one of the hardest drug habits to break.

People who become addicted to cocaine lose control over their use of the drug. They feel a strong need for cocaine, even when they know it causes them medical, psychological and social problems. Getting and taking cocaine can become the most important thing in their lives.

Smoking crack, with its rapid, intense and short-lived effects, is most addictive. However, any method of taking cocaine can lead to addiction. The amount of drug used, and how often people use the drug, has an effect on whether people get addicted.

Cocaine causes people to "crash" when they stop using it. When they crash, their mood swings rapidly from feeling high to distress. This brings powerful cravings for more of the drug. Binging to stay high leads quickly to addiction.

Symptoms of cocaine withdrawal can include exhaustion, extended and restless sleep or sleeplessness, hunger, irritability, depression, suicidal thoughts and intense cravings for more of the drug. The memory of cocaine euphoria is powerful, and brings a strong risk of relapse to drug use.

WHAT ARE THE LONG-TERM EFFECTS OF TAKING COCAINE?
Cocaine increases the same chemicals in the brain that make people feel good when they eat, drink or have sex. Regular cocaine use can cause lasting changes in the brain. This may explain the craving and psychiatric symptoms that last even after drug use stops.

ECSTACY

STREET NAME
E, XTC, Adam, the love drug

WHAT IS IT?
The chemical name for ecstasy is 3,4-methylenedioxymethamphetamine, or MDMA. The chemical structure and the effects of MDMA are similar to amphetamine (a stimulant) and to mescaline (a hallucinogen).

What's sold as ecstasy often contains drugs other than MDMA, which may or may not be similar in effect to MDMA. Some of the other drugs include caffeine, ephedrine, amphetamine, dextromethorphan, ketamine or LSD. Ecstasy sometimes contains highly toxic drugs, such as PMA (paramethoxyamphetamine), which can be lethal even in low doses.

MDMA affects the chemistry of the brain, in particular by releasing a high level of serotonin. Serotonin is a chemical in the brain that plays an important role in the regulation of mood, energy level and appetite, among other things.

MDMA was patented in 1913, and has been used experimentally, most notably as a supplement to psychotherapy in the 1970s. It was made illegal to possess, traffic, import or produce in Canada in 1976 and in the United States in 1985.

WHERE DOES ECSTASY COME FROM?
Ecstasy is made in illicit labs with chemicals and processes that vary from lab to lab. What's sold as ecstasy often contains unknown drugs or other fillers.

WHAT DOES ECSTASY LOOK LIKE?
Ecstasy is usually sold as a tablet or capsule that is swallowed. It may also be sold in powder form, or the tablets may be crushed and then snorted. Although rare, there are also some reports that the drug is injected.

Ecstasy tablets come in different shapes, sizes and colours, and are often stamped with a logo, such as a butterfly or clover, giving them a candy-like look. This "branding" of ecstasy tablets should not be mistaken for an indication of quality, as manufacturers may use the same logo, and low-quality copycats are common. Tablets that are sold as ecstasy may not contain MDMA.

"Herbal ecstacy," often promoted as containing only "natural" ingredients, usually contains herbal ephedrine, which has stimulant properties. The abuse of products containing ephedrine has been associated with strokes, heart attacks and deaths.

WHO USES ECSTASY?
The increased use of ecstasy as a recreational drug began in the 1980s in the U.S. The group most commonly associated with ecstasy use is young people at "raves" or all-night dance parties. More recently, ecstasy has attracted a wider range of users, including urban professionals, and is used in a variety of settings, including mainstream nightclubs.

HOW DOES ECSTASY MAKE YOU FEEL?
How ecstasy affects you depends on several things:
- your age and your body weight
- how much you take and how often you take it
- how long you've been taking it
- the method you use to take the drug
- the environment you're in
- whether or not you have certain pre-existing medical or psychiatric conditions
- if you've taken any alcohol or other drugs (illicit, prescription, over-the-counter or herbal).

In low to moderate doses, ecstasy can produce feelings of pleasure and well-being, increased sociability and closeness with others. Like all stimulant drugs, ecstasy can make users feel full of energy and confidence.

Even at low doses, ecstasy can also have strong negative effects. Higher doses are unlikely to enhance the desirable effects, and may intensify the negative effects. These effects include grinding of teeth and jaw pain, sweating, increased blood pressure and heart rate, anxiety or panic attacks, blurred vision, nausea, vomiting and convulsions.

After the initial effects of the drug have worn off, users may also experience after-effects such as confusion, irritability, anxiety, paranoia, depression, memory impairment or sleep problems.

HOW LONG DOES THE FEELING LAST?
The effects of ecstasy usually begin within an hour, and may last four to six hours. The duration of the after-effects cannot be predicted as precisely, though they may last for days or weeks.

IS ECSTASY DANGEROUS?
It can be. Although some people regard ecstasy as a relatively safe drug, a growing number of deaths have been associated with it. As with many illicit drugs, these risks increase with the amount taken and frequency of use.

A major factor in many ecstasy-related deaths is the dehydration and overheating that can result when ecstasy is taken in conjunction with all-night dancing. Ecstasy increases body temperature, blood pressure and heart rate, which can lead to kidney or heart failure, strokes and seizures. Ecstasy may cause jaundice and liver damage.

APPENDIX C: DO YOU KNOW...

People with high blood pressure, heart or liver problems, diabetes, epilepsy or any mental disorder are the most vulnerable to the potential dangers of ecstasy. Part of the danger is that people may not be aware that they have these conditions, and the effects of ecstasy can trigger symptoms.

As with all illegal street drugs, the purity and strength of ecstasy can never be accurately gauged. When you take ecstasy, you don't know what you're taking, or how it will affect you.

Combining ecstasy with other drugs, illicit or prescription, may cause a toxic interaction. There are several prescription medications known to interact with ecstasy. These include a certain kind of antidepressant called monoamine oxidase inhibitors (MAOIs), and ritonavir, a protease inhibitor used to treat HIV.

Driving or operating machinery while under the influence of ecstasy, or any drug, increases the risk of physical injury to the user, and increases the risk of injury to others.

IS ECSTASY ADDICTIVE?
Tolerance to ecstasy builds up very quickly. This means the more often you take ecstasy, the less effect the drug has. Taking more of the drug may not achieve the desired results, as frequent ecstasy use depletes serotonin and other brain chemicals that give the ecstasy "high."

While there is little evidence to indicate that MDMA can produce physical dependence or withdrawal symptoms, it's not uncommon for the drug to take on an exaggerated importance in people's lives.

WHAT ARE THE LONG-TERM EFFECTS OF TAKING ECSTASY?
Animal research has established that ecstasy use can damage the brain cells that release serotonin. Research on humans is limited, but there is some evidence to support that ecstasy can damage the cells and chemistry of the human brain, affecting some functions of the brain, including learning and memory. Research suggests that the risk of damage caused by ecstasy use is linked to the amount taken and the frequency of use.

At this time it is not known how long the damage caused by ecstasy might last, or if it may be permanent. More research is needed to confirm the long-term effects of ecstasy on the human brain.

GHB

STREET NAME
G, liquid ecstasy, liquid x, grievous bodily harm

WHAT IS IT?
GHB (gamma-hydroxybutyrate) is produced naturally in the human body in very small amounts. When taken as a recreational drug, and especially when taken in combination with alcohol or other drugs, GHB can be extremely dangerous.

GHB is a central nervous system depressant. That means it makes you sleepy, and slows down your breathing and heart rate.

GHB was first made in a laboratory in 1960. It has been used experimentally as an anesthetic, and as a treatment for sleep disorders and alcohol withdrawal.

Before it was banned, GHB was widely available in the U.S. in health food stores. Claims were made that it would help build muscles, burn fat and improve sex. Some called it a "safe" alternative to alcohol and conventional sleep aids. Currently GHB is illegal to possess, traffic, import or produce in Canada and the United States.

WHERE DOES GHB COME FROM?
GHB is made in illicit labs. The chemicals and processes used vary from lab to lab, as does the strength and purity of the final product.

WHAT DOES GHB LOOK LIKE?
In its liquid form, GHB looks like water. It has no smell, and is tasteless or has a slightly salty or solvent taste that can be easily masked. It is usually sold as a liquid in small vials. GHB is also available as a white powder or capsule.

WHO USES GHB?
In recent years, GHB has gained popularity as a "club drug" among young people for its euphoric and sedative effects. Some bodybuilders continue to use it, believing it stimulates growth hormones. GHB has also been used to facilitate sexual assault.

HOW DOES GHB MAKE YOU FEEL?
How GHB affects you depends on several things:
- your age and your body weight
- how much you take and how often you take it
- how long you've been taking it
- the method you use to take the drug

APPENDIX C: DO YOU KNOW...

- the environment you're in
- whether or not you have certain pre-existing medical or psychiatric conditions
- if you've taken any alcohol or other drugs (illicit, prescription, over-the-counter or herbal).

The way you feel when you take GHB is similar to the way some people feel when they drink alcohol. At a low dose, users usually feel more sociable, less inhibited and lightheaded. A slightly higher dose intensifies these effects or makes you drowsy and dizzy. A little more may cause nausea and vomiting, and a higher dose can make you slip into a deep coma-like sleep. An overdose can result in difficulty breathing, a lowered heart rate, convulsions and even death.

With GHB there is only a slight difference between a dose that produces the desired effects, and a dose that puts the user at risk. If you have a little too much GHB, the consequences can be fatal.

HOW LONG DOES THE FEELING LAST?
The effects of GHB can generally be felt between 10 and 20 minutes after you take it, and can last up to four hours, depending on the dose. There have been some reports of dizziness lasting for days.

IS GHB DANGEROUS?
Yes, GHB is dangerous in a number of ways.

Since GHB is illegal, there are no controls over the strength and purity of the drugs produced. What's sold as GHB often contains unknown drugs or other fillers, which may be toxic. You don't know how much GHB is in the solution or what dose is safe.

With GHB it's easy to take too much, or overdose. When taken with alcohol or other drugs, the effects of GHB are more intense, and the risk of toxic effects and overdose increases.

GHB is a potent sedative, causing users to fall into a deep coma-like sleep from which they might not be aroused for several hours. They may vomit while they're sleeping and choke. When in a GHB sleep, convulsions can occur, often alarming others into rushing the user to the hospital for emergency care.

GHB's liquid form allows it to be slipped into drinks, and its sedative effects prevent victims from resisting sexual assault. For this reason, it has been referred to in the media as a "date rape" drug. GHB can also cause amnesia, meaning that when people recover from the drug's effects, they may not remember what happened. Take caution at parties and bars—watch your drink.

GHB may interact dangerously with some medications, such as protease inhibitors used to treat HIV.

Driving or operating machinery while under the influence of GHB, or any drug, increases the risk of physical injury to the user, and increases the risk of injury to others.

IS GHB ADDICTIVE?
Regular use of GHB can cause physical dependence. Stopping abruptly can result in anxiety, tremors, inability to sleep and other unpleasant, potentially dangerous side-effects, including paranoia with hallucinations and high blood pressure. Dependent users should seek medical help to ease withdrawal.

WHAT ARE THE LONG-TERM EFFECTS OF USING GHB?
Because very little research has been done in this area, the long-term effects of using GHB are not known.

HEROIN

STREET NAMES
junk, H, smack, horse, skag, dope

WHAT IS IT?
Heroin is a dangerous and illegal drug with a high addictive potential. It is also an effective painkiller.

Heroin belongs to the opioid family of drugs. Also in the opioid family are the "opiates," such as morphine and codeine, which are natural products of the opium poppy; and "synthetic" opioids, such as Demerol® and methadone, which are chemically manufactured. Heroin is a "semi-synthetic" opioid; it is made from morphine that has been chemically processed, giving it a stronger and more immediate effect. Heroin is converted back into morphine in the brain.

When heroin was first introduced in the late 19th century, it was promoted as a pain reliever and cough suppressant. By the early 20th century, the dangers of heroin were recognized. Laws were introduced throughout North America and Europe to restrict the production, distribution and use of heroin. In some countries, there are circumstances where heroin may be prescribed by physicians. In Britain, for example, doctors may prescribe heroin for extreme pain. This treatment is usually reserved for patients who are ter-

APPENDIX C: DO YOU KNOW...

minally ill. Although Canadian drug regulations were changed
in the 1980s to allow heroin to be prescribed, it is rarely used. In
Britain, the Netherlands and Switzerland, a small number of people
who are heroin-dependent, and who have not responded to other
treatments, receive heroin by prescription in carefully monitored
maintenance programs.

WHERE DOES IT COME FROM?

Most heroin is produced in Asia and Latin America, where opium
poppies are grown. Morphine is extracted from the opium gum
in laboratories close to the fields, and then converted into heroin in
labs within or nearby the producing country.

WHAT DOES IT LOOK LIKE?

In its pure form, heroin is a fine, white, bitter-tasting crystalline powder
that dissolves in water. When it is sold on the street, its colour and
consistency vary, depending on the manufacturing process and what
additives it has been mixed, or "cut," with. Street heroin may come
in the form of a white powder, a brown, sometimes grainy substance
or a dark brown sticky gum. The purity of heroin varies from batch
to batch, and can range from two to 98 per cent.

Some additives, such as sugars, starch or powdered milk are used
to increase the weight for retail sale, or other drugs may be added to
increase the effects of the heroin. Quinine may be added to imitate
heroin's bitter taste, making it difficult to determine the purity of
the drug.

HOW IS IT USED?

The most common ways of using heroin are:

- injection—either into a vein ("mainlining," intravenous or I.V.
  use), into a muscle (intramuscular or I.M. use) or under the skin
  ("skin-popping" or subcutaneous use)
- snorting—inhaling the powder through the nostril
  (also called sniffing)
- inhaling or smoking—this method is also referred to as "chasing
  the dragon," and involves gently heating the heroin on aluminum
  foil and inhaling the smoke and vapours through a tube.

Injection may be chosen because this method gives the greatest
and most immediate effect for the least amount of drug. People
who are dependent on heroin may inject two to four times a day.
The drug is more likely to be snorted or smoked when heroin of high
purity is available, or by occasional users who prefer not to inject.

WHO USES HEROIN?

Heroin use is found among a range of people, from a variety of cultural, social, economic and age groups. Twice as many males as
females use heroin. First-time users tend to be young, in their
teens or 20s, but most people who use heroin regularly are over 30.

HOW DOES HEROIN MAKE YOU FEEL?

The way heroin, or any drug, affects you depends on many
factors, including:

- your age
- how much you take and how often you take it
- how long you've been taking it
- the method you use to take the drug
- the environment you're in
- whether or not you have certain pre-existing medical or psychiatric conditions
- if you've taken any alcohol or other drugs (illicit, prescription,
  over-the-counter or herbal).

When heroin is injected into a vein, it produces a surge of euphoria,
or "rush." This effect is felt in seven to eight seconds, and lasts
from 45 seconds to a few minutes. The initial effect with snorting or
smoking is not as intense. Following the rush comes a period of
sedation and tranquillity known as being "on the nod," which may
last up to an hour. When heroin is injected under the skin or into a
muscle, the effect comes on more slowly, within five to eight minutes.

New users often experience nausea and vomiting. The desired effects
include detachment from physical and emotional pain and a feeling
of well-being. Other effects include slowed breathing, pinpoint
pupils, itchiness and sweating. Regular use results in constipation,
loss of sexual interest and libido, and an irregular or stopped menstrual cycle in women.

Heroin use causes changes in mood and behaviour. People who are
dependent on heroin may be docile and compliant after taking heroin,
and irritable and aggressive during withdrawal.

HOW LONG DOES THE FEELING LAST?

Regardless of how it is used, the effects of heroin generally last for
three to five hours, depending on the dose.

People who are dependent on heroin must use every six to 12 hours to
avoid symptoms of withdrawal. The initial symptoms are intense, and
include runny nose, sneezing, diarrhea, vomiting, restlessness and a

persistent craving for the drug. Also associated with withdrawal are goose bumps and involuntary leg movements, leading to the expressions "cold turkey" and "kicking the habit." Withdrawal symptoms peak within a couple days, and usually fade within five to 10 days. Other symptoms, such as insomnia, anxiety and craving, may continue for some time. Heroin withdrawal is not life-threatening, but can be extremely uncomfortable.

IS HEROIN DANGEROUS?

Yes. Heroin is dangerous in a number of ways. Overdose is the most immediate danger of heroin use. Heroin depresses the part of the brain that controls breathing. In an overdose, breathing slows down, and may stop completely. A person who has overdosed is unconscious and cannot be roused, and has skin that is cold, moist and bluish. A heroin overdose can be treated at a hospital emergency room with drugs, such as naloxone, which blocks heroin's depressant effects.

The risk of overdose is increased by:
- The unknown purity of the drug. Ironically, many overdoses are due to increases in the quality of the drug sold on the street.
- Injection, because the drug reaches the brain more quickly than by other ways of taking the drug, and because the dose is taken all at once.
- Combining heroin with other sedating drugs, such as alcohol, benzodiazepines and methadone.

Other dangers associated with heroin use include:
- Injection: injection drug use puts the user at high risk of bacterial infection, blood poisoning, abscesses, endocarditis (an infection of the lining of the heart) collapsed veins and overdose. Sharing needles greatly increases the risk of becoming infected with, or spreading, HIV and hepatitis B or C.
- Unknown content of the drug: the unknown purity and potency of the drug makes it difficult to determine the correct dose and to protect from overdose. In addition, heroin is often cut with additives, which may be poisonous, such as strychnine, or that do not dissolve (and can clog blood vessels), such as chalk.
- Combining heroin with other drugs, such as cocaine (speedballs): when drugs interact inside the body, the results are unpredictable, and sometimes deadly.
- Dependence: the constant need to obtain heroin, and the repeated use of the drug, can result in criminal involvement or other high-risk behaviour, breakdown of family life, loss of employment and poor health.

- Pregnancy: women who use heroin regularly often miss their periods; some mistakenly think that they are infertile, and become pregnant. Continued use of heroin during pregnancy is very risky for the baby.

IS HEROIN ADDICTIVE?

Yes. Regular use of heroin, whether it is injected, snorted or smoked, can lead to physical and psycho-logical dependence within two to three weeks.

Not all people who experiment with heroin become dependent. Some use the drug only on occasion, such as on weekends, without increasing the dose. With regular use, however, tolerance to the effects of the drug develop, and more and more heroin is needed to achieve the desired effect. Continuous use of increasing amounts of the drug inevitably leads to dependence.

Once dependence is established, stopping use can be extremely difficult. People who have used heroin for a long time often report that they no longer experience any pleasure from the drug. They continue to use heroin to avoid the symptoms of withdrawal, and to control the powerful craving for the drug, which is often described as a "need." Cravings may persist long after the drug is discontinued, making relapse, or beginning to use again, difficult to avoid.

WHAT ARE THE LONG-TERM EFFECTS OF USING HEROIN?

Heroin dependence, and the medical, social and legal complications that often result from heroin use, can be devastating to the lives of the people who use the drug.

Research using brain scans has revealed that long-term regular use of heroin results in changes in the way the brain works. While the effect of these changes is not fully understood, this research has shown that it may take months or years for the brain to return to normal functioning after heroin use is stopped.

Methadone maintenance treatment, which prevents heroin withdrawal and reduces or eliminates drug cravings, is the most effective treatment for heroin dependence currently available. (For more information on methadone, see *Do You Know...Methadone*.)

APPENDIX C: DO YOU KNOW...

INHALANTS

STREET NAMES
glue, gas, sniff (solvents); whippets (nitrous oxide); poppers, room odourizers, VCR cleaner—some sold under "brand" names such as Rush, Bolt, Kix (nitrites)

WHAT ARE INHALANTS?
The term "inhalants" refers to chemical vapours or gases that produce a "high" when they are breathed in. Most of the substances used as inhalants, such as glue, gasoline, cleaning solvents and aerosols, have legitimate everyday uses, but they were never meant for human consumption. Inhalants are cheap, legal and easy to get. They have a high potential for abuse—especially by children and young adults.

There are hundreds of different kinds of inhalants, roughly dividing into four different types:

- Volatile solvents: These are the most commonly abused type of inhalants. "Volatile" means they evaporate when exposed to air, and "solvent" means they dissolve many other substances. Examples of solvents used as inhalants include benzene, toluene, xylene, acetone, naptha and hexane. Products such as gasoline, cleaning fluids, paint thinners, hobby glue, correction fluid and felt-tip markers contain a mixture of different types of solvents.
- Aerosol or spray cans: Hair spray, spray paint, cooking spray and other aerosol products contain pressurized liquids or gases such as fluorocarbon and butane. Some aerosol products also contain solvents.
- Gases: This includes some medical anesthetics, such as nitrous oxide ("laughing gas"), chloroform, halothane and ether, as well as gases found in commercially available products, such as butane lighters and propane tanks.
- Nitrites: Amyl nitrite, butyl nitrite and cyclohexyl nitrite (also known as "poppers") are different from other inhalants in effect and availability. They are sold as "room odourizer" or "video head cleaner." Amyl nitrite is used medically to treat cyanide poisoning; butyl nitrite is an illegal substance in the United States.

WHERE DO INHALANTS COME FROM?
Many inhalants are widely available as commercial products. It is hard to prevent their use because these products are found in many homes and workplaces. Some manufacturers taint their products to try to make them less appealing to use as inhalants, but this has not prevented use. Stores may refuse to sell certain products to minors or people who are intoxicated, but there are no laws that enforce this in Ontario.

WHAT DO INHALANTS LOOK LIKE, AND HOW ARE THEY USED?
Solvent and aerosol products—on the store shelf, in the kitchen cupboard or in the workshop—would not be noticed by most people as dangerous drugs.

When solvents are used as drugs, they are either inhaled directly from the container ("sniffed"), from a soaked rag held to the face ("huffed") or from a bag ("bagged"). Sometimes people spray aerosols into a bag or balloon and then inhale the gas.

Nitrous oxide or other anesthetic gases intended for medical use are contained in a gas tank; nitrous oxide is also found in whipped cream dispensers. Because nitrous oxide is pressurized and can be very cold, it is often inhaled from a balloon.

Nitrites are clear yellow liquids that are inhaled directly from the bottle or from a cloth.

WHO USES INHALANTS?
Most of the people who use solvents and aerosols are young— between 10 and 16 years old. Many try inhalants only once or twice, or use them only on occasion. But some people use heavily and may continue using into adulthood. Chronic solvent users are usually in their 20s.

Solvent use is associated with poverty, difficulty at school, lack of opportunity, problems at home and a high incidence of substance use in the family.

An ongoing survey of drug use among Ontario students in grades 7 to OAC reported that student use of solvents one or more times in the past year increased from 2.6 per cent in 1997 to 7.3 per cent in 1999 and decreased to 5.9 per cent in 2001.

Nitrous oxide is a drug of abuse available to many health care workers. Nitrous oxide appears to be gaining popularity among young adults.

Nitrite use is most common among gay men, although U.S. statistics indicate that the rate of nitrite use has fallen.

HOW DO INHALANTS MAKE YOU FEEL?
How inhalants, or any drugs, affect you depends on a number of factors:
- your age
- how sensitive you are to the drug

APPENDIX C: DO YOU KNOW...

- how much you use
- how long and how often you've been using it
- the method you use to take the drug
- the environment you're in
- whether or not you have certain pre-existing medical or psychiatric conditions
- if you've taken any alcohol or other drugs (illicit, prescription, over-the-counter or herbal).

All inhalants are absorbed through the lungs and travel quickly in the blood to the brain. This produces an immediate and brief intoxication. Different types of inhalants produce different effects.

Inhaled solvents usually produce an alcohol-like effect, but with more distortion of perception, such as the shape, size and colour of objects, and distortion of time and space. New users may be initially excited, then become drowsy and fall asleep. People who use solvents more often may feel euphoric, exhilarated and have vivid fantasies. Some feel giddy, outgoing and confident. Physical effects may include dizziness, nausea, vomiting, blurred vision, sneezing and coughing, staggering, slow reflexes and sensitivity to light.

Nitrous oxide produces a dreamy mental state, loss of motor control, hallucinations and an increased threshold for pain.

Nitrites dilate blood vessels and relax muscles. The heartbeat quickens and blood rushes to the head, creating a "rush." Nitrites also cause headaches, dizziness, nausea and flushing. Some men use nitrites during sex for the drugs' capacity to relax muscles and promote blood flow.

HOW LONG DOES THE FEELING LAST?

Several breaths of solvents will produce a high within a few minutes of use. This high may last up to 45 minutes, if no more breaths are taken. Some people continue to take additional breaths to sustain the effects for several hours. As the effects wear off, the person may feel drowsy and have a hangover with a mild-to-severe headache for up to several days.

The effects of nitrous oxide and nitrites are immediate, and wear off within a few minutes.

ARE INHALANTS DANGEROUS?

Yes. Inhalant use is dangerous in many ways:

Solvents and aerosols

- Suffocation: Solvents are often sniffed from a plastic bag, which is held firmly around the nose and mouth. People who use solvents sometimes pass out with the bag still in place, and suffocate due to lack of oxygen. Choking on vomit when unconscious is another major cause of inhalant-related death.
- Recklessness: Sniffing reduces inhibition and affects the way people feel about themselves and the world around them. It makes some people feel powerful, which has led to dangerous and destructive behaviour that caused serious harm. Others don't get "high" when they sniff; they get depressed. Self-destructive or suicidal behaviour are common among people who use solvents. Most inhalants are highly flammable; recklessness with lit cigarettes and flames while using inhalants has caused tragic accidents.
- Sudden sniffing death (SSD): Prolonged sniffing of highly concentrated inhalants can cause a rapid and irregular heartbeat, leading to death from heart failure. SSD can occur after only one sniffing session, and when stress or strenuous exercise follows several deep inhalations.
- Serious health problems: People who use solvents regularly for a long time can damage their liver, kidneys, lungs, heart, brain, bones and blood. Sometimes this damage heals when drug use is stopped; sometimes it is permanent.
- Fetal solvent syndrome: Use of solvents during pregnancy, especially chronic use, can result in premature birth, birth defects or stillbirth.

Nitrous oxide

- Lack of oxygen: Sniffing pure nitrous oxide starves the body of oxygen. Some people have died this way.
- Loss of motor control: People who use nitrous oxide while standing can fall and hurt themselves.
- Frostbite: The gas is extremely cold as it is released from the cylinder and can freeze skin. In addition, pressure in the tank can damage the lungs.
- Nerve damage: High levels of nitrous oxide use, even with adequate oxygen, has been shown to damage nerves. This can cause numbness, weakness and loss of balance.

APPENDIX C: DO YOU KNOW...

Nitrites

- Unsafe sexual practices: An increased risk of contracting HIV and hepatitis is associated with nitrite use.
- Weakened immune system: Recent animal research shows that nitrites may impair the immune system that protects against infectious diseases.

ARE INHALANTS ADDICTIVE?

They can be.

Most inhalant use is experimental and occasional. However, people who use inhalants regularly can develop "tolerance." This means that more and more of the substance is needed to produce the same effects. Regular use also leads to a persistent craving for the high, which makes it hard to stop using. When regular use is stopped, withdrawal symptoms may include nausea, loss of appetite, tremors, anxiety, depression and paranoia.

WHAT ARE THE LONG-TERM EFFECTS OF USING INHALANTS?

The long-term effects of inhalants vary depending on which inhalant is used. Some of the possible effects are bloodshot eyes, sores on the nose and mouth, nosebleeds, pale skin, excessive thirst and weight loss. People who use inhalants over a long term may also be confused, tired, depressed, irritable, hostile and paranoid and have trouble concentrating, remembering and thinking clearly. Heavy solvent use can result in numbness, weakness, tremors and a lack of co-ordination in the arms and legs.

Some long-term effects may be reversible, but others are permanent. When inhaled, solvents are carried by the blood and stored in fat tissue in the body. Internal organs that have high blood circulation and that are rich in fat tissue, such as the brain, liver and kidney, are particularly affected. If inhalant use is stopped, damage to the liver and kidneys may heal, but damage to the brain is almost always permanent. Studies using scans of people's brains after chronic long-term solvent use show that solvent use can cause the brain to atrophy, or shrink, which can severely affect thinking, memory and movement control.

Inhalant use can also result in permanent hearing loss and damage to bone marrow.

KETAMINE

STREET NAME

special K, K, ket, vitamin K, cat tranquilizers

WHAT IS IT?

Ketamine is a fast-acting anaesthetic and painkiller used primarily in veterinary surgery. It is also used to a lesser extent in human medicine.

Ketamine can produce vivid dreams or hallucinations, and make the user feel as though the mind is separated from the body. This effect is called "dissociation," which is also the effect of the related drug PCP. When ketamine is given to humans for medical reasons, it is often given in combination with another drug that prevents hallucinations.

WHAT DOES KETAMINE LOOK LIKE?

The ketamine that is manufactured for medical use is sold in a liquid form, though it is usually converted into a white powder before it is sold illicitly. The powder is snorted, mixed into drinks or smoked with marijuana or tobacco. The liquid is added to drinks, or injected, usually into a muscle, because injecting it into a vein usually causes loss of consciousness.

WHO USES KETAMINE?

Ketamine is legally available only to veterinarians and medical doctors. It is then stolen or diverted, and sold illegally on the street or in clubs for recreational use.

Ketamine has been used for its psychedelic effects for nearly 30 years. Users include those who take the drug for the feeling that it allows them to enter another reality. A recent increase in the popularity of the drug among young people may be related to its availability as a "club drug" at parties and "raves."

Ketamine dissolves in liquid, allowing it to be slipped into drinks, and its sedative effects have been used to prevent victims from resisting sexual assault. For this reason it has been commonly referred to in the media as a "date rape" drug. Take caution at parties and bars—watch your drink.

APPENDIX C: DO YOU KNOW...

HOW DOES KETAMINE MAKE YOU FEEL?

The way ketamine—or any other drug—affects you depends on many factors, including:

- your age and your body weight
- how much you take and how often you take it
- how long you've been taking it
- the method you use to take the drug
- the environment you're in
- whether or not you have certain pre-existing medical or psychiatric conditions
- if you've taken any alcohol or other drugs (illicit, prescription, over-the counter or herbal).

The effects of ketamine are usually felt between one and ten minutes after taking the drug. Users report a drunken and dizzy feeling and a quick numbness in the body. The range of visual experiences are reported to include blurred vision, seeing "trails," "astral travel" and intense and terrifying hallucinations. Some report feelings of weightlessness, and "out-of-body" or "near-death" experiences.

When ketamine is taken in lower doses, users may feel sleepy, distracted and withdrawn. They may find it more difficult to think clearly, feel confused and have a distorted perception of time and body. At higher doses they may babble, not remember who or where they are, stumble if they try to walk, feel their hearts race and find it difficult to breathe. Too high a dose of ketamine causes loss of consciousness.

HOW LONG DOES THE FEELING LAST?

The effects of ketamine usually last about an hour. Some users may feel low or anxious, have some memory loss and experience flashbacks of their drug experience long after the effects of the drug have worn off.

IS KETAMINE DANGEROUS?

Yes. If it is not used under the care of health professionals in a medical setting, users of ketamine put themselves at risk a number of ways.

Like all anaesthetics, ketamine prevents the user from feeling pain. This means that if injury occurs, the user may not know it. Depending on the amount of drug taken, those under its effects may have difficulty standing up or speaking, resulting in an increased risk of injury.

As with other anaesthetics, ketamine may cause vomiting. Eating or drinking before taking the drug increases the risk of choking on vomit.

When taken in higher doses, ketamine may depress the central nervous system. This can reduce the level of oxygen that gets to the brain, heart and other muscles, and may even cause death.

The ketamine sold at clubs may be mixed with other drugs, which in combination could make it even more dangerous. Combining ketamine with alcohol or other sedatives can be fatal.

Driving or operating machinery while under the influence of ketamine, or any drug, increases the risk of physical injury to the user, and increases the risk of injury to others.

IS KETAMINE ADDICTIVE?

If ketamine is used regularly, the user becomes more tolerant to the effects of the drug; meaning more and more is needed to achieve the same effect. There have been no reports of typical symptoms of drug withdrawal when users stop taking ketamine.

WHAT ARE THE LONG-TERM EFFECTS OF USING KETAMINE?

Since there has been little research about the long-term non-medical use of ketamine, the long-term effects are not known.

LSD

STREET NAMES

acid, blotter, microdot, windowpane

WHAT IS IT?

LSD (lysergic acid diethylamide) is a potent hallucinogen. The term "hallucinogen" describes a drug that can alter a person's perception of reality and vividly distort the senses. LSD was originally derived from "ergot," a fungus that grows on rye and other grains.

The hallucinogenic effect of LSD was first discovered in Switzerland in 1943 by Dr. Albert Hofmann, a research chemist at a pharmaceutical company. Early studies exploring potential use of the drug focused on what insight it might offer into certain kinds of mental illness. In the 1950s, intellectuals such as Aldous Huxley experimented with the drug for its alleged ability to induce a state of "cosmic consciousness." LSD was the subject of numerous research studies in the 1950s and early '60s. These included investigating the therapeutic potential of the "psychedelic" experience in treating chronic alcoholism and mental illness, and in helping patients dying of terminal illnesses to accept death. LSD also captured the attention of the CIA, who tested its potential for use in psychological warfare.

APPENDIX C: DO YOU KNOW...

Recreational use of LSD increased in the 1960s as its "mind-expanding" qualities were promoted by influential role models such as Harvard scientist Timothy Leary and novelist Ken Kesey.

Concerns about the possible long-term effects of LSD led to new laws aimed at restricting its use. The sale, possession for the purpose of selling and distribution of LSD were first made punishable in Canada in 1962. LSD currently has no medical use, and is prohibited under Schedule III of *Canada's Controlled Drugs and Substances Act*.

WHERE DOES LSD COME FROM?
Most LSD is produced in illicit laboratories, with only a very small amount legally manufactured for use in research.

WHAT DOES LSD LOOK LIKE?
Pure LSD is a white, crystalline powder that dissolves in water. It is odourless and has a slightly bitter taste. An effective dose of the pure drug is too small to see (20 to 80 micrograms). LSD is usually packaged in squares of LSD-soaked paper ("blotters"), miniature powder pellets ("microdots") or gelatin chips ("window pane"). Blotters are sometimes printed with illustrations of cartoon characters.

WHO USES LSD?
People who use LSD range from those seeking a high to those seeking a mystical experience. The incidence of LSD use reached its highest peak during the 1960s and '70s, and was closely associated with the "hippie" youth culture of that time. Rates of LSD use dropped in the 1980s and then began to rise again in the 1990s. In a 2001 Ontario survey of drug use among students in grades seven to OAC, 4.5 per cent of the students surveyed reported using LSD in the past year.

HOW IS LSD USED?
LSD is usually taken by mouth and held on the tongue or swallowed, but there have been reports of it being inhaled or injected.

HOW DOES LSD MAKE YOU FEEL?
How LSD affects you depends on several things:
- your age
- how sensitive you are to the drug
- how much you take and how often you take it
- how long you've been taking it
- the method you use to take the drug
- the environment you're in
- whether or not you have certain pre-existing medical or psychiatric conditions
- if you've taken any alcohol or other drugs (illicit, prescription, over-the-counter or herbal).

The physical effects of LSD may include numbness, rapid heartbeat, reduced co-ordination, chills, nausea, tremor, weakness and dilated pupils. Sensations of gravity may be altered, ranging from feeling weighted down, to feeling light and floating. The LSD experience, usually referred to as a "trip," varies widely, and is unpredictable. Individual reactions to the drug can range from ecstasy to terror, even within a single drug-taking experience. People who have used the drug before, and had a positive experience, may have a negative experience if they take it again.

Two factors that influence the way people feel when they take LSD are their "mindset"—their expectations, experience and mood at the time they take the drug—and the setting, or place where they are. For those who use the drug, the possibility of a "bad trip" may be reduced by taking the drug only when already in a positive state of mind, in a relaxed environment and with supportive friends.

LSD produces vivid visual effects. Colours seem to become more intense, halos or rainbows may appear around objects, and shapes may become fluid in form. Rapidly changing, brightly-coloured geometric patterns and other images may be seen, whether the eyes are open or shut. These visual distortions are referred to as "pseudo-hallucinations" because people are aware that what they are seeing is not real, but is due to the effect of the drug. True hallucinations, where people believe that what they are seeing is real, are not as common, but can occur, and can be frightening.

LSD affects your senses, mood, thoughts and how you perceive yourself and the world around you. The drug can produce a wide spectrum of mental states, from a sense of joy, wonder and heightened sensitivity, to panic, confusion and anxiety. Thoughts may seem clear and profound or race rapidly without logic. Sense of time, distance and body image may be distorted. Boundaries between the self and the outside world may seem to dissolve. Some users report a fusion of the senses; for example, "seeing" music or "hearing" colour.

HOW LONG DOES THE FEELING LAST?
The effects of LSD come on gradually within an hour of taking the drug, "peak" at two to four hours and gradually taper off, with the entire trip lasting up to 12 hours. The intensity of the effect depends on the size of the dose.

APPENDIX C: DO YOU KNOW...

Some users feel let down or fatigued for 12 to 24 hours after the trip is over.

IS LSD DANGEROUS?
It can be.

Sometimes people who take the drug feel that the experience gets out of control. They may feel they are losing their identity or are disintegrating into nothingness. Such a reaction can lead to a state of panic. They may try to flee the situation, or become paranoid and frightful and lash out at the people around them. Persons experiencing a dangerous reaction to LSD should, if possible, be kept calm. If the distress continues, they should receive treatment at a hospital emergency room.

No deaths resulting exclusively from an overdose of LSD have been reported. However, LSD affects judgment, which can lead to irrational, sometimes dangerous, behaviour. The drug has made people feel that they could fly, or that they could walk through traffic, and this has resulted in accidental injuries and deaths. In some people, LSD may release underlying psychosis or aggravate anxiety or depression. Long-term psychological problems may follow an adverse reaction, or "bad trip," with LSD. Taking only a small amount, or low dose, of LSD may not reduce the possibility of having a negative reaction. One person may have a "bad trip" on a low dose, while another may take a high dose, and get through it without distress. Higher doses do, however, increase the hallucinogenic effect of the drug.

Because LSD is produced illegally, it varies in purity and strength. Dealers may substitute another drug, such as PCP, or the LSD may include additives such as strychnine. If you take LSD, you can't be sure exactly what or how much you are taking, or how it will affect you.

Because LSD profoundly alters perception, it is highly hazardous to drive a vehicle while under the drug's influence.

IS LSD ADDICTIVE?
People who use LSD regularly do not experience physical withdrawal symptoms when they stop taking the drug. Regular use of LSD, however, will produce "tolerance" to the effects of the drug. This means that if the drug is taken repeatedly over a period of several days, it no longer has the same effect. After several days of not taking the drug, it becomes effective once again.

Although LSD is not physically addictive, it can be psychologically addictive. Some people who use LSD repeatedly feel compelled to take it. The drug takes on an exaggerated importance in their lives, leading to emotional and lifestyle problems.

WHAT ARE THE LONG-TERM EFFECTS OF TAKING LSD?
The use of LSD can result in long-term effects in one-time and regular users of the drug. Possible negative effects are "flashbacks" of the drug experience, as well as prolonged anxiety, depression or psychosis. These reactions usually decrease over time, and end within a few months after LSD was last taken, but may continue for years.

"Flashbacks" are the spontaneous and unpredictable replay of an aspect of the LSD trip, occurring some time after the initial effects of the drug have worn off. Visual or emotional experiences that were originally seen or felt while under the influence of LSD are re-experienced. Flashbacks usually last only a few seconds or minutes, but may happen over and over again. Only some people who take LSD have flashbacks, but frequent users of the drug are said to be at greater risk. Flashbacks may be triggered by smoking marijuana or drinking alcohol, or by emotional stress, fatigue or meditation.

Depression or anxiety may follow a "bad trip." Psychosis may develop after using LSD, although it is thought that this reaction may be more likely to occur in people with latent or underlying mental health problems.

METHADONE

STREET NAMES
juice, meth (also used to refer to methamphetamines)

WHAT IS IT?
Methadone belongs to the opioid family of drugs. It is used most commonly to treat dependence on other opioid drugs such as heroin, codeine and morphine.

Methadone is a "synthetic" opioid, which means that it is made from chemicals in a lab. Other opioid drugs include the "opiates," such as morphine and codeine, which are natural products of the opium poppy, and "semi-synthetic" opioids, such as heroin, which is morphine that has been chemically processed.

Methadone was developed in Germany during the Second World War and was first used to provide pain relief.

Methadone maintenance treatment, which prevents opioid withdrawal and reduces or eliminates drug cravings, was first developed in the

1960s. For many years, Canadian regulations around the prescription of methadone were so restrictive that few doctors offered the treatment. People who wanted methadone treatment often had to wait months or years. In the 1990s, the need to reduce the harm of drug use was more clearly recognized, and changes were made to make it easier for doctors to provide methadone treatment. This has led to an increase in the number of people receiving treatment, and a decrease in the number of heroin-related deaths.

Methadone maintenance is not a "cure": it is a treatment. Through treatment, people who are dependent on opioids receive the medical and social support they need to stabilize and improve their lives. They are encouraged to stay in treatment for as long as it helps them.

WHAT DOES METHADONE LOOK LIKE?
Pure methadone is a white crystalline powder. The powder is dissolved, usually in a fruit-flavoured drink, and is taken orally once a day.

WHO USES METHADONE?
Most people who are prescribed methadone are being treated for dependence on opioid drugs. This includes people who are dependent on illicit opioids, such as heroin, and also prescription opioids, such as codeine.

Women who use opioid drugs regularly and who are pregnant are often treated with methadone to protect the fetus. Short-acting opioids such as heroin must be taken frequently to avoid withdrawal. Opioid withdrawal increases the risk of miscarriage or premature birth. Methadone maintenance, combined with medical care, improves the chances of having a healthy baby. There are no known long-term effects of methadone on the baby.

People who use opioid drugs regularly, and who are infected with HIV or hepatitis C, are prescribed methadone treatment to help protect their health, and to reduce the risk of spreading infection through needle sharing.

Methadone is sometimes used to provide pain relief for people who have severe chronic pain or pain associated with terminal illness.

HOW DOES METHADONE MAKE YOU FEEL?
When people begin methadone treatment, some experience the euphoria and sedation that are common to all opioid drugs. As treatment continues, and a stable dose of methadone is established, tolerance to these effects develops. Those in treatment often describe the feeling of being on methadone as "normal." Methadone treatment does not interfere with their thinking. They can work, go to school or care for family. Methadone also blocks the euphoric effect of heroin and other opioids, and in this way reduces the use of these drugs.

Most people experience some side-effects from methadone treatment. Possible side-effects include sweating, constipation and weight gain.

HOW LONG DOES THE EFFECT LAST?
A person who is opioid-dependent is kept free of withdrawal symptoms for 24 hours with a single dose of methadone. In contrast, a person who uses heroin to avoid withdrawal must use three to four times a day.

Daily treatment with methadone may continue indefinitely. If, however, the person taking methadone and his or her doctor agree to move toward ending treatment, the methadone dose is tapered down gradually over many weeks or months, easing the process of withdrawal.

If methadone is stopped abruptly, symptoms such as stomach cramps, diarrhea and muscle and bone ache will occur. These symptoms begin within one to three days after the last dose, peak at three to five days, and then gradually subside, although other symptoms such as sleep problems and drug cravings may continue for months.

IS METHADONE DANGEROUS?
When methadone is taken as prescribed, it is very safe and will not cause any damage to internal organs or thinking, even when taken daily for many years. On the other hand, methadone is a powerful drug and can be extremely dangerous to people who do not take it regularly, as they have no tolerance for its effects. Even a small amount may be fatal for a child. For this reason, the dispensing of methadone is carefully monitored and controlled.

An important benefit of methadone treatment is that it reduces heroin use. The dangers of heroin use include death by overdose, and becoming infected, through needle sharing, with viruses such as HIV and hepatitis C. Methadone treatment helps to protect people from heroin-related tragedies.

IS METHADONE ADDICTIVE?
Modern definitions of "addiction" look at many factors in assessing a person's drug use. These include "tolerance," or the need to use increasing amounts to achieve the same effect; "physical dependence," resulting in withdrawal symptoms if drug use is stopped; and

APPENDIX C: DO YOU KNOW...

"compulsive use," despite the negative consequences of continuing to use the drug.

Some people say that methadone is just as "addictive" as heroin. People in methadone treatment do become tolerant to certain effects of the drug, and will experience withdrawal if they do not take their regular dose. But methadone fails to meet a full definition of "addictive" when we look at how and why the drug is used.

First of all, methadone maintenance is offered as a medical treatment, and is prescribed only to people who are already dependent on opioid drugs. For these people, methadone provides a safe alternative to the routine danger and desperation of securing a steady supply of street drugs such as heroin. It frees them from the nagging compulsion to use, and allows them a chance to focus on improving their lives.

Methadone is sometimes used as a street drug, but when it is, it is usually taken to prevent symptoms of heroin withdrawal. The effects of methadone come on too slowly and last too long to give it much appeal as a substance of abuse.

WHAT ARE THE LONG-TERM EFFECTS OF METHADONE?
Methadone maintenance is a long-term treatment. Length of treatment varies, from a year or two to 20 years or more. This prolonged treatment with proper doses of methadone is medically safe and is the most effective treatment currently available for opioid dependence.

METHADONE

STREET NAME
speed, meth, chalk, ice, crystal, crystal meth, jib

WHAT IS IT?
Methamphetamine belongs to a family of drugs called amphetamines—powerful stimulants that speed up the body's central nervous system. In the 1930s methamphetamine was marketed as a nasal decongestant, and is still medically available in the U.S. as a treatment for obesity. The medical usefulness of methamphetamine is limited by the severity of its adverse effects, and by its high addictive potential. Methamphetamine is not legally available in Canada.

WHERE DOES METHAMPHETAMINE COME FROM?
The methamphetamine that is produced for recreational use is made in illicit labs with fairly inexpensive, and often toxic or flammable,

ingredients. The chemicals and processes used vary from lab to lab, affecting the strength, purity and effect of the final product.

WHAT DOES METHAMPHETAMINE LOOK LIKE?
Methamphetamine is a white, odourless, bitter-tasting crystalline powder that dissolves easily in water or alcohol and may be snorted, swallowed, smoked or injected. In its smokable form, methamphetamine is called "ice," "crystal," "crank" or "glass" because of its transparent, sheet-like crystals. It is smoked in a pipe like crack cocaine.

WHO USES METHAMPHETAMINE?
In the past, illicit methamphetamine use was most closely associated with biker gangs, and also had a spell of popularity in the hippie culture of the 1960s. More recently, the low cost, ease of manufacture and availability of methamphetamine has led to a rise in use among a variety of people. These users include young people at raves, nightclubs and parties, and cocaine users who substitute methamphetamine for its cocaine-like effects.

HOW DOES METHAMPHETAMINE MAKE YOU FEEL?
The way methamphetamine—or any other drug—affects you depends on many factors, including:

- your age and your body weight
- how much you take and how often you take it
- how long you've been taking it
- the method you use to take the drug
- the environment you're in
- whether or not you have certain pre-existing medical or psychiatric conditions
- if you've taken any alcohol or other drugs (illicit, prescription, over-the-counter or herbal).

Immediately after smoking methamphetamine or injecting it into a vein, the user experiences an intense surge of euphoria, called a "rush" or "flash." Snorting methamphetamine produces effects within three to five minutes; swallowing in about 15–20 minutes.

Methamphetamine makes people feel alert and energetic, confident and talkative. They feel little need for food or sleep. On the other hand, users are also likely to feel the many unwanted effects of the drug, including racing of the heart, chest pain, dryness of the mouth, nausea, vomiting and diarrhea and physical tension. Many report an anxious "wired" feeling of restlessness and irritability. The negative effects of methamphetamine can be extreme and alarming, including paranoid delusions, hallucinations, aggressive behaviour and impulsive violence.

HOW LONG DOES THE FEELING LAST?
When methamphetamine is injected or taken by mouth, the effects of the drug last about six to eight hours. Smoking methamphetamine may produce effects that last from 10–12 hours. After the effects of the drug have worn off, users are left feeling tired and depressed. Some use the drug continuously over a period of days or weeks in a "binge and crash" pattern, inviting serious health risks, and leading to drug dependency.

IS METHAMPHETAMINE ADDICTIVE?
Yes. Tolerance to the effects of methamphetamine builds up quickly in regular users, meaning they need more and more of the drug to achieve the desired effect. When dependent users stop taking methamphetamine, they have strong cravings for the drug, and within a few days will experience withdrawal symptoms, including stomach pain, hunger, headaches, shortness of breath, tiredness and depression.

IS METHAMPHETAMINE DANGEROUS?
Yes. Methamphetamine causes the heart to beat faster and blood pressure to rise. Since the content of the drug sold varies widely, it is difficult to judge the size of dose. An overdose of methamphetamine can result in seizures, high body temperature, irregular heartbeat, heart attack, stroke and death. The risk of overdose is highest when the drug is injected.

Injecting methamphetamine also puts the user at risk of infections from used needles or impurities in the drug, and of hepatitis or HIV if they share needles with others.

Driving or operating machinery while under the influence of methamphetamine, or any drug, increases the risk of physical injury to the user, and increases the risk of injury to others.

WHAT ARE THE LONG-TERM EFFECTS OF USING METHAMPHETAMINE?
When methamphetamine is used regularly over a long period of time, people can develop amphetamine psychosis. The symptoms of amphetamine psychosis include hallucinations, delusions, paranoia and bizarre and violent behaviour.

Research in animals and humans suggests that methamphetamine may cause long-term damage to cells in those areas of the brain associated with thinking, memory and movement. Further research is needed to determine if these effects are permanent.

OPIOIDS

STREET NAMES
junk, H, horse, smack, shit, skag (for heroin); M, morph, Miss Emma (for morphine); meth (for methadone); percs (for Percodan®, Percocet®); juice (for Dilaudid®)

WHAT ARE THEY?
Opioids are a family of drugs that have morphine-like effects. Their primary medical use is to relieve pain. Other medical uses include control of coughs and diarrhea, and the treatment of addiction to other opioids. Opioids can also produce euphoria, making them prone to abuse.

Federal laws regulate the possession and distribution of all opioids. Penalties for the illicit possession and distribution of opioids range from fines to life imprisonment.

WHERE DO OPIOIDS COME FROM?
Some opioids, such as morphine and codeine, occur naturally in opium, a gummy substance collected from the seed pod of the opium poppy, which grows in southern Asia. Other opioids, such as heroin, are made by adding a chemical to morphine. Today, many drugs in the opioid category don't actually come from opium. Instead, they are made synthetically from chemicals. Examples of opioids produced by pharmaceutical companies include oxycodone (Percodan/Percocet), meperidine (Demerol®), hydrocodone (Tussionex®) and hydromorphone (Dilaudid).

WHAT DO OPIOIDS LOOK LIKE?
Prescription opioids come in various forms—tablets, capsules, syrups, solutions and suppositories.

Opium comes in dark brown chunks or powder, and is usually eaten or smoked. Heroin is usually a white or brownish powder. (See *Do You Know... Heroin.*)

WHO USES OPIOIDS?
Doctors and dentists prescribe opioids to people with acute or chronic pain resulting from disease, surgery or injury. Opioids are also prescribed to people with moderate to severe coughs and diarrhea. Opioids such as methadone and buprenorphine are used to treat addiction to other opioids, such as heroin.

APPENDIX C: DO YOU KNOW...

Because of the risk of abuse, opioids are prescribed cautiously for chronic pain. However, opioids are of particular value in controlling pain in the later stages of terminal illness, when the possibility of physical dependence is not significant.

Some people use opioids for their ability to produce a mellow, relaxed "high." Much attention is given to the use of illegal drugs, such as heroin, but some of the most commonly used and abused opioids are prescription drugs, such as codeine-containing Tylenol® (1, 2, 3 and 4), hydromorphone (Dilaudid), oxycodone (Percocet, Percodan), morphine and others.

Sometimes people who are prescribed opioids use them inappropriately. One warning sign is the early renewal of prescriptions. People who abuse opioids sometimes "double doctor," an illegal practice of filling an opioid prescription from more than one doctor, without letting the others know. These drugs are also stolen from pharmacies, and sold on the street.

Health professionals with access to prescription drugs are also at risk of opioid abuse. Some become dependent.

HOW DO OPIOIDS MAKE YOU FEEL?
The way opioids affect you depends on:
- how much you use
- how often and how long you use
- how you take them (e.g., by injection, orally)
- your mood, expectations and environment
- your age
- whether you have certain pre-existing medical or psychiatric conditions
- whether you've taken any alcohol or other drugs (illicit, prescription, over-the-counter or herbal).

Low doses of opioids suppress the sensation of pain and the emotional response to pain. They may also produce euphoria, drowsiness, relaxation, difficulty concentrating, constricted pupils, slight decrease in respiratory rate, nausea, vomiting, constipation, loss of appetite and sweating. With higher doses, these effects are more intense and last longer.

The speed and intensity of the effects of opioids vary depending on how the drugs are taken. When taken orally, the effects come on gradually, and are usually felt in about 10 to 20 minutes. When injected into a vein, the effects are most intense and are felt within a minute.

HOW LONG DOES THE FEELING LAST?
When opioids are taken to relieve pain, how long the effect is felt varies somewhat depending on the type of opioid taken, although a single dose of many opioids can provide pain relief for four to five hours.

ARE OPIOIDS DANGEROUS?
Yes. Opioids can be dangerous if they are used without medical supervision. Here are some of the reasons:
- All opioid drugs, especially heroin, are particularly dangerous when taken in large quantities or when taken with other depressants, such as alcohol or benzodiazepines. Opioids slow down the part of your brain that controls breathing. Signs of overdose include slow breathing, bluish skin and coma. Death can result, usually because breathing stops. If caught in time, overdose can be treated with drugs such as naloxone, which blocks the effects of opioids, including the effect on breathing.
- People who seek the euphoric effects of opioids may take more and more of the drug as they develop tolerance to its effects. As the amount taken increases, so does the risk of overdose. If people with tolerance stop taking the drug, they lose their tolerance. If they then resume taking the same amount they took before they stopped, the risk of overdose is extreme.
- Some people inject opioids to increase the intensity of the euphoric effect. Non-medical injection drug use carries a high risk of infection and disease due to dirty needles, sharing needles and impurities in the drug. The incidence of HIV and hepatitis is particularly high among injection drug users. Street drugs are almost never pure, and pharmaceutical tablets or capsules, when diluted for injection, contain substances that can permanently damage veins and organs.
- Taking short-acting opioids, such as heroin, during pregnancy can result in premature delivery, low birth weight, infant withdrawal and infant death. Pregnant women who are dependent on opioids are treated with the long-acting opioid methadone to prevent withdrawal symptoms. (See *Do You Know... Methadone.*)

ARE OPIOIDS ADDICTIVE?
They can be.

When opioids are used occasionally under medical supervision, there is little risk of addiction. However, people who use opioids regularly for their pleasurable effects soon develop tolerance to these effects. They may then use more of the drug to achieve the original intensity of effect. Chronic use or abuse of opioids can lead to psychological and physical dependence.

People are *psychologically dependent* when a drug is so central to their thoughts, emotions and activities that the need to continue its use becomes a craving or compulsion.

With *physical dependence*, the body has adapted to the presence of the drug, and withdrawal symptoms occur if use of the drug is reduced or stopped abruptly.

The person who is physically dependent will experience withdrawal symptoms about six to 12 hours after last taking a short-acting opioid, such as heroin, and about one to three days after last taking a long-acting opioid, such as methadone. With short-acting opioids, withdrawal comes on quickly and is intense; with longer-acting opioids, withdrawal comes on more gradually, and is less intense.

Symptoms of withdrawal include uneasiness, yawning, tears, diarrhea, abdominal cramps, goose bumps and runny nose. These symptoms are accompanied by a craving for the drug. Symptoms usually subside after a week, although some symptoms, such as anxiety, insomnia and drug craving, may continue for a long time. Unlike alcohol withdrawal, opioid withdrawal is rarely life-threatening.

WHAT ARE THE LONG-TERM EFFECTS OF TAKING OPIOIDS?

Long-term use of opioids can cause mood instability, constricted pupils (impaired night vision), constipation, decreased libido and menstrual irregularities. Addiction to opioids can have devastating long-term social, financial and emotional effects.

ROHYPNOL®

STREET NAME

roofies, roachies, La Roche, rope, rophies, ruffies

WHAT IS IT?

Rohypnol® is the brand name of flunitrazepam, a medication with sedative effects that is produced and marketed outside North America for medical use. In Canada and the U.S., it is illegal to possess, traffic, import or produce Rohypnol.

Rohypnol belongs to a family of medications called benzodiazepines, which also includes diazepam (Valium®) and lorazepam (Ativan®). Benzodiazepines are central nervous system depressants, which decrease anxiety and cause drowsiness, and slow your heart rate,

breathing and thinking. Rohypnol's main medical use is as a short-term treatment for insomnia.

Rohypnol has been referred to in the media as a "date rape" drug. While there is little evidence of Rohypnol use in Canada, there have been reports of drugs being used to facilitate sexual assault. Such cases may have involved other drugs such as GHB, ketamine, alcohol and other benzodiazepines.

WHAT DOES ROHYPNOL LOOK LIKE?

Rohypnol tablets are white and are single or cross-scored on one side, with "ROCHE" and "1" or "2" in a circle on the other. Hoffman-La Roche Inc., the drug company that makes Rohypnol, has recently stopped making the higher strength 2 mg tablet. Rohypnol sold on the street is often still in the original blister packaging, leading to the mistaken belief that the drug is legal and safe. It is usually taken orally, but there are some reports of it being ground up and snorted.

WHO USES ROHYPNOL?

When used non-medically, Rohypnol is rarely taken on its own, and is usually taken to increase the effect of other drugs, especially alcohol, marijuana or heroin. Rohypnol is also taken to decrease the after-effects of other drugs, such as cocaine, ecstasy or amphetamines.

The main recreational users of Rohypnol are teenagers and young adults, who usually combine it with alcohol.

Until recently, Rohypnol's tablets dissolved quickly in liquid, making it easy to slip them into drinks without arousing suspicion. When the drug took effect, the victim was too sedated to resist sexual assault.

Since 1997 the tablets have been made to dissolve more slowly in liquid, turn clear beverages bright blue, and turn darker beverages murky, making it much easier to detect the presence of the drug in a drink. Despite these changes, take caution at parties and bars—watch your drink.

HOW DOES ROHYPNOL MAKE YOU FEEL?

The way Rohypnol affects you depends on many factors, including:

· your age and your body weight
· how much you take and how often you take it
· how long you've been taking it
· the method you use to take the drug
· the environment you're in

APPENDIX C: DO YOU KNOW...

- whether or not you have certain pre-existing medical or psychiatric conditions
- if you've taken any alcohol or other drugs (illicit, prescription, over-the-counter or herbal).

The effects of Rohypnol begin within 30 minutes and peak within two hours. As little as 1 mg can have effect for eight hours. Depending upon how much you take, Rohypnol can make you feel anything from relaxed and calm, to drowsy and clumsy, to unconscious.

Even when Rohypnol is taken without alcohol or other drugs, users can appear "drunk." The effects of Rohypnol include reduced inhibition and judgment, slurred speech, weakness and staggering, dizziness, confusion and severe drowsiness. Users may also experience visual disturbances and amnesia. These effects are intensified when Rohypnol is combined with alcohol, and often result in "blackouts," or periods of time, from eight to 24 hours, for which the person has no memory.

IS ROHYPNOL DANGEROUS?

The most extreme and immediate dangers of Rohypnol are caused by its intoxicating and sedating effects. Recreational drug users who combine Rohypnol with other depressant drugs such as alcohol may find themselves much more stoned and drunk than they had intended. They may be unable to think clearly or protect themselves from harm. If they lose consciousness, they may vomit and choke.

When Rohypnol or other drugs are dissolved in someone's drink without his or her knowledge, the drug becomes a partner in crime. Many assault victims have reported waking naked and bruised, having had unprotected sex, without any memory of what took place.

Driving or operating machinery while under the influence of Rohypnol, or any drug, increases the risk of physical injury to the user, and increases the risk of injury to others.

IS ROHYPNOL ADDICTIVE?

It can be. The addictive potential of Rohypnol depends on how much you take, how long you take it, and whether or not you have been dependent on any other drug.

If Rohypnol is taken daily for more than a few weeks, users may become dependent on it, feeling that they need the drug in order to relax or get to sleep. Those who are dependent on Rohypnol are "tolerant" to its effects, meaning they need more and more of the drug in order to achieve the desired results.

Those who use Rohypnol regularly for more than four weeks should see a doctor for help in managing a gradual withdrawal. Dependent Rohypnol users who stop using the drug can expect withdrawal symptoms, which may be mild to severe, including anxiety, insomnia, nausea, dizziness and depression. Abrupt withdrawal can cause severe symptoms, including convulsions and psychosis.

TOBACCO

WHAT IS IT?

Tobacco is a plant (*Nicotiana tabacum* and *Nicotiana rustica*) that contains nicotine, an addictive drug with both stimulant and depressant effects.

Tobacco is most commonly smoked in cigarettes. It is also smoked in cigars or pipes, chewed as chewing tobacco, sniffed as dry snuff or held inside the lip or cheek as wet snuff. Tobacco may also be mixed with cannabis and smoked in "joints." All methods of using tobacco deliver nicotine to the body.

Although tobacco is legal, federal, provincial and municipal laws tightly control tobacco manufacture, marketing, distribution and use. Second-hand tobacco smoke is now recognized as a health danger, which has led to increasing restrictions on where people can smoke. Violations of tobacco-related laws can result in fines and/or prison terms.

WHERE DOES TOBACCO COME FROM?

Tobacco was cultivated and widely used by the peoples of the Americas long before the arrival of Europeans. Today, most of the tobacco sold in Canada is grown in Ontario. The plant's large leaves are cured, fermented and aged before they are manufactured into tobacco products. Canadian tobacco is commercially packaged and sold to retailers by one of three tobacco companies.

WHO USES TOBACCO?

Greater awareness of the negative health effects of smoking and increased restrictions have led to a steady decline in rates of smoking in Canada. In 1965, almost half of the population smoked. By 2002, this rate had dipped to less than a quarter (23 per cent of men and 20 per cent of women, aged 15 and over). Despite the decline, 5.4 million Canadians still smoke.

Most people who smoke begin between the ages of 11 and 15. An ongoing survey of Ontario students in grades 7 to OAC indicates that cigarette smoking has declined in young people, from 29.2 per cent in 1999, to 23.6 per cent in 2001.

While tobacco use is decreasing in Canada and other developed countries, it is increasing in developing countries.

Tobacco use tends to be more common among people with lower levels of education and income.

Studies show that genetic factors play a role in whether or not a person will become dependent on nicotine.

People with certain psychiatric disorders are more likely to use tobacco. A U.S. survey of people who received psychiatric outpatient services reported that rates of smoking were 88 per cent for people with schizophrenia, 70 per cent for those with mania and 49 per cent for those with depression. Another study found that 85 per cent of people seeking treatment for alcohol dependence also smoked.

HOW DOES TOBACCO MAKE YOU FEEL?

The nicotine in tobacco smoke travels quickly to the brain, where it acts as a stimulant and increases heart rate and breathing. Tobacco smoke also reduces the level of oxygen in the bloodstream, causing a drop in skin temperature. Inexperienced smokers are likely to experience dizziness, nausea and coughing or gagging.

The mood-altering effects of nicotine are subtle, complex and powerful. Some people feel that smoking helps them to be alert and to concentrate, and also that it helps them to feel relaxed. Research has shown that smoking raises levels of dopamine, a chemical in the brain, increasing feelings of pleasure and reinforcing the desire to continue to smoke.

Smoking and second-hand smoke can irritate the eyes, nose and throat. Tobacco smoke may cause headaches, dizziness, nausea, coughing and wheezing, and can aggravate allergies and asthma. Smoking also weakens the sense of taste and smell, reduces hunger and causes the stomach to produce acid.

HOW SMOKING AFFECTS YOU DEPENDS ON

- how much and how often you smoke
- how long you've been smoking
- your mood, expectations and the environment
- your age
- whether you have certain pre-existing medical or psychiatric conditions

- whether you've taken alcohol or other drugs (illicit, prescription, over-the-counter or herbal).

HOW LONG DOES THE FEELING LAST?

When a cigarette is smoked, the effects are felt in less than 10 seconds, and last only a few minutes.

IS TOBACCO DANGEROUS?

Yes. Tobacco use is the primary cause of preventable disease and death in Canada, and is considered our greatest public health concern. One study estimated that more than 45,000 Canadians die each year of smoking-related causes. This includes people who smoke, and people who are exposed to second-hand smoke.

Nicotine itself is extremely toxic. Ingesting about 40 milligrams of pure nicotine, or roughly the amount contained in two cigarettes, is fatal. However, when a cigarette is smoked, most of the nicotine is burned, and only one to four milligrams are absorbed by the smoker.

When tobacco is burned, a dark sticky "tar" is formed from a combination of hundreds of chemicals, including poisons that cause cancers and bronchial disorders. Tar is released in tobacco smoke in tiny particles that damage the lungs and airways and stain teeth and fingers. Tar is the main cause of lung and throat cancers.

Burning tobacco also forms carbon monoxide (CO), a poisonous gas you can't see or smell. When smoke is inhaled, CO replaces oxygen in red blood cells. While nicotine speeds up the heart, making it work harder, CO deprives it of the extra oxygen this work demands. This is one way that smoking contributes to heart disease.

Canadian laws require that levels of tar, nicotine and carbon monoxide appear on cigarette packages. It was once thought that cigarettes with less tar and nicotine might be less harmful to the smoker. However, research has shown that so-called "light" cigarettes are just as likely to cause disease.

IS TOBACCO ADDICTIVE?

Yes. Once a person begins to smoke, particularly at a young age, the chances of becoming addicted are quite high. New smokers quickly develop tolerance to the initial ill effects, and if they enjoy the stimulant and pleasant effects, they may begin to smoke regularly. Regular smokers tend to smoke a consistent number of cigarettes per day. Canadian smokers have, on average, about 16 cigarettes per day.

APPENDIX C: DO YOU KNOW...

Nicotine dependence involves psychological and physical factors. Psychological factors may include feelings of pleasure and alertness. People who smoke regularly may learn to rely on the effects of nicotine to bring about these feelings. They also develop conditioned signals, or "triggers," for cigarette use. For example, some people always smoke after a meal, while working at a certain task or while in certain emotional states, such as feeling depressed or anxious. These triggers lead to behaviour patterns, or habits, which can be difficult to change.

Signs of physical dependence include the urge to smoke within minutes of waking, smoking at regular intervals throughout the day, and ranking the first cigarette of the day as the most important.

People who are dependent on nicotine may become tolerant to the desired effects. They may no longer experience pleasure from smoking, but continue smoking to avoid nicotine withdrawal.

Symptoms of nicotine withdrawal include irritability, restlessness, anxiety, insomnia and fatigue. These symptoms vanish within a couple of weeks. Some people may be unable to concentrate, and have strong cravings to smoke, for weeks or months after quitting smoking.

QUITTING SMOKING

People who quit smoking can generally achieve the same health levels as non-smokers after a few years, especially if they stop while they are young. Quitting smoking can take several attempts, so it is important to keep trying. Stop-smoking aids containing nicotine, such as the patch, gum, inhaler or nasal spray can help to ease withdrawal symptoms and reduce cravings. Such aids work best when the person is highly motivated to quit, and when the person has other supports, such as family, friends, a stop-smoking group or telephone support.

Certain medications that do not contain nicotine can help people to quit smoking. These include bupropion (Zyban®) and nortriptyline (Aventyl®). Both are available by prescription.

For some people, cutting down before quitting helps to lessen the withdrawal symptoms, and allows them to change their smoking behaviours gradually. Strategies for cutting down include delaying cigarettes, smoking fewer cigarettes and smoking less of each cigarette. Although cutting down may reduce some health risks, there is no safe level of smoking; cutting down is not an alternative to quitting.

There are currently more former smokers than smokers in Canada. In 2001, 24 per cent of the population, or about 5.9 million Canadians aged 15 and over, reported they had quit smoking.

WHAT ARE THE LONG-TERM EFFECTS OF USING TOBACCO?

The risk of long-term effects increases with the amount smoked, and the length of time a person smokes.

Smoking:
- is the *main* cause of lung cancer
- increases the risk of cancers of the colon, mouth, throat, pancreas, bladder and cervix
- causes *most* cases of chronic bronchitis and emphysema
- causes smoker's cough
- is a *major* cause of heart disease and stroke
- increases the risk of medical problems for a woman during pregnancy (e.g., miscarriage, bleeding, placenta previa and poor healing) and increases the risk that her baby will be underweight or will die in infancy
- causes osteoporosis (thinning of the bones)
- increases risk of digestive problems
- affects the immune system, making smokers more prone to colds, flus and pneumonia
- decreases the amount of vitamin C in the body, which may cause skin wounds to heal less quickly
- can cause the arteries in the legs to become clogged, resulting in poor circulation, leg pain, gangrene and loss of limb.

Many of the risks and dangers of smoking also apply to people who are exposed to second-hand smoke. Long-term exposure to second-hand smoke:
- has been linked to heart disease and cancer
- (in pregnant women) increases the risk of complications during pregnancy and delivery, and of delivering babies with a low birth weight
- (in young children) has been linked to sudden infant death syndrome, can lead to or worsen respiratory problems such as asthma; also causes middle ear infections.

Use of tobacco products that are not smoked, such as snuff and chewing tobacco, are linked to an increased risk of oral cancers, gingivitis and tooth decay.

APPENDIX D: SCREENING TOOLS

Brief summaries of tools reported in the literature that are youth specific and that can be administered by any experienced professional.

MENTAL HEALTH & SUBSTANCE USE	AGE	COST/ACCESS	SCORING	COMMENTS
Problem Oriented Screening Instrument for Teenagers (POSIT)	12 to 19	National Clearinghouse for Alcohol and Drug Information, Rockville MD 800 729-6686; cost not provided	Hand- or computer-scored	20 to 30 minutes to administer. It is a 139 item yes/no format questionnaire developed by a panel of experts to identify problems in 10 areas including substance use, mental/physical health and social relationships. Scoring uses empirically derived cut-off scores that indicate low, medium or high risk for each problem area. The POSIT is part of the Comprehensive Assessment Battery (CAB).
Drug Use Screening Inventory—Revised (DUSI-R)	Adolescents and adults	Department of Psychiatry, University of Pittsburgh Medical School; $2 per DUSI-R questionnaire, no information printed on cost of manual or computerized version	Hand- or computer-scored	20 to 40 minutes to administer. This is a 159 item questionnaire that documents the level of involvement with a variety of drugs and quantifies severity of consequences associated with drug use. The profile identifies and prioritizes intervention needs and provides an informative method of monitoring treatment course and aftercare. Its purpose is to comprehensively evaluate adolescents or adults who are suspected of using drugs, to identify problem areas and to estimate likelihood of a drug-use problem diagnosis. It covers substance use, health status, psychiatric disorder, social skills, family system, school/work, peer relationships and leisure activities.
MENTAL HEALTH				
Mental Status Checklist—Adolescent (also an adult version for 18 and over)	13 to17	Psychological Assessment Resources (PAR); $50 for 25 checklists	no scoring required	20 minutes to administer. It is designed to assess adolescent mental health status and covers a wide variety of psychological, health, alcohol/drug, memory and personality problems based on the client's self-report (e.g., self-reported symptoms of anxiety, depression), as well as interviewer observations and clinical impressions. Clients respond to a series of questions asked by an interviewer or it can be self-administered.
Personal Problems Checklist—Adolescent (also an adult version for 18 and over)	13 to 17	Psychological Assessment Resources (PAR); $50 for 25 checklists	no scoring required	20 minutes to administer. It is designed to identify areas that might be problematic, including social, job, home, school, money, religion, emotions, appearance, family, dating, health, attitudes and crises. Clients respond to a series of questions asked by an interviewer or it can be self-administered. Published in 1984.

APPENDIX D: SCREENING TOOLS

Brief summaries of tools reported in the literature that are youth specific and that can be administered by any experienced professional.

MENTAL HEALTH	AGE	COST/ACCESS	SCORING	COMMENTS
Problem Behavior Inventory—Adolescent Screening Inventory (adult version available)	Under 18	Western Psychological Services; $50 for 25 carbonized Auto Score forms	Hand-scored	10 to 15 minutes to administer. The inventory lists over 100 symptoms related to DSM-IV diagnostic categories. The client checks symptoms he/she is experiencing.
Adolescent Psychopathology Scale—Short Form (APS—SF) (the RAASI is a briefer screener for the APS)	12 to 19	Canadian Skill Builders; $250 for manual, 25 test booklets and key disk	Computer-scored only	20 minutes to administer. This is the screener for the parent instrument Adolescent Psychopathology Scale (APS). The APS—SF is comprised of 115 items related to DSM-IV. It consists of 12 clinical scales and 2 validity scales. 6 of the clinical scales focus on symptoms associated with conduct disorders, oppositional defiant disorder, depression, anxiety, PTSD and substance use problems. The other 6 scales evaluate related domains of adolescent psychosocial problems and competencies (e.g., eating disturbance, anger, self-concept, etc.). The computer-scoring program generates T-scores for each scale and a general clinical report.
Reynolds Adolescent Adjustment Screening Inventory (RAASI)	12 to 19	Canadian Skill Builders; $200, for manual and 50 tests booklets	Hand-scored	5 minutes to administer. This is a brief screening measure to identify adolescents in need of psychological evaluation. Comprised of 32 items from the parent Adolescent Psychopathology Scale (APS), it yields scores on 4 scales using T-scores: anti-social behaviour, anger control, emotional distress, and positive self image, as well as a Total Adjustment Score.
Symptom Assessment—45 (SA—45)	13 and older	MHS; $71 for starter kit (SA—45 manual and 25 Quick Score forms)	Hand- or computer-scored	10 minutes to administer. This is a short form of the Symptom Checklist 90—R (SCL—90—R) that provides a brief assessment of symptomatology across 9 symptom dimensions: somatization, obsessive-compulsive disorder (OCD), interpersonal sensitivity, depression, anxiety, hostility, phobias, paranoid ideation and psychosis. It is comprised of 45 items on a 5-point scale. Normative data is available for outpatient and in-patient adolescents and adults. An independent review indicated "the SA—45 is a psychometrically sound screening measure, with greater support for its use with adults than adolescents (due to the small adolescent standardization sample). The benefits of the SA—45 over the 53-item BSI appear limited (they share 78% of items)." Published in 1996 and 1998.

APPENDIX D: SCREENING TOOLS

Brief summaries of tools reported in the literature that are youth specific and that can be administered by any experienced professional.

MENTAL HEALTH	AGE	COST/ACCESS	SCORING	COMMENTS
Brief Symptom Inventory (BSI) (also a "briefer" BSI for adults 18 and over)	13 to 17	MHS; $215 for starter kit for adolescents (BSI manual and 50 forms); $215 for starter kit for adults (BSI manual and 50 forms)	Hand- or computer-scored	8-10 minutes to administer. This is a short form of the Symptom Checklist—90—R (SCL—90—R). Comprised of 53 items, it evaluates psychological distress in medical and psychiatric patients in 9 symptom dimensions: somatization, OCD, interpersonal sensitivity, depression, anxiety, hostility, phobias, paranoid ideation, and psychosis. Normative data is available for 4 populations: non-patient adolescent, non-patient adult, outpatient psychiatric and in-patient psychiatric.
Holden Psychological Screening Inventory (HPSI)	14 and older	MHS; $67 for complete kit (HPSI manual and 25 Quick Score forms)	Hand- or computer-scored	5 to 7 minutes to administer. Comprised of 36 items on a 5-point scale, it measures 3 major dimensions of psychopathology: psychiatric symptomatology; social symptomatology and depression. Normative data is available for high school and university students, general adult and psychiatric adult populations. An independent review concluded that "the scoring materials are user friendly" and "the HPSI meets its primary goal as an efficient method for clinical screening." Developed in Canada and published in 1996.
Behaviour and Symptom Identification Scale (BASIS—32)	Adolescents (and adults)	McLean Hospital, Department of Mental Health Services Research www.basis-32.org/index.html	Hand-scored	10 minutes to administer. This is a 32-item questionnaire using a 5-point scale to identify difficulties in life functioning areas. There are 5 scales: relations to self/others, daily living, depression/anxiety, impulsive/addictive, and psychosis, as well as an overall average score. Results are presented as a bar graph with ratings from "no difficulty" to "extreme difficulty."
ALCOHOL USE				
Adolescent Drinking Index (ADI)	12 to 17	Psychological Assessment Resources; $100 for manual and 25 test booklets	Hand-scored	5 minutes to administer. This is a 24-item rating scale to screen for alcohol use problems with adolescents who have psychological, emotional or behavioural problems. Scores are converted to T-scores.
Rutgers Alcohol Problem Index (RAPI)	12 to 21	Center for Alcohol Studies, Rutgers University; in the public domain, no cost for use	Hand-scored	10 minutes to administer. This is a 23-item rating scale to screen for adolescent problem drinking. Scores are converted to T-scores.

APPENDIX D: SCREENING TOOLS

Brief summaries of tools reported in the literature that are youth specific and that can be administered by any experienced professional.

ALCOHOL AND OTHER DRUGS	AGE	COST/ACCESS	SCORING	COMMENTS
Substance Abuse Subtle Assessment Inventory (SASSI)	Adolescents	SASSI Institute, $75 for starter kit: $55 for manual; $45 for 25 test booklets	Hand- or computer-scored	20 minutes to administer. It is an 81-item questionnaire consisting of 55 true/false and 26 direct questions regarding frequency of substance use. Measures 5 areas: alcohol, drugs, obvious attributes, subtle attributes and defensiveness.
Personal Experience Screening Questionnaire (PESQ)	12 to 18	Western Psychological Services; $125 for manual and 25 Auto Score test forms	Hand-scored	10 minutes to administer. This is a 40-item questionnaire that is divided into 3 sections: problem severity, psychosocial items and drug use history. There are 2 validity scales (faking good and faking bad). Its purpose is to "identify teenagers who may be chemically dependent" and "to screen briefly for select psychosocial problems."

SUBSTANCE USE	AGE	COST/ACCESS	SCORING	COMMENTS
Psychoactive Drug Use History (DHQ) (See Appendix F)	Adolescents and adults	CAMH marketing@camh.net	Structured interview; no scoring required	10 to 30 minutes to administer depending on client. It provides a description of the client's pattern of use. Client responds to a series of questions regarding frequency and quantity of use for 14 different drugs or drug categories.
Adverse Consequences of Use (See Appendix F)	Adolescents and adults	CAMH marketing@camh.net	Structured interview; no scoring required	10 minutes to administer. It is designed to provide a quick review of consequences due to alcohol or drug use in 7 areas: physical health, memory, mood, relationships, school/work, legal and financial.
Adolescent Drug Abuse Diagnosis (ADAD)	Adolescents	In the public domain, no cost for use		This is a 150-item instrument used as a structured interview. It is comprehensive, covering 9 life areas: medical, school, work, social relationships, family, psychological, legal, alcohol and drug use. Each life problem area is rated for problem severity on a 10-point scale by the interviewer. According to the authors, it has proven useful in school settings, youth agencies and mental health facilities
SUBSTANCE USE & MENTAL HEALTH				
Adolescent Diagnostic Interview	Adolescents	Dr. Ken Winters Western Psychological Services Cost: $75 per kit (manual and 5 administration booklets	Scored by interviewer, clinician, or trained para-professional, using a straightforward item-scoring format	30 to 90 minutes to administer. This is a structured diagnostic interview schedule designed to assess DSM-IV criteria for substance use problems. It also screens for several coexisting mental/behavioural disorders.
Personal Experience Inventory (PEI)	12 to 18	Western Psychological Services; $300 for manual and 25 computerized uses; computer uses can be purchased separately following purchase of the manual	Computer-scored only, either from disk or through mail-in service	50 to 60 minutes to administer either by paper and pencil or computer screen. This is a 300-item questionnaire administered as a 2-part test: Part 1 is focussed on alcohol and drug use and Part 2 is focussed on psychosocial functioning, including 8 personal risk factor scales and 4 environmental factor scales. There are also several validity indexes. Results are presented as a narrative report along with T-scores for the scales.

SUBSTANCE USE & MENTAL HEALTH	AGE	COST/ACCESS	SCORING	COMMENTS
Adolescent Self-Assessment Profile (ASAP)	Adolescents	Center for Addictions Research and Evaluation, Colorado, USA 303 421-1261; $100 for 100 administrations; manual provided; pricing dependent on volume	Hand or computer scored	30 to 60 minutes to administer depending on client's situation. This is a 225-item questionnaire comprising 20 basic scales and 15 supplementary scales that measure 6 risk-resilience factors and drug use involvement in 9 drug categories, including alcohol. Its purpose is to provide assessment of the adolescent's psychosocial adjustment and substance use involvement. It provides a "broad-based assessment of major risk factors and in-depth assessment of substance use." Areas include family, mental health, peer influence, school, conduct problems, attitudes towards, and pattern of drug use. Raw scores are converted into percentile scores and several normative groups are available. Several scales can be used to measure treatment outcomes.
Hilson Adolescent Profile (HAP)	9 to 19	Hilson Research Inc; New York, USA 800 926-2258; $20 per administration	Computer scored only by mail-in to Hilson Research	45 minutes to administer. It consists of 310 true/false items grouped into 16 scales that correspond to psychiatric diagnostic categories. The HAP questions adolescents directly about their behaviours rather than inferring them from statistically or theoretically derived indicators. It is designed to assess the presence and extent of adolescent behaviour problems including alcohol/drug use, school difficulties, legal, frustration tolerance, anti-social behaviour, rigidity/obsessiveness, interpersonal difficulties, family conflict, social/sexual adjustment, health, anxiety, and depression.
The Child and Adolescent Functional Assessment Scale (CAFAS)		www.cafasinontario.ca	It is not administered. A trained rater chooses from a list of behavioural descriptions.	This is a rating scale that assesses a youth's degree of impairment in day-to-day functioning due to emotional, behavioural, psychological, psychiatric or substance use problems.

APPENDIX F: YOUTH ASSESSMENT INSTRUMENTS

The following assessment tools are draft youth versions adapted from the adult instruments in: Cross, S. & Sibley, L.B. (2001). *The Standardized Tools and Criteria Manual: Helping Clients Navigate Addiction Treatment in Ontario. Toronto*: Centre for Addiction and Mental Health.

ADVERSE CONSEQUENCES
PSYCHOACTIVE DRUG HISTORY QUESTIONNAIRE
READINESS FOR CHANGE

ADVERSE CONSEQUENCES OF USE

(Note to Clinician: Code only the most severe level of consequences for each problem)

As a result of your substance use, have you experienced:	EVER	PAST 90 DAYS	CLINICAL COMMENTS
a. Problems with your physical health (including overdose, poisoning, illness or accident, vomiting, rashes, significant weight change, passing out, difficulty sleeping) 0 None 1 Self-identified/other person concerned 2 Health care professional warning 3 Medical treatment for physical problem (illness or accident related to substance abuse)	__ 0 __ 1 __ 2 __ 3 __ 8 __ 9	__ 0 __ 1 __ 2 __ 3 __ 8 __ 9	If ever, when:
b. Blackouts or memory problems, forgetting, confusion, difficulty thinking 0 None 1 5 or fewer occasions 2 more than 5 occasions	__ 0 __ 1 __ 2 __ 8 __ 9	__ 0 __ 1 __ 2 __ 8 __ 9	If ever, when:
c. Mood changes, personality changes, substance-related psychosis such as: irritability, mood swings, anxious or panicky, depressed, nervous, paranoia, seeing/hearing things, flashbacks when using 0 None 1 minor (impairment had no serious consequences on daily functioning) 2 major (impairment had adverse consequences on daily functioning)	__ 0 __ 1 __ 2 __ 8 __ 9	__ 0 __ 1 __ 2 __ 8 __ 9	If ever, when:
d. Problems with friends, family, teachers or co-workers/ community (relationship issues) 0 None 1 minor (tension, arguments, mistrust 2 major (relationship broken off or about to be broken, forced to leave home, lost friends)	__ 0 __ 1 __ 2 __ 8 __ 9	__ 0 __ 1 __ 2 __ 8 __ 9	If ever, when:

8 = Refused, 9 = Missing

		If ever, when:		If ever, when:

e.
- 0   none
- 1   been verbally aggressive/abusive/threatening or bullying when using
- 2   been physically aggressive/abusive/threatening or bullying when using
- 8
- 9

If ever, when: 0 / 1 / 2 / 8 / 9   0 / 1 / 2 / 8 / 9

f. School or work problems:
- 0   None
- 1   performance affected (loss of time from work or school, turning in school assignments late or not at all, skipping school/job or not attending at all, receiving complaints on performance by teacher or supervisor
- 2   suspensions/expulsions from school, fired/terminated from job or being threatened of job loss
- 3   n/a no job and not in school
- 8
- 9

If ever, when: 0 / 1 / 2 / 3 / 8 / 9   0 / 1 / 2 / 3 / 8 / 9

g. Trouble with the law (substance related)
- 0   None
- 1   charged only (case pending, dropped, diversion)
- 2   convicted – community service, open/closed custody, probation
- 8
- 9

If ever, when: 0 / 1 / 2 / 8 / 9   0 / 1 / 2 / 8 / 9

h. Financial problems due to substance use
- 0   None
- 1   minor – spending too much, selling personal items
- 2   major – use associated with significant debt, forging cheques, stealing, selling drugs to support
- 8
- 9

If ever, when   0 / 1 / 2 / 8 / 9   0 / 1 / 2 / 8 / 9

8 = Refused, 9 = Missing

PSYCHOACTIVE DRUG HISTORY QUESTIONNAIRE

Drug Type	Used in past 12 months	# days used in past 90 days	How long since last drug use? *	Typical amount on each day of use in last 90 days **	Clinical Comments
(1) None					
(2) Alcohol: beer/liquor/wine	___ 1 ___ 2 ___ 8 ___ 9				
(3) Cocaine/Crack: coke	___ 1 ___ 2 ___ 8 ___ 9				
(4) Amphetamines/Other Stimulants: crystal, speed, crank, Ritalin	___ 1 ___ 2 ___ 8 ___ 9				
(5) Cannabis: hash, weed, grass, pot, marijuana, oil	___ 1 ___ 2 ___ 8 ___ 9				
(6) Benzodiazepines: GHB, Rohypnol, valium	___ 1 ___ 2 ___ 8 ___ 9				
(7) Barbituates: sleeping pills	___ 1 ___ 2 ___ 8 ___ 9				
(8) Heroin/Opium	___ 1 ___ 2 ___ 8 ___ 9				
(9) Prescription Opioids: painkillers	___ 1 ___ 2 ___ 8 ___ 9				
(10) Over-the-counter codeine preparations: cough medicines	___ 1 ___ 2 ___ 8 ___ 9				

1 = Yes; 2 = No; 8 = Refused; 9 = Missing

* How long since last used: 1 = <24 hrs; 2 = 1-3 days; 3 = within last week; 4 = within last month; 5 = more than a month ago

** See guidelines for describing amount of each drug

(11) Hallucinogens: LSD, acid, shrooms, ecstasy, (E)	___ 1 ___ 2 ___ 8 ___ 9		
(12) Glue/other inhalants: cooking spray, gas	___ 1 ___ 2 ___ 8 ___ 9		
(13) Tobacco	___ 1 ___ 2 ___ 8 ___ 9		
(14) Other psychoactive drugs: ketamine (K), anti-depressants, anti-psychotics; gravol, steroids	___ 1 ___ 2 ___ 8 ___ 9		

1 = Yes; 2 = No; 8 = Refused; 9 = Missing

* How long since last used: 1 = <24 hrs; 2 = 1-3 days; 3 = within last week; 4 = within last month; 5 = more than a month ago

** See guidelines for describing amount of each drug

READINESS FOR CHANGE

Name_____

Date_____

WHICH STATEMENT BEST DESCRIBES YOUR SITUATION:

Part one (check off one)

___ I chose to attend services today.

___ I'm okay with being here today even though_____suggested that I come.

___ I did not choose to attend. I was told by_____that I had to come.

Part two (check off the one that best describes the reason you are here today)

1. ___ I am not prepared to change at this time. I am not thinking about changing my use of drugs and/or alcohol.

2. ___ Sometimes I think about changing my use of drugs and/or alcohol and sometimes I think that I don't have to.

3. ___ My drug and/or alcohol use is causing me some problems. I am thinking about making changes.

4. ___ I am feeling ready to begin to make some changes in my use of drugs and/or alcohol. I am here to get some help with these changes.

5. ___I have made changes already in my use of drugs and/or alcohol and feel that it would be helpful to have a place to check in and make sure that I am doing okay.

6. ___ I have made changes but I am concerned that I might go back to my old ways of thinking and/or using

PLEASE USE THE STATEMENTS BELOW IF NONE OF THE ABOVE APPLY TO YOUR SITUATION
____ I have made changes and I don't feel that I need any help.
____ None of these statements apply to my situation.

Rating for Part 2:
1. Precontemplative
2. Contemplative
3. Preparing for Action
4. Action
5. Maintenance
6. Relapse Concern

APPENDIX G: PSYCHIATRIC MEDICATIONS
TABLE 1: ANTIDEPRESSANTS

ANTIDEPRESSANT CLASS	DRUG	SIDE EFFECTS	THESE MEDICATIONS SHOULD NOT BE USED WITH…
Selective Serotonin Reuptake Inhibitors (SSRI)	citalopram (Celexa®), fluoxetine (Prozac®), fluvoxamine (Luvox®), paroxetine (Paxil®), sertraline (Zoloft®)	nausea, insomnia, headaches, sexual dysfunction, akathisia, dry mouth, drowsiness	St. John's Wort, MAOI; alcohol can increase side effects; caffeine can increase anxiety/insomnia
Non-selective Cyclic Antidepressants/ Tricyclics (TCA)	amitriptyline (Elavil®), clomipramine (Anafranil®), desipramine (Norpramin®), doxepin (Sinequan®), imipramine (Tofranil®), nortriptyline (Aventyl®), trimipramine (Surmontil®)	dry mouth, sedation, constipation, blurred vision, dizziness, weight gain, urinary retention	alcohol can increase side effects; caffeine can increase anxiety/ insomnia
Monoamine Oxidase Inhibitors (MAOI)	phenelzine (Nardil®), tranylcypromine (Parnate®)	sedation, insomnia, blurred vision, constipation, tremor, orthostatic hypotension, nausea	all other antidepressants (including St. John's Wort), foods containing tyramine (must follow special restrictive diet), meperidine, over-the-counter cough and cold products
Reversible Inhibitors of Monoamine Oxidase (RIMA)	moclobemide (Manerix®)	insomnia, headache, dry mouth, blurred vision	meperidine, dextromethorphan (DM cough syrup), St. John's Wort
Serotonin Norepinephrine Reuptake Inhibitor (SNRI)	venlafaxine (Effexor®, Effexor XR®)	sedation, insomnia, headache, dry mouth, constipation, sweating, dizziness, nausea, sexual dysfunction, increased blood pressure	MAOI; alcohol can increase side effects; caffeine can increase anxiety/insomnia; use with caution in hypertensive patients
Norepinephrine Dopamine Reuptake Inhibitor (NDRI)	bupropion (Wellbutrin®, Zyban®)	tremor, insomnia, headaches, dry mouth, nausea	MAOI; stimulants; increased seizure risk in epileptic patients
Serotonin-2 Antagonists/ Reuptake Inhibitor (SARI)	trazodone (Desyrel®)	sedation, headache, nausea, dry mouth, blurred vision, constipation, orthostatic hypotension, dizziness	use caution in combination with some benzodiazepines; alcohol can increase side effects; caffeine can increase anxiety/insomnia
Noradrenergic/Specific Serotonergic Antidepressant (NaSSA)	mirtazapine (Remeron®)	sedation, fatigue, dry mouth, constipation, increased appetite, weight gain	MAOI; dosage adjustment required with carbamazepine; alcohol can increase side effects

APPENDIX G : PSYCHIATRIC MEDICATIONS
TABLE 2: MOOD STABILIZERS

DRUG	SIDE EFFECTS	THESE MEDICATIONS SHOULD NOT BE USED WITH...
carbamazepine (Tegretol®)	drowsiness, headache, tremor, blurred vision, nausea, weight gain, rash, photosensitivity, blood dyscrasias	interacts with several medications, therefore patient should always check with physician or pharmacist; alcohol can increase side effects
gabapentin (Neurontin®)	drowsiness, dizziness, blurred vision, tiredness, weight gain	alcohol can increase side effects
lamotrigine (Lamictal®)	dizziness, drowsiness, headache, nausea, vomiting, rash (can be serious—contact physician immediately)	must be used with caution with valproate (increased risk of serious rash); alcohol can increase side effects
lithium (Carbolith®, Duralith®, Lithane®)	tremor, dizziness, confusion, nausea, rash, vomiting, sedation, weight gain; long-term use can cause thyroid and kidney dysfunction	use caution in combination with diuretics and other antihypertensives; ibuprofen can cause increased lithium level; alcohol can increase side effects
oxcarbazepine (Trileptal®)	headache, drowsiness, dizziness, ataxia, tiredness, nausea	interacts with fewer medications than carbamazepine, but oral contraceptives may have decreased efficacy; alcohol can increase side effects
topiramate (Topamax®)	nausea, tremor, drowsiness, dizziness, weight loss	oral contraceptives may have decreased efficacy; alcohol can increase side effects
valproic acid/divalproex (Depakene®, Epival®)	nausea, sedation, weight gain, hair loss, menstrual disturbances, elevated liver enzymes	interacts with several medications, therefore patient should always check with physician or pharmacist; alcohol can increase side effects

TABLE 3: ANXIOLYTICS/SEDATIVES/HYPNOTICS

TYPES OF MEDICATIONS	DRUG	SIDE EFFECTS	THESE MEDICATIONS SHOULD NOT BE USED WITH...
Benzodiazepines	alprazolam (Xanax®), bromazepam (Lectopam®), chlordiazepoxide (Librium®), clonazepam (Rivotril®), diazepam (Valium®), flurazepam (Dalmane®), lorazepam (Ativan®), nitrazepam (Mogadon®), oxazepam (Serax®), temazepam (Restoril®), triazolam (Halcion®)	tolerance, dependence, withdrawal upon discontinuation, dizzinesss, sedation, confusion, memory impairment, impaired co-ordination	alcohol can increase side effects, especially drowsiness; use with caution in combination with other CNS drugs since it can cause increased sedation and other side effects
Miscellaneous	buspirone (Buspar®); zopiclone (Imovane®); zaleplon (Starnoc®)		

APPENDIX G : PSYCHIATRIC MEDICATIONS
TABLE 4: ANTIPSYCHOTICS

SUBTYPES	DRUG	SIDE EFFECTS	THESE MEDICATIONS SHOULD NOT BE USED WITH...
First generation (typical, conventional) antipsychotics	chlorpromazine (Largactil®), flu-penthixol (Fluanxol®), fluphenazine (Modecate®), fluspirilene (IMAP®), haloperidol (Haldol®), loxapine (Loxapac®), mesoridazine (Serentil®), pericyazine (Neuleptil®), perphenazine (Trilafon®), pimozide (Orap®), pipotiazine (Piportil®), prochlorperazine (Stemetil®), thiori-dazine (Mellaril®), thiothixene (Navane®), trifluoperazine (Stelazine®), zuclopenthixol (Clopixol®)	sedation, Parkinson-like symptoms (tremor, muscle stiffness, unco-ordi-nated spastic muscle movements, staggering gait, motor restlessness, pacing, loss of facial expression), hypotension, constipation, dizziness, weight gain, decreased sex drive, irregular heart beat, menstrual irregularities, tardive dyskinesia	alcohol can increase side effects; caffeine can increase anxiety and agitation; use with caution in combi-nation with other CNS drugs that can increase side effects; always check with physician or pharmacist before taking other medications
Second generation (atypical, novel) antipsychotics	clozapine (Clozaril®), olanzapine (Zyprexa®), quetiapine (Seroquel®), risperidone (Risperdal®)	sedation, weight gain, impaired glucose tolerance/diabetes and sexual dysfunction are the most common side effects; can also have same side effects as typical agents, but usually more likely at higher doses; clozapine can cause agranulocytosis (life-threatening low white blood cell count) in 1% of patients, therefore all clozapine patients must get weekly or biweekly blood monitoring	alcohol can increase side effects; caffeine can increase anxiety and agitation; use with caution in combi-nation with other CNS drugs, that can increase side effects; always check with physician or pharmacist before taking other medications

FIRST CONTACT:

A BRIEF TREATMENT FOR YOUNG SUBSTANCE USERS WITH MENTAL HEALTH PROBLEMS

Elsbeth Tupker, MSW

Clinical Services Consultant

Education and Publishing Department

Centre for Addiction and Mental Health

Centre for Addiction and Mental Health

Centre de toxicomanie et de santé mentale

FIRST CONTACT: A BRIEF TREATMENT FOR YOUNG SUBSTANCE USERS WITH MENTAL HEALTH PROBLEMS

Copyright © 2004 Centre for Addiction and Mental Health

ISBN # 0-88868-476-2

Printed in Canada

For professional advice to help your client with an alcohol or drug problem, please call:
Addiction Clinical Consultation Service, 9 a.m. to 5 p.m. Monday to Friday
1 888 720-ACCS
416 595-6968 in the Toronto area

For information on other Centre for Addiction and Mental Health resource materials or to place an order, please contact:
Marketing and Sales Services
Centre for Addiction and Mental Health
33 Russell Street
Toronto, Ontario
Canada M5S 2S1
Tel: 1 800 661-1111 or 416 595-6059 in Toronto
E-mail: marketing@camh.net
Web site: www.camh.net

Disponible en français sous le titre
Premier contact : Traitement de courte durée pour les jeunes usagers d'alcool et de drogues ayant des problèmes de santé mentale

ACKNOWLEDGEMENTS

First Contact: A brief treatment for young substance users with mental health problems was developed and written by:

Elsbeth Tupker

This manual is an adaptation of the first edition of the *First Contact: A brief treatment for young substance users* developed and written by:

Curtis Breslin   Elsbeth Tupker

Kathy Sdao-Jarvie   Shelly Pearlman

We gratefully acknowledge the following agencies that field tested *First Contact* and the counsellors who gave us valuable suggestions for adapting the program so that it may be used for young drug users who also have mental health problems.

Royal Ottawa Hospital

Sheldon Box

Terry Levesque

Richard Voss

Centre David Smith Centre, Ottawa

Ginette Chouinard

Lyne Monpetit

Marie Taylor

Open Doors for Lanark Children and Youth, Carleton Place

Nicki Collins

Steve Martin

Karen Moore

Tri-County Addiction Services, Smith Falls

Marleen MacDonald

David North

Maryvale Adolescent and Family Services, Windsor

Morana Sijan

Tricia Ethelstone

Alternatives for Youth, Genesis Program, Sault Ste. Marie

Phil Jones

Jeff Lefave

Centre for Addiction and Mental Health

Bruce Ballon

Sukhi Bubbra

Maria Carinelli

Gloria Chaim

Joanna Henderson

Colleen Kelly

Megan McCormick

Helen McGee

George Papatheodorou

Solomon Shapiro

Joanne Shenfeld

Tracey Skilling

Christine Wekerle

The field test was co-ordinated by:

Angela Barbara

The art therapy modules were developed by:

Beth Merriam

The feedback at assessment graphs were developed by:

Angela Barbara   Abby Goldstein

The CAMH Project Team

Jane Fjeld   Brian Mitchell

Kathy Kilburn   Elsbeth Tupker

Louise LaRocque-Stuart   Darryl Upfold

FIRST CONTACT:

A BRIEF TREATMENT FOR YOUNG SUBSTANCE USERS WITH MENTAL HEALTH PROBLEMS

INTRODUCTION

In this manual, the original *First Contact: A Brief Treatment for Young Substance Users* has been adapted to help you integrate the treatment of drug use with co-existing mental health problems. Since so many youth present with concurrent mental health and substance use problems, we have provided you with a brief, first step intervention that focuses on drug use in the context of other mental health problems. It incorporates motivational interviewing, cognitive behavioural and harm reduction approaches discussed in the earlier chapters of the resource. It can be implemented in the various settings where youth present—addiction services, mental health services, social services and education programs—as a first step to more extensive treatment or as a stand-alone intervention with youth who do not need or want more treatment. It can also be offered concurrently with treatment for mental health or family issues. *First Contact* is suitable for youth aged 14 to 25 and is mostly used with groups of youth, but may be used in sessions with individuals.

The materials cover Feedback at Assessment and four subsequent treatment sessions: Decision to Change; Triggers, Consequences and Alternatives; Things that Are Important to Me; and Stages of Change.

The adaptations were developed with the help of mental health agency staff and clients who field-tested the original *First Contact* and gave feedback about how to integrate mental health issues into the exercises that focus on drug use. They also made suggestions about how the exercises could be more user-friendly for younger clients and youth who struggle with mental health issues. The original written exercises require literacy skills and conceptual and communication abilities that are not always present among youth who seek treatment. It was suggested that the four sessions be presented in three different modalities: written exercises, activity-based exercises, and art therapy exercises to allow therapists to choose the modality most suited to their clients. The manual suggests activities for only two of the sessions, and we encourage counsellors to make up their own activities that correspond to the goals of a particular session. In our field tests, clients who were younger, less schooled and/or had ADHD or other behaviour problems were better suited for the activity-based exercises, while youth with social skill or conceptual deficits or psychotic disorders, such as first episode, did well with the art therapy modality.

The materials in this manual are still in draft form. CAMH is evaluating the efficacy of the written modality and will update and disseminate the new material when the research has been completed. In the meantime, we invite you to use the materials and provide us with feedback, if you have suggestions for improvements, or wish to share with us how *First Contact* is being used in your setting.

Elsbeth Tupker, MSW
Clinical Services Consultant
Education and Publishing Department
Centre for Addiction and Mental Health
elsbeth_tupker@camh.net

GIVING PERSONALIZED FEEDBACK AT ASSESSMENT

Assessment not only functions as a means to determine a client's appropriateness for *First Contact*, but also as an opportunity to engage the client in the therapy process. The *First Contact* materials for personalized feedback at assessment are intended to give the counsellor additional opportunities to engage and inform the client.

Providing personalized feedback on substance use and mental health to clients at assessment serves two distinct purposes. First, it incorporates information on substance use in the general population of youth and provides a normative standard for clients to compare their use. Normative information serves as a way of correcting client misconceptions such as "everyone uses." This allows for the development of discrepancy, which is believed to increase motivation (Miller & Rollnick, 2002). Second, the information on the relationship between substance use and specific mental health indicators, such as depression, psychological distress and conduct problems, sets the stage for greater awareness of the interrelationship of drug use and mental health symptoms.

To aid in comparing clients' use to normative data, the counsellor should collect information on the quantity and frequency of use for the types of drugs for which *First Contact* provides survey data, as well as screen for mental health problems.

Discussing the client's drug use in comparison with survey data is the next step, thereby increasing the relevance of this feedback. The normative data used in *First Contact* are from the 2001 Ontario Students Drug Use Survey (Adlaf et al, 2002) of students in grades 7 to OAC. The graphs are specific to youth age 15 and younger or 16 and older. They show prevalence of alcohol and other drug use in the past year as well as the co-occurrence of substance use and mental health indicators such as psychological distress, depression and conduct problems. Generally, youth who use are more likely to experience these mental health indicators than youth who do not use drugs or alcohol. In most cases, the more a youth uses, the more likely that he or she will experience mental health symptoms.

GOALS FOR PERSONALIZED FEEDBACK AT ASSESSMENT

1. Following completion of the assessment, increase client's interest in participating in treatment by:
- eliciting reasons for change from the client
- presenting normative information on youth substance use and its relationship to mental health indicators
- making drug education pamphlets available
- clearly describing the purpose and format of the *First Contact* program.

2. Discuss and address barriers to attending the program.

GUIDELINES FOR THE COUNSELLOR

1. Give normative information and other summary information gathered at assessment. Review the graphs with the client that are relevant to the client's age, drugs used and mental health indicators.

"This graph shows you how many students age 15 and younger (or 16 and older) reported using (substance name; e.g., cannabis). This information came from a survey of students in grades 7 to 13 in Ontario done in 2001. The other graph is from the same survey and shows you what percentage of students who use (substance name) experience mental health concerns such as psychological distress, depression or behaviour problems compared to those who do not use (substance name). Generally, youth who use (substance name) are more likely to experience these mental health concerns."

To personalize this information, ask:
· "What do you think about this?"
· "Does this make sense to you? If not, why not?"
· "Does this information surprise you?"

2. Offer the drug education pamphlets.
"Some people may want more information on the effects; for example, physical effects, of the drugs they use. If you are interested in taking any of these pamphlets to read more, please help yourself."

Youth may be uncomfortable taking the pamphlets in front of the counsellor. You may want to have the pamphlets available in a waiting area or outside the counsellor's office. *Do You Know...* brochures can be ordered from CAMH by e-mail at marketing@camh.net, or by phone toll-free at 1 800 661-1111, or 416 595-6059 in Toronto

3. Introduce *First Contact* if appropriate.

4. Examine barriers to treatment.
"What would stop you from coming to the group on May 15?"

5. Introduce individual counsellors or group facilitators (if not the same person as the assessor) and give their phone numbers and appointments.

FACTS ABOUT *FIRST CONTACT*

WHAT IS THE PROGRAM ABOUT?

First Contact:

· is for young people who are willing to look at the impact of their alcohol and/or drug use on their lives, generally, and on their mental health, specifically

· helps youth understand that they are not alone, others are dealing with some of the same concerns

· offers treatment in an accepting atmosphere

· encourages youth to make their own choices and decisions about their lives

· is based on the belief that the first few appointments are important in getting the change process started

· can refer you to additional treatment and follow-up.

HOW DOES IT WORK?

· You will meet with a counsellor to help get a picture of your current situation.

· You will look at the pros and cons of your alcohol or drug use and its effect on your mental health and decide what changes you want to make.

· You will be actively involved in setting your own goals.

· You will identify risky drinking or drug use situations and develop alternative ways of dealing with them.

· Members receive encouragement and suggestions from other youth dealing with many of the same issues.

· How much you participate is up to you. You will not be "put on the spot."

· Please arrive alcohol and drug-free for your weekly sessions.

You have an appointment with _____

on _____ at _____.

If, for any reason, you cannot keep your appointment, please call.

ALCOHOL USE—YOUTH AGE 15 AND YOUNGER*

< HANDOUT >

ALCOHOL—THE BIG PICTURE

Next to caffeine, alcohol is the drug that is most widely used by adults. Alcohol is a depressant; if abused, it can impair your ability to think, make decisions and function in day-to-day life.

The graphs show how much students age 15 and younger use alcohol. How does your alcohol use compare?

The student survey also looked at indicators of mental health such as psychological distress, depression and behaviour problems.

The more you drink alcohol, the more likely you are to experience these mental health concerns.

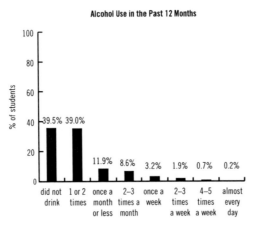

Alcohol Use in the Past 12 Months

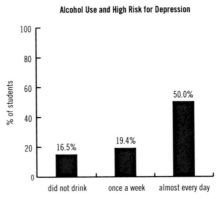

Alcohol Use and High Risk for Depression

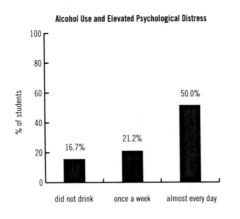

Alcohol Use and Elevated Psychological Distress

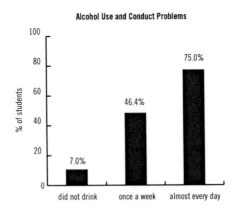

Alcohol Use and Conduct Problems

* Findings From the 2001 Ontario Student Drug Use Survey (Adlaf, Paglia, & Beitchman, 2002)
Copyright © 2004, Centre for Addiction and Mental Health

ALCOHOL USE—YOUTH AGE 16 AND OLDER*

< HANDOUT >

ALCOHOL—THE BIG PICTURE

Next to caffeine, alcohol is the drug that is most widely used by adults. Alcohol is a depressant; if abused, it can impair your ability to think, make decisions and function in day-to-day life.

The graphs show how much students age 16 and older use alcohol. How does your alcohol use compare?

The student survey also looked at indicators of mental health such as psychological distress, depression and behaviour problems.

The more you drink alcohol, the more likely you are to experience these mental health concerns.

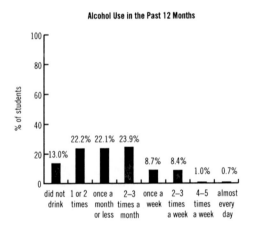

Alcohol Use in the Past 12 Months

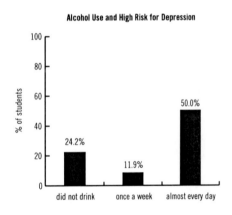

Alcohol Use and High Risk for Depression

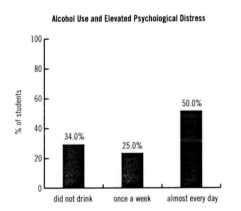

Alcohol Use and Elevated Psychological Distress

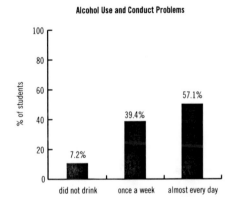

Alcohol Use and Conduct Problems

* Findings From the 2001 Ontario Student Drug Use Survey (Adlaf, Paglia, & Beitchman, 2002)
Copyright © 2004, Centre for Addiction and Mental Health

CANNABIS USE—YOUTH AGE 15 AND YOUNGER*

CANNABIS (HASH, WEED, POT)—THE BIG PICTURE

Cannabis is the most widely used illegal drug in Canada. As much as 22 per cent of Canadians between the ages of 15 and 24 have used marijuana or other forms of cannabis at least once in the past year. The graphs below show how often students in Ontario have used cannabis.

"Where do you fit in?"

The student survey also looked at indicators of mental health such as psychological distress, depression and behaviour problems.

The more cannabis you use, the more likely you are to experience these mental health concerns.

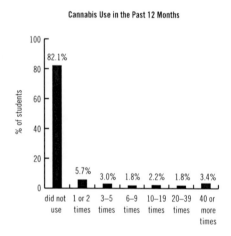

Cannabis Use in the Past 12 Months

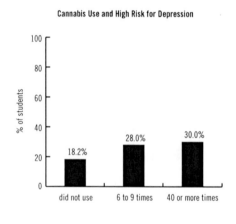

Cannabis Use and High Risk for Depression

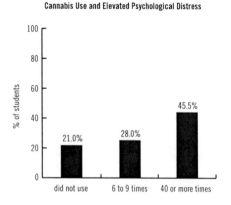

Cannabis Use and Elevated Psychological Distress

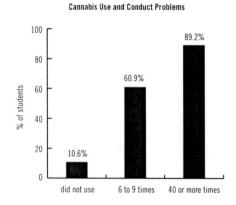

Cannabis Use and Conduct Problems

* Findings From the 2001 Ontario Student Drug Use Survey (Adlaf, Paglia, & Beitchman, 2002)
Copyright © 2004, Centre for Addiction and Mental Health

< HANDOUT >

CANNABIS USE—YOUTH AGE 16 AND OLDER*

CANNABIS (HASH, WEED, POT)—THE BIG PICTURE

Cannabis is the most widely used illegal drug in Canada. As much as 22 per cent of Canadians between the ages of 15 and 24 have used marijuana or other forms of cannabis at least once in the past year. The graphs below show how often students in Ontario have used cannabis.

"Where do you fit in?"

The student survey also looked at indicators of mental health such as psychological distress, depression and behaviour problems.

The more cannabis you use, the more likely you are to experience these mental health concerns

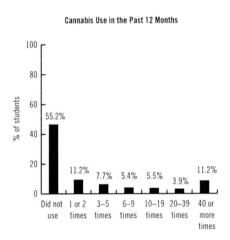

Cannabis Use in the Past 12 Months

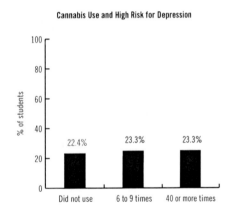

Cannabis Use and High Risk for Depression

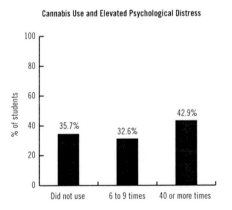

Cannabis Use and Elevated Psychological Distress

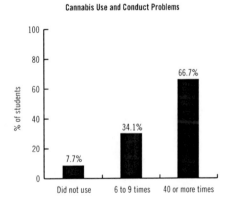

Cannabis Use and Conduct Problems

* Findings From the 2001 Ontario Student Drug Use Survey (Adlaf, Paglia, & Beitchman, 2002)
Copyright © 2004, Centre for Addiction and Mental Health

BARBITUATE OR TRANQUILIZER USE—YOUTH AGE 12–15*

Barbiturate or Tranquilizer Use in the Past 12 Months

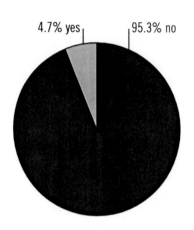

4.7% yes   95.3% no

Mental Health Problems Among Users Vs. Non-Users

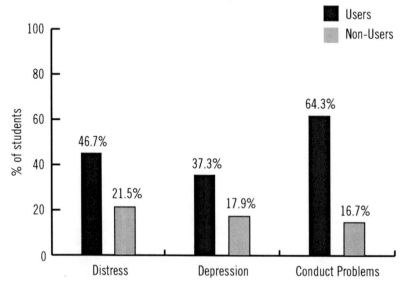

■ Users
▨ Non-Users

Distress: 46.7% / 21.5%
Depression: 37.3% / 17.9%
Conduct Problems: 64.3% / 16.7%

% of students

* Findings From the 2001 Ontario Student Drug Use Survey (Adlaf, Paglia, & Beitchman, 2002)
Copyright © 2004, Centre for Addiction and Mental Health

< HANDOUT >

BARBITUATE OR TRANQUILIZER USE—YOUTH AGE 16–19*

< HANDOUT >

Barbiturate or Tranquilizer Use in the Past 12 Months

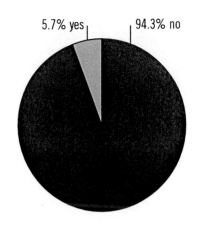

5.7% yes   94.3% no

Mental Health Problems Among Users Vs. Non-Users

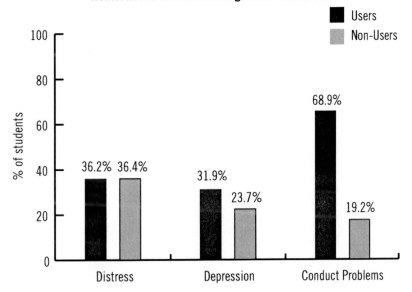

* Findings From the 2001 Ontario Student Drug Use Survey (Adlaf, Paglia, & Beitchman, 2002)
Copyright © 2004, Centre for Addiction and Mental Health

CLUB DRUG USE—YOUTH AGE 12–15*

ECSTASY, ICE, GHB, ROHYPNOL

< HANDOUT >

Club Drug Use in the Past 12 Months**

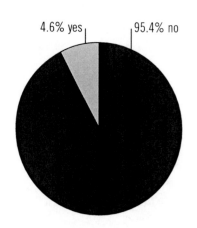

4.6% yes   95.4% no

Mental Health Problems Among Users Vs. Non-Users**

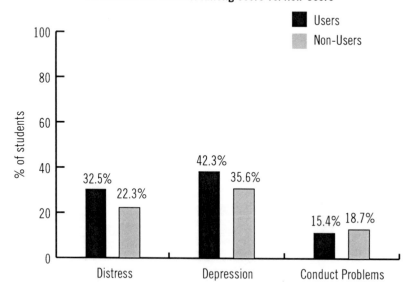

** Findings From the 2001 Ontario Student Drug Use Survey (Adlaf, Paglia, & Beitchman, 2002)
Copyright © 2004, Centre for Addiction and Mental Health

CLUB DRUG USE—YOUTH AGE 16–19*

ECSTASY, ICE, GHB, ROHYPNOL

Club Drug Use in the Past 12 Months**

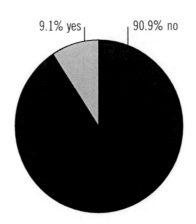

9.1% yes   90.9% no

Mental Health Problems Among Users Vs. Non-Users**

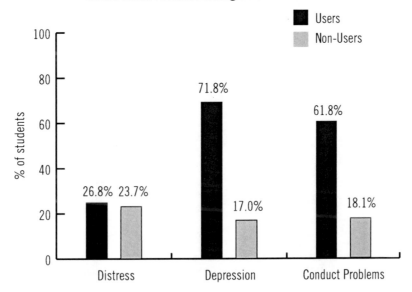

** Findings From the 2001 Ontario Student Drug Use Survey (Adlaf, Paglia, & Beitchman, 2002)
Copyright © 2004, Centre for Addiction and Mental Health

< HANDOUT >

CRACK/COCAINE USE—YOUTH AGE 12–15*

< HANDOUT >

Crack/Cocaine Use in the Past 12 Months

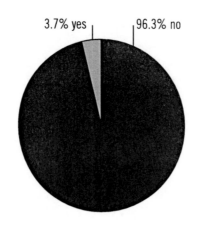

3.7% yes   96.3% no

Mental Health Problems Among Users Vs. Non-Users

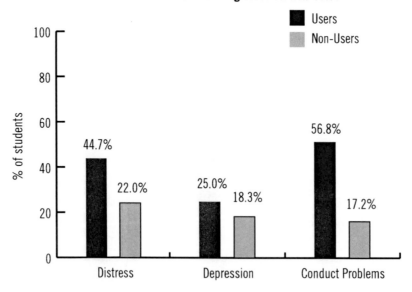

■ Users
■ Non-Users

* Findings From the 2001 Ontario Student Drug Use Survey (Adlaf, Paglia, & Beitchman, 2002)
Copyright © 2004, Centre for Addiction and Mental Health

CRACK/COCAINE USE—YOUTH AGE 16–19*

Crack/Cocaine Use in the Past 12 Months

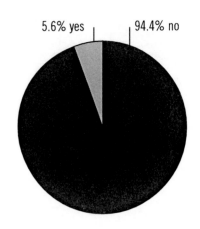

5.6% yes   94.4% no

Mental Health Problems Among Users Vs. Non-Users

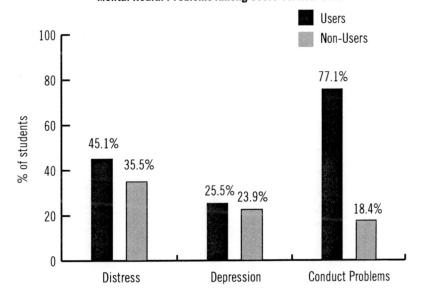

* Findings From the 2001 Ontario Student Drug Use Survey (Adlaf, Paglia, & Beitchman, 2002)

Copyright © 2004, Centre for Addiction and Mental Health

GLUE OR SOLVENT USE—YOUTH AGE 12-15*

< HANDOUT >

Glue or Solvent Use in the Past 12 Months

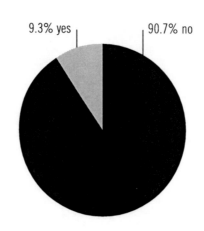

9.3% yes   90.7% no

Mental Health Problems Among Users Vs. Non-Users

■ Users
▨ Non-Users

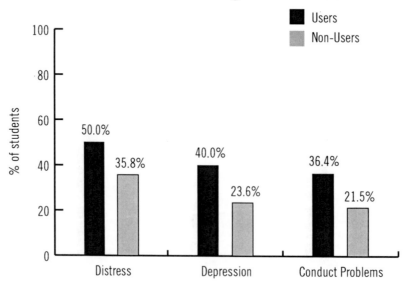

* Findings From the 2001 Ontario Student Drug Use Survey (Adlaf, Paglia, & Beitchman, 2002)
Copyright © 2004, Centre for Addiction and Mental Health

GLUE OR SOLVENT USE—YOUTH AGE 16–19*

Glue or Solvent Use in the Past 12 Months

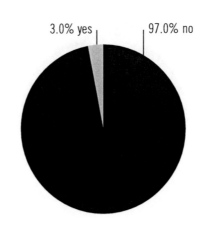

3.0% yes   97.0% no

Mental Health Problems Among Users Vs. Non-Users

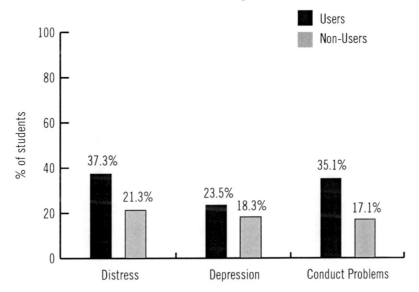

* Findings From the 2001 Ontario Student Drug Use Survey (Adlaf, Paglia, & Beitchman, 2002)

< HANDOUT >

HALLUCINOGEN USE—YOUTH AGE 12–15*

LSD, PCP, MUSHROOMS

< HANDOUT >

Hallucinogen Use in the Past 12 Months

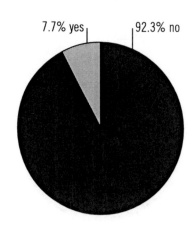

7.7% yes   92.3% no

Mental Health Problems Among Users Vs. Non-Users

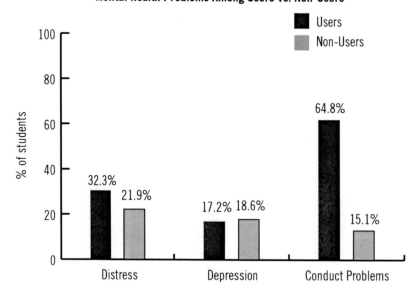

* Findings From the 2001 Ontario Student Drug Use Survey (Adlaf, Paglia, & Beitchman, 2002)
Copyright © 2004, Centre for Addiction and Mental Health

HALLUCINOGEN USE—YOUTH AGE 16–19*

LSD, PCP, MUSHROOMS

Hallucinogen Use in the Past 12 Months

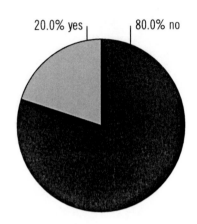

20.0% yes   80.0% no

Mental Health Problems Among Users Vs. Non-Users

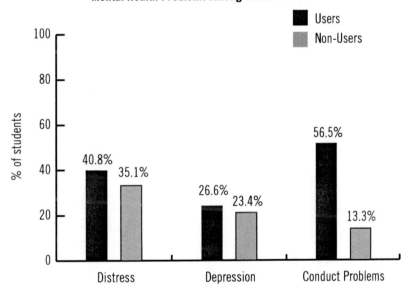

* Findings From the 2001 Ontario Student Drug Use Survey (Adlaf, Paglia, & Beitchman, 2002)
Copyright © 2004, Centre for Addiction and Mental Health

< HANDOUT >

HEROIN USE—YOUTH AGE 12–15*

< HANDOUT >

Heroin Use in the Past 12 Months

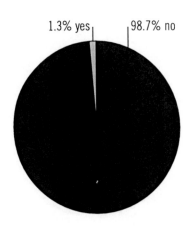

1.3% yes   98.7% no

Mental Health Problems Among Users Vs. Non-Users

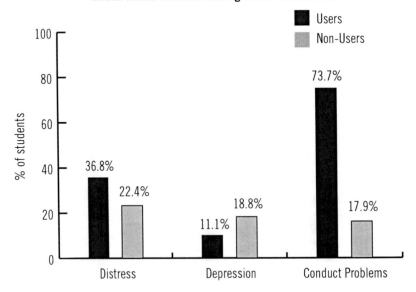

* Findings From the 2001 Ontario Student Drug Use Survey (Adlaf, Paglia, & Beitchman, 2002)
Copyright © 2004, Centre for Addiction and Mental Health

HEROIN USE—YOUTH AGE 16–19*

Herion Use in the Past 12 Months

0.6% yes   99.4% no

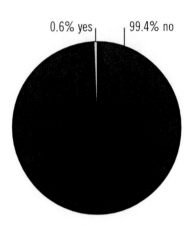

Mental Health Problems Among Users Vs. Non-Users

■ Users
▨ Non-Users

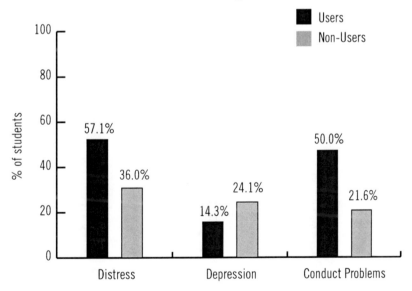

* Findings From the 2001 Ontario Student Drug Use Survey (Adlaf, Paglia, & Beitchman, 2002)

< HANDOUT >

STIMULANT USE—YOUTH AGE 12–15*

METHAMPHETAMINES, SPEED, UPPERS, DIET PILLS

< HANDOUT >

Stimulant Use in the Past 12 Months

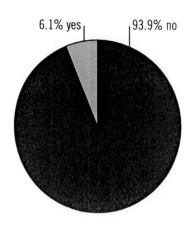

6.1% yes   93.9% no

Mental Health Problems Among Users Vs. Non-Users

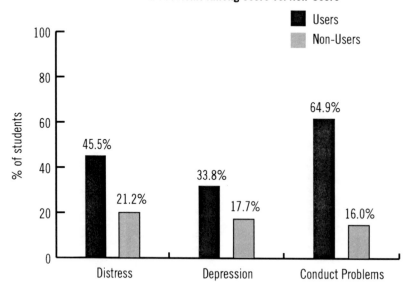

* Findings From the 2001 Ontario Student Drug Use Survey (Adlaf, Paglia, & Beitchman, 2002)
Copyright © 2004, Centre for Addiction and Mental Health

STIMULANT USE—YOUTH AGE 16–19*

METHAMPHETAMINES, SPEED, UPPERS, DIET PILLS

Stimulant Use in the Past 12 Months

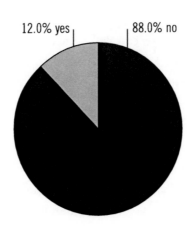

12.0% yes   88.0% no

Mental Health Problems Among Users Vs. Non-Users

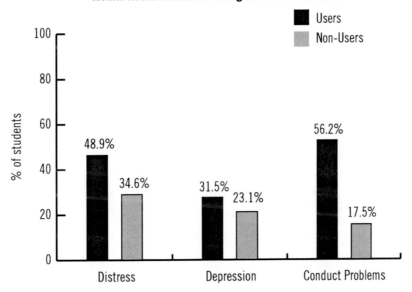

■ Users
▨ Non-Users

% of students

Distress — 48.9% / 34.6%
Depression — 31.5% / 23.1%
Conduct Problems — 56.2% / 17.5%

* Findings From the 2001 Ontario Student Drug Use Survey (Adlaf, Paglia, & Beitchman, 2002)
Copyright © 2004, Centre for Addiction and Mental Health

< HANDOUT >

SESSION 1: THE DECISION TO CHANGE

The *Decision to Change* exercise provides a way to discuss and address clients' ambivalence to change by asking clients to identify the pros and cons of using alcohol and/or drugs and the pros and cons of changing their drug use. The primary goal is to increase clients' awareness of changing their use as a decision wherein some trade-offs are made. Just being aware of the possible pros and cons and asking clients to prioritize them facilitates self re-evaluation, a process that is crucial to increasing one's readiness to change. The *Decision to Change* exercise gives clients a way to talk about the difficulties of changing as well as the consequences of not changing.

While a counsellor may have the urge to talk about how to solve the problems or overcome the obstacles presented, first it is important to acknowledge the obstacles and what would be lost by changing. In a group, members will talk about their own experiences with obstacles to change. You will need to use some clinical judgment in situations where a client seems to be getting discouraged by the obstacles to change. To help a client gain perspective, provide (or have the group provide) some encouraging words and support self-efficacy. For example, it is sometimes useful to affirm a client's decision to seek help, or to draw parallels between a previous accomplishment that took time and effort and his or her present situation. In this way, the counsellor highlights the client's resources for change without taking on the teacher role.

GOALS FOR SESSION I

1. Provide a clear understanding of the purpose, format and goals of *First Contact*.

2. Facilitate group formation by:
- introducing group leaders and clients
- establishing group rules, norms and expectations
- beginning to highlight commonalities among group members to foster support.

3. Create a comfortable, accepting atmosphere using an "ice breaker" and encourage discussion of what brought the clients to the program and what they hope to get out of treatment.

4. Complete the *Decision to Change* exercise with the following goals:
- Help the client to become aware of the decision to change process.
- Provide a forum to talk about the difficulties of changing.
- Highlight the consequences of changing and not changing.
- Acknowledge what would be lost by changing.
- Introduce the idea of choice and control with regard to drug use.

5. Introduce *Check-in* (weekly use/goal monitoring).

GUIDELINES FOR THE COUNSELLOR

1. Introduce the program.

"This group is for young people age 15 and younger (or 16 and older). You will meet for two hours, once a week for four weeks. After four weeks, this group will end and you can decide where you want to go from there."

"The purpose of the group is to look at the impact that drugs and alcohol have on your lives and to explore how your drug use and mental health problems affect each other. This is your group and you are here to help each other out; therefore, what you have to say to each other is very important. We (the therapists) are here to help build some trust and encourage you to participate. We also have some problem-solving tools to share with you. In addition to this group, some of you will also be attending appointments to help you with your mental health concerns."

"Some of you are in different places when it comes to your drug use:
· Some of you have no intention of changing your drug use.
· Some of you are here to deal with your mental health issues.
· Some of you have very mixed feelings about changing your drug use.
· Some of you are thinking about changes but don't know where to start.
· Some of you have already made some changes."

2. Discuss participation in the group and confidentiality.

"This group is a place where you can start solving some of the problems you're facing. So, the more you share, the more you are going to get out of the group. We will have a chance in the group to talk about your life goals and your drug use goals, but what you actually decide to do is up to you. Because people are going to be sharing things, it is important that we all agree that what is said in the group stays in the group."

"Something that is important for us to talk about is your confidentiality. What is said in here stays in this room. We need your permission to talk to or release information to others. However, there are some limits to confidentiality. If you are going to harm yourself or others, or if child abuse is an issue, then, legally, we need to break confidentiality. But aside from those exceptions, your confidentiality is maintained."

3. Introduce clients.

"In this group, we are going to be talking a lot and getting to know one another better. As a way to begin, we can do an ice breaker…"

Icebreaker—the 4 corners

Purpose

· To relieve some of the tension around being in a group for the first time or attending a group with people you do not know.

· To highlight for the clients some of the things they have in common with other group members and to help everyone acknowledge that there are differences between members. This can serve as a good starting point for talking about group norms and how to make everyone feel safe, given that there are many similarities and differences.

Method

Everyone stands in the middle of the room. Group leaders will give instructions to group members to go to different corners (or the middle) of the room according to their answers to specific questions. E.g., Anyone who woke up today before 6 a.m. go to that corner; everyone who woke up between 6 and 7 a.m. go to that corner; everyone who woke up between 7 and 8 a.m. go to that corner; and anyone who woke up later than 8 a.m. go to that corner. If the room is large, it may not be a good idea to use all the corners since people will be too far away from each other. You can use sitting, standing, being by the door, etc.

Time should be given for everyone to find the appropriate corner and allow for conversation to be initiated between members within each corner. Group leaders can then foster more cohesion by saying, "Now, suppose it was a Saturday, where would everyone be standing?" These exercises can be tailored to the needs of the group using them, such as who lives near water or a park, who goes hunting, fishing, snowmobiling, skiing, etc.

Group leaders go through a series of questions so members are constantly shifting themselves throughout the room and joining up with new people. People can be asked to notice whether they are often in the same corner with another person or who they have the most in common with, and, conversely, who they have the least in common with.

Topics can get increasingly focused on clients' attendance at group, using questions such as whether they would like to make changes to their drug use, alcohol use, or both. Another suggestion is to instruct clients, "If you are here because you want to be, go to this corner; if you did not want to come today, go to that corner; if you are not sure why you are here, etc.

This can lead into a discussion about respect for different interests, goals and reasons for attending group.

4. Introduce the *Decision to Change* exercise.

"We'd like to talk about some of the issues you may be struggling with in deciding to stop or reduce your use. What will you gain—and lose—by changing? What about not changing?"

Ways to encourage discussion in this exercise:
· "Which cost (or benefit) is most important?"
· "Why are you concerned about that cost?"
· "How mixed are your feelings about changing your use?"
· "What are some of the fears or hopes you have right now?"

Participants can fill out their own exercise sheet and then discuss their responses with the group, or it can be done with the group as a whole, noting the responses on a flip chart. In residential settings, with clients who are not using, it may be appropriate to only do the second part of this exercise, though most clients find it helpful to reflect back on what it was like for them when they were using.

5. Introduce *Check-in* exercise.

Finally, although the *Check-in* exercise will be completed in Session 2 and at the start of each subsequent session, it is worthwhile to introduce this exercise at the end of the first session. Previewing the *Check-in* exercise gets clients thinking about monitoring use, urges and coping during the coming week so that this information will be easier to recall in Session 2. "This sheet is what we will be using each week as a way of you telling the group what went well during the week and what did not go well. Over the next week, think about what your drug-use goal will be. Also, try to remember when you used, when you craved, and how you dealt with it. In addition, try to recall how your mental health was during the week. Those are the things that we will talk about next week."

6. Wrap up.
· "What's one thing you will do this week to meet your substance-use goal?"
· "Was the group what you expected? Do you have any questions?"
· "What will you be saying to each other on the way back to the elevator? It is important to say it here in the group."
· "What stood out for you in this session? What would you say to someone else about today's group?"

DECISION TO CHANGE EXERCISE

< HANDOUT >

In making a decision to change your drug use, it helps to think about the good and not-so-good things about using. List what is good and what is not so good about your drug use. Look at the Prompts for Exercises on page 255.

Good things about using	Not-so-good things about using

It also helps to think about the good things and not-so-good things about reducing or stopping your drug use. List the pros and cons of changing your use.

Good things about changing my use	Not-so-good things about changing

GOAL SETTING

Early in the treatment process, clients should clarify their intentions about stopping or reducing substance use. Many clients may not choose a goal of abstinence. *First Contact* takes a pragmatic approach by assisting clients to establish and work towards their substance use goals. In the short term, this strategy seeks to decrease the adverse impact of substance use in a style that supports clients' autonomy. In the long term, setting and reviewing goals for reducing or stopping use can be a process whereby clients build the motivation and skills needed for minimal or no use.

Research supports the notion of providing goal choice in that:
· There appears to be no basis for expecting that the therapist assigning treatment goals to clients will affect outcome (Sanchez-Craig, Annis, Bornet & MacDonald, 1984).
· Clients will be more likely to comply with treatment when they themselves have made the decision to pursue that strategy (Sobell & Sobell, 1993).

In discussing substance-use goals, it is important to make clear to the client that allowing goal choice does not mean that the counsellor is condoning or encouraging substance use; in particular, the use of alcohol by anyone who is under legal drinking age and the use of illicit substances by youth of any age. In the spirit of informed choices, this point can be made by stating that the most effective way to eliminate the chance of negative substance-related consequences is to not use at all. For those clients who do not choose a goal of abstinence, however, it is important to provide the message that reduction can decrease substance use-related harms. The *First Contact* program is as relevant for people with non-abstinence goals as it is for those who are prepared to quit altogether.

When clients consider reducing their use, the counsellor should emphasize the feasibility and reasonableness of the chosen goal. For example, when there are reasons why substance use would be too great a risk (e.g., if it would lead to serious legal problems or loss of family relationships), it is an opportunity for the counsellor to determine how the client perceives the potential risks involved, even with reduced use, and the benefits of an abstinence goal.

Because most clients will not know what goal is most realistic for them at first, weekly review of clients' goals is recommended. A reduced substance use goal should be clearly defined so that:
· The client has specific, well-thought-out rules about drinking or drug-use limits when he or she encounters a possible high-risk situation.
· The substance use goal does not change over time in a way that leads to the pre-treatment substance-use pattern.

CHECK-IN

< HANDOUT >

MY WEEK WAS   LOUSY   OK   FANTASTIC

FELT LIKE USING (DRUG) _____ ○ MON ○ TUES ○ WED ○ THU ○ FRI ○ SAT ○ SUN

USED (DRUG) _____ ○ MON ○ TUES ○ WED ○ THU ○ FRI ○ SAT ○ SUN

1. WHAT WAS GOING ON?
○ MY FEELINGS
○ MY THOUGHTS
○ MY ACTIVITES
○ MY RELATIONSHIPS
○ MY SCHOOL/WORK
○ MY MEDICATION/TREATMENT

○ MY LEGAL SITUATION

○ OTHER

2. HOW DID YOU HANDLE IT?
○ DID SOMETHING ELSE
○ THOUGHT OF CONSEQUENCES
○ GOT OUT OF THE SITUATION
○ TALKED TO SOMEONE
○ JUST USED
○ OTHER

4. MY GOALS FOR THE NEXT WEEK
○ NOT TO USE
○ REDUCE USE
○ DEAL WITH MY ISSUES
○ WORK ON ONE OF MY LIFE GOALS
○ UNDERSTAND THE CONNECTION BETWEEN MY LIFE GOALS
   AND MY FEELINGS
○ OTHER

3. WHAT HAPPENED?
○ FELT GOOD/BAD
○ HAD A GOOD TIME/BAD TIME
○ USED LESS/MORE
○ OTHER

SESSION 2: TRIGGERS, CONSEQUENCES AND ALTERNATIVES

GOALS FOR SESSION 2

1. Continue to clarify mental health and drug-use goals.

2. Continue to promote the ideas of choice and control with regard to use.

3. Continue to provide a comfortable and supportive forum to talk about the difficulties and rewards of changing.

4. For groups, continue to highlight commonalities and build group cohesion.

5. Complete the weekly *Check-in* exercise with the following goals:
· Monitor progress.
· Highlight successes.
· Aid in goal-setting (e.g., drug use, mental health and other life goals).
· Increase awareness of urges, cravings and strategies.
· Increase awareness of interactions of drug use, mental health symptoms and medication.
· Search for exceptions to usual patterns.
· Expand on clean time.
· Share strategies.
· Identify high-risk situations.

6. Complete the *Triggers, Consequences and Alternatives* exercise. Its goals are the following:
· Generate clients' options.
· Create awareness of triggers and consequences.
· Explore barriers to change.
· Increase self-efficacy by identifying what clients are already trying.
· Identify relevant successes in past (e.g., "mining the past").
· Help clients understand their use patterns.
· Emphasize the connection between consequences and triggers.
· Address the differences between long and short-term consequences (positive vs. negative).

CHECK-IN

The *Check-in* exercise is a way to reinforce and elaborate on themes introduced in Session 1. Part of the check-in is to ask clients to recall their use and/or their urges to use substances during the past week and keep track of their mental health symptoms and issues. Rather than focus on every day over the past week, you might ask that clients do the exercise for a good day and for a not-so-good day. For youth with concurrent disorders, the check-in is a time to explore mental health antecedents to drug use such as mood, behaviour, psychosis and medication effects.

In the first quadrant, clients identify the circumstances surrounding a craving or a use. This increases awareness of situations when they are likely to use. For clients with mental health problems, it is important to explore how their mental health symptoms trigger cravings or use and how use affects mental health symptoms. In quadrant 2, clients recall the various strategies that they used when they felt like using. This allows the counsellor to highlight what works for them, even if they are simply reducing the quantity or frequency of use. The counsellor should explore incidents of success carefully to ensure that clients actually understand how they succeeded. In quadrant 3, clients recall the consequences of their actions, which can be negative or positive. For clients with concurrent disorders, it is useful to explore how cravings, drug use or abstinence affect their specific mental health issues. Discussion about what they can do to turn a negative outcome into a more positive one is useful. Finally, in quadrant 4, clients are asked to set goals for the coming week with respect to drug use as well as other life areas, including mental health issues.

There are a number of ways to do the check-in. Clients can complete the exercise on their own and then discuss their responses with the group. Or the discussion can take place in dyads. To avoid literacy issues the counsellor can go through the exercise verbally with the client, or use the art therapy module described on page 266.

GUIDELINES FOR THE COUNSELLOR

1. Explain the purpose of the *Check-in* exercise.

"This check-in sheet is a way for you to tell the group what went well during the week and what did not go well."

Define a craving: A craving can be anything from a thought, such as, "I wouldn't mind a joint right now," to a more physical experience, such as palms sweating or difficulty sitting still.

Discuss progress over the last week:
- "Tell us about a situation you handled well."
- "Tell us about your clean time last week…how can you get more of that?"
- "Was anything easier/better last week?"

Help clients support each other:
- "What are other people's reactions to seeing friends?"
- "You were nodding when he/she was speaking, what were you thinking about?"

Help clients set goals for next week:
- "What are you going to do more of next week?"

2. Introduce the *Triggers, Consequences and Alternatives* exercise.

"This exercise follows from some of the things that we talked about during the check-in. It will help you to think about the patterns of your use, what the triggers, payoffs and consequences are. Understanding these connections is the first step to you taking control of your use."

Explain triggers, behaviours and consequences—begin by discussing triggers:
- "When we talk about triggers, we are talking about the situations that lead to use. Triggers can be people, places, things, times and feelings. The behaviour is the drug use. The consequences are the things that happen after you use. They can be both positive and negative. Who can give me some examples of triggers?" (Suggestion: have one of the clients at a flipchart writing client responses down.)
- "What triggers happened last week (refer to check-in)?"
- "What other triggers can you think of?"

Discuss consequences:

- "What is some of the stuff that happens after use? Is there anything you notice about the timing of the consequences?"
- "Some clients have said that using was really fun in the beginning but that now it is not as much fun. Has anyone experienced that?"
- "Some consequences are hidden, some are lost opportunities. Has anyone experienced missing out on something because they were using?"

Discuss alternatives to use:

- "On non-using days, what has worked for you?"
- "What is going to help you not use?"
- "What might be frightening about doing something different when you want to use?"
- "What would be the easiest thing to do differently?"

3. Wrap up.

Look at ways that the *Triggers, Consequences and Alternatives* exercise could apply to daily life outside the session:

- "What is one alternative to substance use that you can try this week to help you not to use?"

EXPLORING PATTERNS OF USE

The *Triggers, Consequences and Alternatives* exercise can help clients understand their use patterns by emphasizing the link between the triggers/antecedents of use and the resulting positive and negative consequences. This exercise can also help the client explore the relationship between drug use and mental health symptoms. Many of the goals of this exercise are drawn from issues raised during the check-in, such as how to identify triggers and generating alternatives to use. Sometimes clients maintain that there are no triggers to their use. What usually helps in this situation is to go over the potential list of people, places and things (e.g., emotions, time of day) that can serve as triggers. Also, clients may have mentioned something during the *Check-in* exercise that provides a clue as to what triggers are salient to them.

It is important to talk about the timing of the consequences of use if the subject does not naturally come up in discussion. On one hand, when people drink or use drugs, they are seeking the positive consequences (e.g., temporary relaxation) that can occur during or shortly after use. On the other hand, the negative or harmful consequences are often delayed and are difficult to link with the actual substance use. For instance, a gradual decline in the quality of one's schoolwork could be a long-term result of substance use that would not be directly related to any single occasion of use.

STRATEGIES FOR CHANGE

After discussing the clients' triggers and alternatives to substance use, the counsellor encourages them to select one alternative that they are willing to try during the coming week. Sometimes clients do not feel confident about engaging in new activities in high-risk situations and these concerns need to be explored. Two useful strategies to increase clients' self-efficacy in trying alternatives are:

· identifying what clients are already doing to reduce their use. Clients sometimes fail to realize that they already engage in some activities that deal with urges or remove them from high-risk situations. Even simple things like keeping busy, listening to music, or spending time with family or friends who do not use drugs should be acknowledged and encouraged.

· drawing parallels with a previous accomplishment (e.g., "mining" the past). It is also helpful to find out if clients have tried to reduce or quit in the past and how they did so. Even if their strategies were only temporarily successful, discussing how those strategies can be modified or supplemented can be a fruitful way to build on the clients' existing resources.

< HANDOUT >

TRIGGERS, CONSEQUENCES AND ALTERNATIVES EXERCISE

Triggers	Use/Craving Drug?/How much?/ How often?	Consequences Positive	Negative	Alternatives
feelings: physical/mood				
thoughts/activities/ situations				
friends and family				
school/work				
mental health				
therapy/medication				
legal				

PROMPTS FOR EXERCISES

Below are common triggers and consequences for use. Which ones apply to you?

Feelings	Physical	Thoughts	Mental health	Situations
○ frustrated	○ tired	○ I'm no good	○ voices	○ with friends
○ relaxed	○ awake	○ No one likes me	○ confused	○ alone
○ confused	○ sleepy	○ I'm…	○ paranoid	○ party
○ clear	○ alert	○ They're…	○ anxious	○ celebration
○ angry	○ hurt	○ waste of time	○ depressed	○ camping
○ content	○ well	○ What's the use?	○ manic	○ having fun
○ anxious	○ hungry	○ I want to feel…	○ binge eating	○ taking risks
○ calm	○ full	○ I can control it	○ purging	○ in trouble
○ sad	○ hungover	○ I don't fit in	○ not eating	○ at school
○ happy	○ healthy	○ Things are great	○ flashbacks	○ after school
○ scared	○ weak	○ No one can touch me	○ feeling calm	○ at work
○ excited	○ strong	○ I love…	○ thinking clearly	○ after work
○ disappointed	○ restless		○ concentrating	○ having money
○ bored	○ peaceful		○ hyper	○ weekend
○ lonely	○ slow		○ in control	○ court
○ overwhelmed	○ hyper		○ out of control	○ fight
○ mellow	○ horny			○ sports
	○ in pain			

ALTERNATIVES

Below are possible alternatives to using drugs

Avoid people or places that trigger cravings or thoughts about using.	Remember the positive things about using healthy coping skills.	Read something inspiring!
Identify and avoid high-risk situations—situations in which you'd be likely to use (e.g, bars, clubs, raves).	Remember the negative consequences of using alcohol or other substances.	Ask yourself what you are feeling. (Go through a list of your common feeling triggers—am I sad, angry, anxious, stressed?)
Take a friend, someone you trust, when going to a risky place/situation.	Remind yourself that feelings, even difficult and unpleasant ones, are normal!	Give yourself permission to feel emotions without judging them.
Leave situations that seem risky or limit how long you stay.	Distract yourself by thinking about something else.	Express your feelings (cry, smile, laugh, frown, etc.).
If you're feeling triggered, call someone for support.	Recognize when you are making negative statements about yourself (i.e., I am such a loser).	Ask for support.
Go for a walk.	Plan ahead for any risky situations or obstacles to your plan.	Talk to someone about your feelings.
Read a book, magazine or go on the Internet.	Think about your future goals and how you can achieve them.	Find ways to express your feelings creatively—play some music, draw or write a poem.
Exercise or do something physical— go for a run, bike, or skateboard.	Make a commitment to yourself to fulfil a goal and remind yourself of it.	Start keeping a journal and write about yourself.
Clean up your room, take out the garbage, do some household chores.	Remind yourself that you are in charge of whatever decisions you make.	Take time to soothe yourself.
Do volunteer work.	Tell yourself that you are doing well and don't want to interfere with the progress.	Praise yourself for the progress you have made—give yourself some credit!

< HANDOUT >

SESSION 3: THINGS THAT ARE IMPORTANT TO ME

GOALS FOR SESSION 3

1. Reassess treatment/use goals.

2. Find out whether clients tried any new alternative responses since the last session.

3. Continue to explore the connection between triggers and consequences.

4. For groups, continue to highlight commonalities and build group cohesion.

5. Complete the *Things that Are Important to Me* exercise with the following goals:
- Help clients talk about the future (i.e., hopes and expectations).
- Create discrepancy.
- Explore the role of use in achieving goals.
- Review goal achievement:
  - status six months ago
  - current status
  - anticipated progress in six months.
- Try to determine plans and next steps to achieve goals.

CHECK-IN

Session 3 starts out again with the *Check-in* exercise. Although asking about triggers and alternatives to use is always an integral part of this exercise, a counsellor can probe these issues in more detail based on what was discussed in the *Triggers, Consequences and Alternatives* exercise during Session 2.

LIFE GOALS AND VALUES

Session 3 includes the *Things that Are Important to Me* exercise, which relates to clients' life goals and values. Several therapeutic approaches, such as solution-focused and motivational interviewing, support the usefulness of exploring life goals and values. Clarifying what life goals a client wants to achieve and assessing where he or she is now helps develop discrepancy, one of the key elements of Motivational Interviewing (Miller & Rollnick, 2002). Discussing the things that are important to them helps clients acknowledge their aspirations, strengths and competencies, rather than focusing exclusively on problematic areas of their lives, reflecting a solution-focussed perspective.

Understanding clients' life goals also allows for a discussion of how use affects progress towards such goals. Clients may think that drug use helps them to reach some goals, such as being popular. However, most clients will acknowledge that alcohol and other drug use impairs their ability to achieve life goals to some degree (e.g., completing school or being healthy).

The *Things that Are Important to Me* exercise should also include a discussion of what concrete steps clients can take to start progressing toward their goals. The "Top 10 Ways of Achieving Your Goals" is included in this exercise to help clients decide what the next steps are to achieving their goals. However, it is important for the counsellor to help in translating the life goals into concrete steps or activities for the client to work on, ideally, within the next week. Counsellors can assist in this part of the exercise by helping clients select short-term goals that are realistic and measurable.

GUIDELINES FOR THE COUNSELLOR

1. Check-in.

Discuss progress over the past week. For tips, see *Check-in* in Session 1.

Help clients see patterns in their use or change strategies:
· "What strategies from last week's triggers, consequences and alternatives exercise did you try?"
· "How have these last few weeks been for you—better, worse or about the same?"

Help clients to use strategies other than avoidance:
· "Avoiding triggers is the first step for a lot of people. What are the good things and not-so-good things about doing that?"
· "What is the next step?"

2. Introduce the *Things that Are Important to Me* exercise.

"This exercise is about finding out what you want from your life. Read through the whole list and pick the top 10 things that are important to you or that you want to work towards." (For larger groups, have them pick out 10, but discuss only the top two or three items.)

Affirmation: "It looks like you want to make some changes in your life and that you know what you want."

Make steps towards goals more concrete:
· "When you picture yourself doing that, what are you doing?"
· "What are the steps to get there?"

Look at the impact of drug use on achievement of goals:

- "How do drugs fit into your goals?"
- "Where were you six months ago in relation to your goals?"
- "Where do you see yourself six months from now?"
- "What about your use?"

3. Wrap up.

Integrating life goals:

- "What is one thing you can do this week that would help you move a step closer to one of your life goals?"

THINGS THAT ARE IMPORTANT TO ME EXERCISE

Choose the top 10 things that are important to you

Friends
have close, supportive friends

Hope
maintain a positive and
optimistic outlook

Feel good about myself
like myself just as I am

Get things done
accomplish and achieve

Relaxation
reduce and manage stress

Fame
be known and recognized

Humour
see the humorous side of myself
and the world

Loved
be loved by those close to me

Loving
give love to others

Romance
have an intense, exciting love
relationship

Understand myself
have a deep, honest understanding
of myself

Belonging
fit in with others

Attractiveness
be physically attractive

Trustworthy
be reliable and trusted

Flexibility
adjust to new or unusual
situations easily

Fun
play and have fun

Health
be physically and mentally healthy

Independence
be free from dependence on others

Leisure
take time to relax and enjoy

Balance
avoid extremes and find a
middle ground

Pleasure
enjoy good things

Popularity
be well-liked

Self-control
be in charge of my own actions

Sex
have an active and satisfying sex life

Wealth
have plenty of money

Contribution
make a difference

Creativity
have new and original ideas

Generosity
give to others

Loyalty
be there for others

Risk
try new things

Family
have a happy, loving family

God's will
follow the will of God

Inner peace
experience personal peace

Knowledge
learn and possess valuable
knowledge

Structure
have a life that is well-organized

Grounded
be realistic and practical

Safety
be safe and secure

Simplicity
live life simply, with minimal needs

Honesty
be open and straightforward

Adventure
have new and exciting experiences

Respectful
be polite and considerate to others

Forgiveness
be forgiving of others

Persistence
work hard and not give up

Stability
have a life that stays fairly
consistent

Spirituality
grow spiritually

Tolerance
accept and respect those different
from me

< HANDOUT >

Adapted from Miller, W.R. & C'deBaca, J. (1994)

TOP 10 WAYS OF ACHIEVING YOUR GOALS

1. **Desire**: Pick a goal that you really want to achieve.

2. **Belief**: Pick a goal that is challenging but realistic, one that you believe you can achieve.

3. **Benefits**: List the benefits that will come from achieving your goal—the more benefits, the more motivated and persistent you will be.

4. **Obstacles**: Identify some of the obstacles and think about how you are going to deal with them—there are always obstacles to achieving a worthwhile goal.

5. **Knowledge**: Find out what you need to know to achieve your goal.

6. **People**: Identify the people that can help you achieve your goal.

7. **Current status**: Figure out where you are now on your way to achieving your goal—for example, if you want to improve your self-esteem, ask yourself, on a scale of 1 to 10, "where am I now?" and "what one small step can I take to move a little closer to my goal?"

8. **Plan**: Make a plan, break things down into small manageable steps, make the steps concrete and be willing to revise your plan. Remember, no first plan is perfect.

9. **Timeline**: Set an overall timeline to achieve your goal. Then think about how much time it will take to complete the first step

10. **Persistence**: Keep in mind that mistakes and disappointments can occur, but that you can make it. It's not always smooth sailing.

< HANDOUT >

SESSION 4: STAGES OF CHANGE

GOALS FOR SESSION 4

1. Review progress and emphasize success, especially overcoming barriers to change.

2. Continue to discuss use goals in the context of life goals.

3. Discuss future treatment planning.

4. Review *First Contact* treatment and the changes made in all life areas.

5. For groups, review group process—emphasize sharing in group as positive risk-taking.

6. Acknowledge completion of *First Contact* cycle (i.e., success and achievement).

7. Complete the *Stages of Change* exercise with the following goals:
· Increase awareness of change as a process.
· Identify clients' stage of change.
· Make more concrete changes during *First Contact* treatment.
· Identify more concrete ways of getting to the next stage.

REVIEW OF CHANGE PROCESS

Session 4 is the last session in the *First Contact* program. Consequently, the primary goals for clients in this session are to review progress and affirm whatever positive changes have taken place in their lives (even if it is only increased awareness), and, if the counsellor is leading a *First Contact* group, to review group process and emphasize the sharing and support that have occurred. Because many of these young clients have difficulty completing things, it is also worthwhile to acknowledge their success in completing the *First Contact* program. Show that you recognize the motivation and courage that it takes for them to examine the impact of substance use on their lives.

The *Stages of Change* exercise is included to increase clients' understanding of change as a process and offer a long-term perspective on change. The *Stages of Change* exercise does not include the original terms used by Prochaska & DiClemente (1984). Instead, the terms for the stages have been modified, using everyday language that is more appealing to young clients.

Clients are asked to identify what stage they were in when they started *First Contact* and where they are now. This exercise highlights the changes and what they have done to make those changes. It is also helpful to talk about concrete ways to maintain gains and get to the next stage (for clients not in the maintenance stage).

TREATMENT NEEDS AND OPTIONS FOR THE FUTURE

This session is also the time to talk with the client about treatment needs after *First Contact*. The recommended treatment plan will depend on the characteristics of the client, the response to treatment and the options available. For those who have responded well and have no other urgent treatment needs, continuing care is a common suggestion. For those with additional needs, such as individual, family or specific skills (e.g., anger management), treatment should also be considered. For those who have not responded to treatment, case management and referral to a more intensive intervention (e.g., community day program) may be suggested.

GUIDELINES FOR THE COUNSELLOR

1. *Check-in.*

Discuss progress over the past week: For tips, see *Check-in* exercise from Session 1.

Help clients to consolidate change:
· "Over the course of the last four weeks, what strategies have been the most helpful?"
· "Is this pattern of use (or abstinence) something you can keep up?"

2. Introduce *Stages of Change Exercise Handout.*

Review and consolidate progress

This exercise is a way of figuring out where you are. Change is like taking a journey. Some people aren't interested; others are uncertain and are just thinking about it; and others are preparing themselves, and so on.

Look over the stages of change and tell us:
· "Where were you when you came in?"
· "Where are you now?"
· "What led to the change (if any)?"
· "What are the next steps (i.e. coping strategies, treatment referrals)?"

3. Discuss additional treatment options.

Look at future treatment planning:
· "What kind of additional help might be useful at this point?"
· "What would you like to work on in the next month or two?"

4. Wrap up.

Highlight changes and progress, review treatment process, and obtain feedback:
- "What led to changes (if any)?"
- "What are the next steps (e.g., coping strategies)?"
- "What did you think about being here for the past four weeks?"
- "What was the first group session like for you?"
- "How did things change for you in the group over the four weeks?" (Emphasize the ability to stick with it despite initial discomfort.)
- "What was most helpful about the program?"
- "Do you have any suggestions about how to improve these groups?"

STAGES OF CHANGE EXERCISE

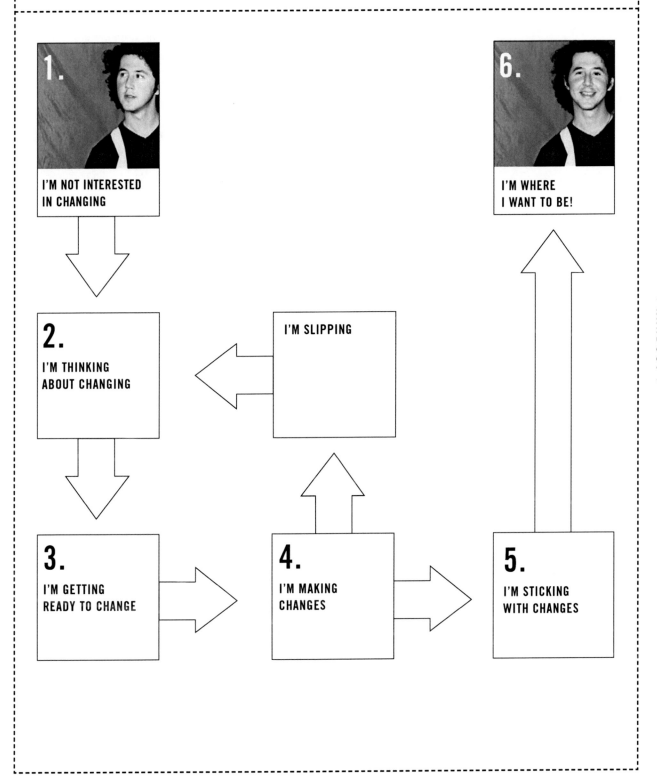

1.
I'M NOT INTERESTED
IN CHANGING

6.
I'M WHERE
I WANT TO BE!

2.
I'M THINKING
ABOUT CHANGING

I'M SLIPPING

3.
I'M GETTING
READY TO CHANGE

4.
I'M MAKING
CHANGES

5.
I'M STICKING
WITH CHANGES

< HANDOUT >

INTRODUCTION TO ART THERAPY MODALITY

One of the central features of art therapy is its ability to help people communicate better about their issues, feelings, conflicts and preoccupations. Art provides a means for the participant to illustrate his or her various problems and channel emotions, concerns and problems associated with substance use to objectively explore the situation and find more appropriate solutions. Art therapy exercises can facilitate self-reflection. Participants can work constructively on a problem rather than internalizing it in an unhealthy way or acting out in self-destructive ways.

Youth who might benefit most from an art therapy modality include youth:
· who have difficulty focusing or a short attention span (they might benefit from an activity-based art program)
· whose verbal expression is compromised; for example, during a period of vulnerability because of mental illness
· who are withdrawn and have difficulty expressing feelings verbally (they might find art a safer way to communicate)
· who express themselves more easily through visual images, who will, therefore, feel comfortable with this mode of expression.
· who intellectualize and might be able to lower their defenses through art.
· with a language barrier, who might feel more competent in a group where visual communiction is emphasized and pictures are used as a visual aid for discussions.

GOALS AND OBJECTIVES OF ART THERAPY

The art therapy instructions that accompany each session of *First Contact* are designed to enhance the learning experience and meet the needs of the youth involved. The goal is to use the art activity to reduce barriers to awareness and facilitate their ability to look objectively at their substance use. This can occur in a number of ways:
· Encourage autonomy and self-determination while lessening dependency. Art is a hands-on activity and there are benefits from active participation. Treatment in art therapy involves doing something—art. This helps participants realize that they can examine their substance use through the process of assembling and forming art. The art itself becomes the means for self-expression around a specific problem or situation as well as the arena for further exploration.
· Accentuate time and the need to focus. Creating artwork is an easy and enjoyable activity that encourages attention; seeing shapes and colours on a piece of paper tends to help people focus. The completed image helps participants separate what is important from what is unimportant. Seeing one's substance use in this concrete form helps the individual to view it with greater objectivity and perspective.

- Foster individual growth. Art is a non-verbal activity that can overcome verbal resistance. Participants can express and find details in their artwork that they may not usually be aware of or consider. The process of making sense of the imagery, through careful inquiry and discussion, encourages this reflection. There is a sense of accomplishment, which further improves self-esteem and confidence.
- Encourage new and different perspectives through a non-verbal modality. A person's first response to treatment is often expressed in artwork as anger, confusion, panic, fear or helplessness. The person is encouraged to acknowledge and examine these emotional responses and generate new and healthy alternative views.

GUIDELINES TO HELP FACILITATORS RESPOND TO A CLIENT'S ART IN A SUPPORTIVE WAY THAT WILL ADVANCE THE GOALS OF *FIRST CONTACT*

Materials

Always use good quality materials that will withstand heavy pressure without breaking and try to have an ample supply of materials so that everyone has a choice. Suggested materials are broad-tip markers, oil pastels, pencil crayons and graphite pencils. Have pencil sharpeners, erasers and rulers available as well as good quality scissors and glue sticks for collage. Provide large sheets of paper (18" x 24") that are strong enough not to tear. Construction or cartridge paper in white or neutral colours is recommended. Have pictures from magazines cut out before the group. Images should include people representing a variety of ages, cultures and races as well as people involved in a variety of activities and expressing a range of human emotions. Include images of animals, places and things.

When looking at art and talking about art:

- Never force a participant to talk if he or she does not want to.
- Try to avoid interpreting the art by having participants describe their own work.
- Have each participant share the experience of making the picture.
- Ask what his or her feelings were about approaching and continuing the task. How would you describe the picture? What would be the title of the picture?
- Promote self-discovery by asking each participant to elaborate on parts of the picture. Ask questions that encourage the participant to project more into the art. What part of the picture do you like best (least)? Why?
- Focus on certain parts of a picture that suggest a theme, or that are distorted or exaggerated. What is the person in the picture doing? What is the person in the picture thinking or feeling? What do these colours mean to you?
- Encourage reflection. Do you ever feel that way? Do you ever do that? Does that fit with your life in any way?

SESSION 1: DECISION TO CHANGE

Art materials
· One sheet of 18" x 24" white drawing paper
· Coloured pencils, oil pastels, chalk pastels
· Magazines for collage, scissors, glue

Getting started
"Spend a few minutes considering your drug and alcohol use. What are the benefits, the good things about using, and what are the costs, the not-so-good things? If you reduce or stop your use of substances, what are the good and not-so-good things that would result?"

Art-making instructions
"Fold the sheet of paper in half. On one side make a picture about the good things about using, and on the other side, a picture about the not-so-good things.

Take a second sheet of paper, folded in half. On one side make a picture of the good things about reducing or stopping your drug use, and on the other side, a picture of the not-so-good things."

Looking at art and talking about art
"Describe your pictures and what is happening in each picture. How do they differ? What are the good things about using and the not-so-good things about using? What do you like in each picture and what don't you like?"

CHECK-IN

Art materials
· One sheet of 18" x 24" white drawing paper
· Coloured pencils, oil pastels, chalk pastels
· Magazines for collage, scissors, glue

Getting started
"Spend a few minutes to think about a good day and a not-so-good day this past week when you felt like using or you used. Where were you at the time? Were you with someone or were you alone? What was going on? What were you feeling?"

Art-making instructions

"Divide the page in the middle and on one side make a picture about a good day, and on the other side, a not-so-good day when you felt like using or used alcohol or drugs. Put as much detail as you can about where you were and what time it was. How were you feeling at the time and what was going on?"

Looking at, and talking about art.

"Describe your picture. What is happening in the picture? What made you think about using and then what happened? Did you use? What could have been an alternative to using at the time?"

- -

SESSION 2: TRIGGERS, CONSEQUENCES AND ALTERNATIVES

Art materials
·   One sheet of 18" x 24" white drawing paper
·   Coloured pencils, oil pastels, chalk pastels
·   Magazines for collage, scissors, glue

Getting started

"Spend a few minutes to think about a time when you thought about using this week. Where were you at the time? Were you alone or with someone? What was going on? How were you feeling?"

Art-making instructions

"Make a picture about a time this week when you thought about using alcohol or drugs. Put as much detail as you can about where you were and what time it was. How were you feeling at the time and what was going on?"

Looking at, and talking about art

"Describe your picture. What is happening in the picture? What made you think about using and what happened? Did you use? What could have been an alternative to using at the time?"

SESSION 3: THINGS THAT ARE IMPORTANT TO ME

Art materials
- One sheet of 18" x 24" white drawing paper
- Coloured pencils, oil pastels, chalk pastels
- Magazines for collage, scissors, glue

Getting started

"Think about where you would like to be in a year or two. How would you like your life to look? What would you like to accomplish? Is there someone you admire that you would want to be like?"

Art-making instructions

"Make a picture of how you would like people to see you in the future."

Looking at, and talking about art

"Talk about the picture: who you are, where you are and what you are doing. What is one thing you could do to get to where you are in the picture?"

SESSION 4: STAGES OF CHANGE

Art materials
- One sheet of 18" x 24" white drawing paper
- Coloured pencils, oil pastels, chalk pastels
- Magazines for collage, scissors, glue

Getting started

"Think about what brought you to this group and what you have learned about yourself."

Art-making instructions

"Draw a line down the middle of the page. On one side, make a picture about you when you came into the program, on the other side, a picture of where you are at right now."

Looking at, and talking about art

"Compare the pictures and describe what is different. What has changed? What other changes do you think there will be in the near future?"

ACTIVITY MODALITY

SESSION 1: DECISION TO CHANGE ACTIVITY

Materials

· A bowl of small treats like popcorn, jelly beans or smarties
· Two paper plates or cups per person. One is labelled "good things," the other, "not-so-good things"
· One copy per person of the *Decision to Change* exercise
· One copy of the list of prompts

Getting started

The group sits in a circle with the two plates in front of each person. The therapist has a *Decision to Change* exercise sheet for each person in the group and will record participants' answers on their sheet.

Introduce the activity

We would like to talk about some issues you may be struggling with in deciding to change (reduce or stop) your drug use. What will you gain or lose by changing? What about not changing?

The activity

Pass the bowl around the circle. As each person receives the bowl, they talk about a good thing about their drug use, take a treat from the bowl and place it on the "good things" plate. The therapist records each person's response on their exercise sheet. If clients have difficulty generating good things or not-so-good things, refer to the prompts list. Keep going around until everyone has talked about all the good things about their use that are important to them. Next, go around the group to have clients talk about the not-so-good things about use, and put a treat on their "not-so-good things" plate. Again, keep going around until everyone has had a chance to talk about as many not-so-good things about their drug use as they can think of.

Repeat the activity for the good things and not-so-good things about changing your drug use. In residential settings, with youth who are not using you may just want to do this part of the activity, although many of them may find it helpful to reflect on the pros and cons when they were using.

Discussion

- "When you compare the number of treats on each plate, how mixed are your feelings about making a change?"
- "Which costs (or benefits) are most important? Why are you concerned about those costs?"
- "What are some of the fears or hopes that you have right now?"

SESSION 4: STAGES OF CHANGE ACTIVITY

Getting started

Designate places in the room for each stage of the change process.

Introduce the activity

"This exercise is a way of figuring out where you are at. Change is like taking a journey. Some people aren't interested; others are uncertain and are just thinking about it; and others are preparing themselves, and so on. Let's look over the stages of change." (Read out loud each of the stages.)

The activity

Go to the spot that reflects the stage you were in when you first came to the group. Now go to the spot that reflects the stage you are in now.

Discussion

- "What led to the change (if any)?"
- "What are the next steps (e.g., coping strategies, treatment referrals)?"

REFERENCES

Addiction Research Foundation and Health and Welfare Canada. (1991). *Youth & Drugs: An Education Package for Professionals.* Toronto: Addiction Research Foundation.

Addington, J. & Addington, D. (2001). Impact of an Early Psychosis Program on Substance Use. *Psychiatric Rehabilitation Journal, 25 (1)*, 60-67.

Addington, J. & Addington, D. (1998). Effects of Substance Misuse in Early Psychosis. *British Journal of Psychiatry, 172 (supplement 33)*, 134-136.

Adlaf, E.M. & Paglia, A. (2001). *Drug Use Among Ontario Students 1977–2001.* CAMH Research Document Series No. 10. Toronto: Centre for Addiction and Mental Health.

Adlaf, E.M., Paglia, A. & Beitchman, J.H. (2002). *The Mental Health and Well-Being of Ontario Students: Findings from the OSDUS 1991–2001.* CAMH Research Document Series No. 11. Toronto: Centre for Addiction and Mental Health.

American Psychiatric Association. (1994). *Diagnostic and Statistical Manual of Mental Disorders*, (4th ed.). Washington, DC.

Annis, H.M. & Martin, G. (1985). *Inventory of Drug-Taking Situations.* Toronto: Addiction Research Foundation.

Baer, J.S. & Peterson, P.L. (2002). Motivational Interviewing with Adolescents and Young Adults. In W.R. Miller, & S. Rollnick (Eds.), *Motivational Interviewing: Preparing People for Change* (2nd ed.) (pp.320-332). New York and London: The Guilford Press.

Ballon, B.C. (in press). Concurrent Disorders in Young People. In W.J.W. Skinner & P. Smith (Eds.), *Concurrent Disorders Handbook.* Toronto: Centre for Addiction and Mental Health.

Ballon, B.C., Courbasson, C.M.A. & Smith, P.D. (2001). Physical and Sexual Abuse Issues Among Youths with Substance Use Problems. *Canadian Journal of Psychiatry, 46*, 617-621.

Barbara, A.M., Chaim, G. & Doctor, F. (2002). *Asking the Right Questions: Talking about sexual orientation and gender identity during assessment for drug and alcohol concerns.* Toronto: Centre for Addiction and Mental Health.

Bois, C. & Graham, K. (1997). Case Management. In S. Harrison and V. Carver (Eds.), *Alcohol and Drug Problems* (2nd ed.). (pp. 61-76). Toronto: Addiction Research Foundation.

Boudreau, R.J. (in press). Substance Use Problems and the Family. In S. Harrison & V. Carver (Eds.), *Alcohol and Drug Problems* (3rd ed.). Toronto: Centre for Addiction and Mental Health.

Boudreau, R., Chaim, G., Pearlman, S., Shenfeld, J. & Skinner, W. (1998). *Working with Couples and Families: Skills for Addiction Workers. Trainer's Guide.* Toronto: Addiction Research Foundation.

Brands, B., Sproule, B. & Marshman, J. (1998). *Drugs & Drug Abuse* (3rd ed.). Toronto: Addiction Research Foundation.

Braverman, M.T. (2001). Applying Resilience Theory to the Prevention of Adolescent Substance Abuse. *Youth Development Focus* (Invited monograph series). University of California, Davis: 4-H Center for Youth Development [Obtained on-line]. Available on Internet: http://ucce.ucdavis.edu/freeform/4hcyd/documents/CYD_Focus1190.pdf

Brent, D.A., Holder, D., Kolko, D., Brimaher, B., Baugher, M., Roth, C., Iyengar, S. & Johnson, B.A. (1997). A Clinical Psychotherapy Trial for Adolescent Depression Comparing Cognitive, Family and Supportive Therapy. *Archives of General Psychiatry, 54 (9)*, 877-885.

Browne, G., Brown, C., Levine, M. & Kertyzia, J. (April 2001). *The Current Status of Mental Health Services for School-Aged Children and Youth of Ontario.* Toronto: Government of Ontario [Obtained on-line]. Available on Internet: http://www.fhs.mcmaster.ca/slru/paper/Current_ Status_of_Mental_Health.pdf.

Bukstein, O., Dunne, J.E., Ayres, W., Arnold, V., Benedek, E., Benson, R.S., Bernet, W., Berstein, G., Gross, R.L., King, R., Kinlan J., Leonard, H., Licamele W., McClellan, J., Shaw, K., Sloan, L.E. & Miles, C.M. (1997). Practice Parameters for the Asssessment and Treatment of Children and Adolescents with Substance Use Disorders. *Journal of the American Academy of Child and Adolescent Psychiatry, 36 (10): Supplement*, October 1997.

Bukstein, O.G. & Van Hasselt, V.B. (1993). Alcohol and Drug Abuse. In A.S. Bellack & M. Hersen (Eds.), *Handbook of Behavior Therapy in the Psychiatric Setting* (pp. 453-475). New York: Plenum.

Campbell, M. & Malone, R. (1991). Mental Retardation and Psychiatric Disorders. *Hospital Community Psychiatry, 42*, 374-389.

Canadian Centre on Substance Abuse and Centre for Addiction and Mental Health (1999). *Canadian Profile: Alcohol, Tobacco and Other Drugs*, 1999. Ottawa: Canadian Centre on Substance Abuse.

Catalano, R.F., Hawkins, J.D., Wells, E.A. (1991-1992). Evaluation of the Effectiveness of Adolescent Drug Abuse Treatment: Assessment of Risk for Relapse, and Promising Approaches for Relapse Prevention. *International Journal of Addictions, 25*, 1085-1140.

Centre for Addiction and Mental Health. (2002a). *Substance Use and Mental Health Concerns in Youth*. Youth Scoop Sheet #4. Toronto: Centre for Addiction and Mental Health.

Centre for Addiction and Mental Health. (2002b). *CAMH Position on Harm Reduction: Its Meaning and Applications for Substance Use Issues* [Obtained on-line]. Available on Internet: http://www.camh.net/best_advice/harm_reduction_pos0602.html.

Centre for Addiction and Mental Health (2001). *Cultural Competence for Social Workers. Module One*. Toronto: Education and Training Services, Centre for Addiction and Mental Health.

Centre for Addiction and Mental Health and Canadian Mental Health Association. (2001). *Talking about Mental Illness: A guide for developing an awareness program for youth*. Toronto: Centre for Addiction and Mental Health.

Chaim, G. & Shenfeld, J. (in press). Concurrent Disorders: A Framework for Working with Couples and Families. In W.J.W. Skinner & P. Smith (Eds.), *Concurrent Disorders Handbook*. Toronto: Centre for Addiction and Mental Health.

Chaim, G., Shenfeld, J. & Long, D. (in press). Working with Youth. In S. Harrison & V. Carver (Eds.), *Alcohol and Drug Problems*, (3rd ed.). Toronto: Centre for Addiction and Mental Health.

Children's Mental Health Ontario. (2001a). *Evidence Based Practices for Depression in Children and Adolescents*. Toronto: Children's Mental Health Ontario [Obtained on-line]. Available on Internet: http://www.cmho.org/pdf_files/MDD_W3_Full_Document.pdf.

Children's Mental Health Ontario (2001b). *Evidence Based Practices for Conduct Disorder in Children and Adolescents*. Toronto: Children's Mental Health Ontario [Obtained on-line]. Available on Internet: http://www.cmho.org/pdf_files/CD_W3_Full_Document.pdf.

Collin, K. & Paone, M. (2002). *Cocktails: Facts for Youth About Mixing Medicine, Booze and Street Drugs*. Children's and Women's Health Centre of British Columbia.

Connors, G.J., Donovan, D.M. & DiClemente, C.C. (2001). *Substance Abuse Treatment and the Stages of Change*. New York and London: The Guilford Press.

Cross, S. & Sibley, L.B. (2001). *The Standardized Tools and Criteria Manual: Helping Clients Navigate Addiction Treatment in Ontario*. Toronto: Centre for Addiction and Mental Health.

DiClemente, C.C. & Velasquez, M.M. (2002). Motivational Interviewing and the Stages of Change. In W.R. Miller & S. Rollnick (Eds.), *Motivational Interviewing: Preparing People for Change* (2nd ed.) (pp.201-216). New York and London: The Guilford Press.

Dishion, T.J. & Kavanagh, K. (2001). An Ecological Approach to Family Intervention for Adolescent Substance Use. In E.F. Wagner & H.B. Waldron (Eds.), *Innovations in Adolescent Substance Abuse Interventions* (pp.127-142). New York: Pergamon.

Dixon, L. (1999). Dual Diagnosis of Substance Abuse in Schizophrenia: Prevalence and Impact on Outcomes. *Schizophrenia Research, 35*, S93-S100.

Donahue, B. & Azrin, N. (2001). Family Behavior Therapy. In E.F. Wagner & H.B. Waldron (Eds.), *Innovations in Adolescent Substance Abuse Interventions* (pp.205-227). New York: Pergamon.

Drake, R.E. & Mueser, K.T. (2000). Psychosocial Approaches to Dual Diagnosis. *Schizophrenia Bulletin, 26*, 105-118.

Drake, R.E. & Osher F.C. (1997). Treating Substance Abuse in Patients with Severe Mental Illness. In S.W. Henggeler & A.B. Santos (Eds.), *Innovative approaches for difficult-to-treat populations* (pp.191-207). Washington, DC: American Psychiatric Press.

Edgerton, R.B. (1986). Alcohol and Drug Use by Mentally Retarded Adults. *American Journal of Mental Deficiency, 90*, 602-609.

Godley, S.H., Godley, M.D. & Dennis, M.L. (2001a). The Assertive Aftercare Protocol for Adolescent Substance Abusers. In E.F. Wagner & H.B. Waldron (Eds.), *Innovations in Adolescent Substance Abuse Interventions* (pp. 313-331). New York: Pergamon.

Godley, S.H., Meyers, R.J., Smith, J.E., Karvinen, T., Titus, J.C., Godley, M.D., Dent, G., Passetti, L. & Kelberg, P. (2001b). *The Adolescent Community Reinforcement Approach for Adolescent Cannabis Users*, Cannabis Youth Treatment Series, Volume 4. Center for Substance Abuse Treatment [Obtained on-line]. Available on Internet: ftp://ftp.health.org/pub/ncadi/govpubs/bkd387.pdf.

Griffens, D.M., Stavrakaki, C. & Summers, J. (Eds.). (2002). *Dual Diagnosis: An Introduction to the Mental Health Needs of Persons with Developmental Disabilities*. Sudbury, ON: Habilitative Mental Health Resource Network.

Hamilton, N.L., Brantley, L.B., Tims, F.M., Angelovich, N. & McDougall, B. (2001). *Family Support Network for Adolescent Cannabis Users*. Cannabis Youth Treatment (CYT) Series, Volume 3. Center for Substance Abuse Treatment. [Obtained on-line]. Available on Internet: http://www.health.org/govpubs/bkd386/cyt3.pdf.

Hansen, N.D. & Pepitone-Areola-Rockwell, A.F. (2000). Multicultural Competencies: Criteria and Case Examples. *Professional Psychology: Research and Practice. 31(6)*, 652-660.

Harrison, S. & Carver, V. (1997). *Alcohol and Drug Problems: A Practical Guide for Counsellors* (2nd ed.). Toronto: Addiction Research Foundation.

Haskell, L. (2001). *Bridging Responses: A front-line worker's guide to supporting women who have post-traumatic stress*. Toronto: Centre for Addiction and Mental Health.

Health Canada. (2002). *Best Practices Concurrent Mental Health and Substance Use Disorders*. Ottawa: Minister of Public Works and Government Services Canada.

Health Canada. (2001). *Best Practices Treatment and Rehabilitation for Youth with Substance Use Problems*. Ottawa: Minister of Public Works and Government Services.

Health Canada. (2000). *Straight Facts About Drugs and Drug Abuse*. Ottawa: Minister of Public Works and Government Services.

Health Canada. (1999). *Best Practices Substance Abuse Treatment and Rehabilitation*. Ottawa: Minister of Public Works and Government Services Canada.

Jenson, J.M., Howard, M.O. & Yaffe, J. (1995). Treatment of Adolescent Substance Abusers: Issues for Practice and Research. *Social Work in Health Care, 21*, 1-18.

Kaminer, Y. (2001). Psychopharmacological Therapy. In E.F. Wagner & H.B. Waldron (Eds.), *Innovations in Adolescent Substance Abuse Interventions* (pp. 285-311). New York: Pergamon.

Kaminer, Y., Burleson, J.A. & Bouchard, L. (1998). Cognitive Behavioral Therapy Versus Interactional Therapy for Adolescents: 15-month follow-up (abstract). *Alcoholism: Clinical and Experimental Research, 22 (3, suppl.)*, 74A.

Lewinsohn, P.M., Clarke, G.N., Hops, H. & Andrews, J. (1990). Cognitive-Behavioral Treatment for Depressed Adolescents. *Behavior Therapy, 21*, 385-401.

Liddle, H.A. (2002). *Multidimensional Family Therapy for Adolescent Cannabis Users*, Cannabis Youth Treatment Series, Volume 5. (DHHS Pub. No. 02-3660). Rockville, MD: Center for Substance Abuse Treatment, Substance Abuse and Mental Health Services Administration.

Liddle, H.A. & Hogue, A. (2001). Multidimensional Family Therapy For Adolescent Substance Abuse. In E.F. Wagner & H.B. Waldron (Eds.), *Innovations in Adolescent Substance Abuse Interventions* (pp.229-261). New York: Pergamon.

Longo, L. (1997). Alcohol Abuse in Persons with Developmental Disabilities. *The Habilitative Mental Health Care Newsletter, 16(4)*, 61-64.

Mangham, C., McGrath, P., Reid, G. & Stewart, M. (1995). *Resiliency: Relevance to Health Promotion.* Discussion Paper submitted to Office of Alcohol, Drugs and Dependency Issues, Health Canada. Ottawa: Ministry of Supply and Services, 1995 [Obtained on-line]. Available on Internet: http://www.hc-sc.gc.ca/hecs-secs/cds/publications/resiliency/print3.htm.

March, J. & Mulle, K. (1996). Banishing Obsessive-Compulsive Disorder. In E. Hibbs & P. Jensen, (Eds.), *Psychosocial Treatments for Child and Adolescent Disorders* (pp. 82-103). Washington, DC: American Psychological Press.

March, J.S., Amaya-Jackson, L. & Murray, M.C. (1998). Cognitive-Behavioral Psychotherapy for Children and Adolescents with Post-traumatic Stress Disorder after a Single-Incident Stressor. *Journal of the American Academy of Child and Adolescent Psychiatry, 37*, 585-593.

Marlatt, G.A. (1998). *Harm Reduction: Pragmatic Strategies for Managing High-Risk Behaviours.* New York: The Guilford Press.

Marlatt, G.A. & Gordon, J.R. (1985). *Relapse Prevention.* New York: Guilford Press

Masten, A. S. (2001). Ordinary Magic: Resilience Processes in Development. *American Psychologist, 56 (3)*, 227-238.

Miller, E.T., Kilmer, J.R., Kim, E.L., Weingardt, K.R. & Marlatt. G.A. (2001). Alcohol Skills Training for College Students. In P.M. Monti, S.M. Colby, & T.A. O'Leary, (Eds.), *Adolescents, Alcohol and Substance Abuse* (pp.183-215). New York and London: The Guilford Press.

Miller, E.T., Turner, A.P. & Marlatt, G.A. (2001). The Harm Reduction Approach to the Secondary Prevention of Alcohol Problems in Adolescents and Young Adults: Considerations across a Developmental Spectrum. In P.M. Monti, S.M. Colby & T.A. O'Leary (Eds.), *Adolescents, Alcohol and Substance Abuse* (pp. 58-79). New York and London: The Guilford Press.

Miller, W.R. (2001). Foreword. In P.M. Monti, S.M. Colby & T.A. O'Leary (Eds.), *Adolescents, Alcohol and Substance Abuse* (pp. x-xiii). New York and London: The Guilford Press.

Miller, W.R. & C'deBaca, J. (1994). Quantum change: Toward a psychology of transformation. In T. Heatherton & J. Weinberger (Eds.), *Can personality change?* (pp 253-280). Washington DC: American Psychological Association.

Miller, W.R. & Rollnick, S. (Eds.). (2002). *Motivational Interviewing: Preparing People for Change* (2nd ed.). New York and London: The Guilford Press.

Mirza, K.A.H. (2002). Adolescent Substance Use Disorder. In S. Kutcher (Ed.), *Practical Child and Adolescent Psychopharmacology* (pp. 328-381). Cambridge, UK: Cambridge University Press.

Monti, P.M., Colby, S.M. & O'Leary, T.A. (Eds.). (2001). *Adolescents, Alcohol and Substance Abuse*. New York and London: The Guilford Press.

Myers, M.G. (2001). Cigarette Smoking Treatment for Substance-Abusing Adolescents. In E.F. Wagner & H.B. Waldron (Eds.), *Innovations in Adolescent Substance Abuse Interventions* (pp.263-283). New York: Pergamon.

Myers, M.G., Brown, S.A. & Kelly, J.F. (2000). A Cigarette Smoking Intervention for Substance-Abusing Adolescents. *Cognitive and Behavioral Practice, 7*, 64-82.

Myers, M.G., Brown, S.A., Tate, S., Abrantes, A. & Tomlinson, K. (2001). Toward Brief Interventions for Adolescents with Substance Abuse and Comorbid Psychiatric Problems. In P.M. Monti, S.M. Colby & T.A. O'Leary (Eds.), *Adolescents, Alcohol and Substance Abuse* (pp. 275-296). New York and London: The Guilford Press.

National Crime Prevention Centre (2000). *Policy Framework for Addressing Crime Prevention in Children Ages 0 to 12*. Ottawa: NCPC.

National Institute on Drug Abuse. (1997). *Preventing Drug Use Among Children and Adolescents: A research-based guide*. Rockville, MD: National Institute on Drug Abuse.

Offord, D., Boyle, M. & Racine, Y. (1989). *Ontario Child Health Study: Children at Risk*. Toronto: Ontario Ministry of Community and Social Services, Queen's Printer for Ontario.

Ontario Substance Abuse Bureau and Ontario Addiction Services Advisory Council. (2000). *Admission and Discharge Criteria*. Toronto: Ontario Ministry of Health.

Parks, G.A., Anderson, B.K. & Marlatt, G.A. (2000). Harm Reduction Therapy for Co-occurring Disorders. *The Dual Network, 1 (3), Winter*, 6-7.

Patterson, J.M. (2002). *Risk and Protective Factors Associated with Children's Mental Health*. Maternal and Child Health Program, School of Public Health, University of Minnesota [Obtained on-line]. Available on Internet: http://www.epi.umn.edu/mch/resources/hg/hg_mentalhealth.pdf.

Pickrel, S.G., Hall, J.A. & Cunningham, P.B. (1997). Interventions for Adolescents who Abuse Substances. In S.W. Henggeler and A. B. Santos (Eds.), *Innovative approaches for difficult-to-treat populations* (pp. 99-116). Washington, DC: American Psychiatric Press.

Prochaska, J.O., & DiClemente, C.C. (1984). *The Transtheoretical Approach: Crossing Traditional Boundaries of Therapy*. Homewood, IL: Dow Jones/Irwin.

Prochaska, J.O., & DiClemente, C.C. (1982). Transtheoretical Therapy: Toward a more integrative model of change. *Psychotherapy: Theory, Research and Practice, 19 (3),* 276-288.

Riggs, P.D. & Whitmore, E.A. (1999). Substance Use Disorders and Disruptive Behaviour Disorders. In R.L. Hendren (Ed.), *Disruptive Behavior Disorders in Children and Adolescents, 18 (2), Review of Psychiatry Series* (pp. 133-173). Washington, DC: American Psychiatric Press.

Rotgers, F & Graves, G. (2001). *Motivational Enhancement Treatment Manual: Institutional and Community Volume.* Augusta, Maine: Maine Office of Substance Abuse.

Ruf, G. (1999). Addiction Treatment for People with Mental Retardation and Hearing Disabilities: Why We Need Specialized Services. *The National Association of Developmental Disabilities Bulletin, 2 (3),* 95-101.

Sampl, S. & Kadden, R. (2001). *Motivational Enhancement Therapy and Cognitive Behavioral Therapy for Adolescent Cannabis Users: 5 Sessions.* Cannabis Youth Treatment (CYT) Series, Volume 1. Centre for Substance Abuse Treatment (CSAT) [Obtained online]. Available on Internet: http://www.health.org/govpubs/bkd384/.

Sanchez-Craig, M., Annis, H. M., Bornet, A. R. & MacDonald, K.R. (1984). Random assignment to abstinence and controlled drinking: Evaluation of a cognitive-behavioural program for problem drinkers. *Journal of Consulting and Clinical Psychology, 52,* 390-403.

Schwartz, G. (1997). *Kids are Kids: Exploring the Connection between Substance Abuse & Mental Health in Adolescents.* Toronto: Ontario Ministry of Community and Social Services and Ontario Ministry of Health.

Skinner, H., Maley, O., Smith, L., Chirrey, S. & Morrison, M. (2001). New Frontiers: Using the Internet to Engage Teens in Substance Abuse Prevention and Treatment. In P.M. Monti, S.M. Colby & T.A. O'Leary (Eds.), *Adolescents, Alcohol and Substance Abuse* (pp. 297-318). New York and London: The Guilford Press.

Skinner, W.J.W. & Toneatto, T. (2001). *Helping Clients with Concurrent Disorders.* Powerpoint presentation. Toronto: Education and Training Services, Centre for Addiction and Mental Health.

Slesnick, N., Meyers, R. J., Meade, M. & Sedelken, D.H. (1999). Bleak and Hopeless No More: Engagement of Reluctant Substance-Abusing Runaway Youth and their Families. *Journal of Substance Abuse Treatment, 19,* 215-222 .

Sobell, M. B. & Sobell, L. C. (1993). *Problem Drinkers: Guided Self-change Treatment.* New York: Guilford Press.

Stavrakaki, C. (2002). Substance-Related Disorders in Persons with Developmental Disabilities. In D.M. Griffens, C. Stavrakaki & J. Summers (Eds.), *Dual Diagnosis:*

An Introduction to the Mental Health Needs of Persons with Developmental Disabilities (pp. 456-481). Sudbury, ON: Habilitative Mental Health Resource Network.

Stavrakaki, C. (1999). Depression, Anxiety and Adjustment Disorders in People with Developmental Disabilities. In N. Boudras (Ed.), *Psychiatric and Behavioral Disorders in Developmental Disabilities and Mental Retardation* (pp. 175-187). Boston, MA: Cambridge University Press.

Stavrakaki, C. & Mintsioulis, G. (1997). Anxiety Disorders in Persons with Mental Retardation: Diagnostic, Clinical, and Treatment Issues. *Psychiatric Annals, 27*, 182-189.

Stavrakaki, C. & Mintsioulis, G. (1995). Pharmacalogical Treatment of Obsessive-Compulsive Disorders in Down's Syndrome Individuals: Comparison with Obsessive-Compulsive Disorders of Non-Down's Mentally Retarded Persons. In *Proceedings of the International Congress II on the Dually Diagnosed* (pp. 52-56). Boston, MA.

Szapocznik, J., Kurtines, W.M., Foote, F., Perez-Vidal, A. & Hervis, O. (1986). Conjoint Versus One-Person Family Therapy: Further Evidence for the Effectiveness of Conducting Family Therapy through One Person with Drug-Abusing Adolescents. *Journal of Consulting & Clinical Psychology, 54(3)*, 395-7.

Trupin, E. & Boesky, L.M. (2001). *Working Together for Change: Co-occurring Mental Health and Substance Use Disorders among Youth Involved in the Juvenile Justice System: An On-line Tutorial for Juvenile Justice, Mental Health and Substance Abuse Treatment Professionals.* New York: Policy Research Associates. [Obtained on-line]. Available on Internet: http://www.gainsctr.com/curriculum/juvenile/.

U.S. Department of Health and Human Services, Public Health Service, Substance Abuse and Mental Health Services Administration & Center for Substance Abuse Treatment (CSAT). (1999). *Screening and Assessing Adolescents for Substance Use Disorders.* Treatment Improvement Protocol (TIP) Series 31. Rockville, MD: Center for Substance Abuse Treatment.

Van Hasselt, V.B., Null, J.A., Kempton, T. & Bukstein, O.G. (1993). Social Skills and Depression in Adolescent Substance Abusers. *Addictive Behaviors, 18*, 9-18.

Wagner, E.F., Brown, S.A., Monti, P.M., Myers, M.G. & Waldron, H.B. (1999). Innovations in Adolescent Substance Abuse Intervention. *Alcoholism: Clinical and Experimental Research, 23 (2)*, 236-249.

Wagner, E.F., Kortlander, E. & Morris, S.L. (2001). The Teen Intervention Project: A School-Based Intervention for Adolescents with Substance Use Problems. In E.F. Wagner & H.B. Waldron (Eds.), *Innovations in Adolescent Substance Abuse Interventions* (pp. 189-203). New York: Pergamon.

Wagner, E.F. & Waldron, H.B. (Eds). (2001). *Innovations in Adolescent Substance Abuse Interventions*. New York: Pergamon.

Waldron, H.B. (1997). Adolescent Substance Abuse and Family Therapy Outcome: A Review of Randomized Trials. In T.H. Ollendick & R.J. Prinz (Eds.), *Advances in Clinical Child Psychology, Vol. 19* (pp. 199-234). New York: Plenum.

Waldron, H.B., Brody, J.L. & Slesnick, N. (2001). Integrative Behavioral and Family Therapy for Adolescent Substance Abuse. In P.M. Monti, S.M. Colby & T.A. O'Leary (Eds.), *Adolescents, Alcohol and Substance Abuse* (pp. 216-243). New York and London: The Guilford Press.

Webb, C., Scudder, M., Kaminer, Y. & Kadden, R. (2002). *The Motivational Enhancement Therapy and Cognitive Behavioral Therapy Supplement: 7 Sessions of Cognitive Behavioral Therapy for Adolescent Cannabis Users.* Cannabis Youth Treatment (CYT) Series, Volume 2. (DHHS Pub. No. [SMA] 02-3659). Rockville, MD: Center for Substance Abuse Treatment (CSAT), Substance Abuse and Mental Health Services Administration.

Westermeyer, J., Phaoblong, T. & Neither, J. (1988). Substance Use and Abuse Among Mentally Retarded Persons: A Comparison of Patients and a Survey Population. *American Journal of Drug and Alcohol Abuse, 14*, 109-123.

Wilford, B.B. (1981). *Drug Abuse: A Guide for the Primary Care Physician*. Chicago, Ill.: American Medical Association.

Winters, K.C. (1999). Treating Adolescents with Substance Use Disorders: An Overview of Practice Issues and Treatment Outcomes. *Substance Abuse, 20 (4)*, 203-225.

Winters, K. C. (2001). Assessing Adolescent Substance Use Problems and Other Areas of Functioning: State of the Art. In P.M. Monti, S.M. Colby & T.A. O'Leary (Eds.), *Adolescents, Alcohol and Substance Abuse* (pp. 80-108). New York and London: The Guilford Press.

Winters, K.C., Latimer, W.W. & Stinchfield, R. (2001). Assessing Adolescent Substance Use. In E.F. Wagner & H.B. Waldron (Eds.), *Innovations in Adolescent Substance Abuse Interventions*, (pp. 1-29). New York : Pergamon.

Lightning Source UK Ltd.
Milton Keynes UK
UKOW012300030912

198397UK00001BA/73/P